IMPERIALISM
AND ITS CONTRADICTIONS

IMPERIALISM
AND ITS CONTRADICTIONS

■ **V. G. Kiernan** ■

edited & introduced by HARVEY J. KAYE

Routledge · New York & London

Published in 1995 by

Routledge
29 West 35th Street
New York, NY 10001

Published in Great Britain by

Routledge
11 New Fetter Lane
London EC4P 4EE

Library of Congress Cataloging-in-Publication Data

Kiernan, V. G. (Victor Gordon), 1913–
    Imperialism and its contradictions / V.G. Kiernan ; edited and
introduced by Harvey J. Kaye.
        p.   cm. — (American radicals)
    Collection of previously published essays.
    Includes bibliographical references and index.
        ISBN 0-415-90796-9 (acid-free paper). — ISBN 0-415-90797-7 (acid-free paper)
        1. Imperialism. 2. Colonies.   I. Kaye, Harvey J.   II. Title.   III. Series.
JC359.K525   1994
325'.32—dc20
                                                                        94-14828
                                                                        CIP

British Library Cataloguing-in-Publication Data also available.

To the memory of George Rudé (1910–1993),
who firmly believed that all history must be studied afresh.

CONTENTS

England has to fulfill a double mission in India: one destructive, the other regenerating—the annihilation of old Asiatic society, and the laying of the material foundations of Western society in Asia. . . .

The Indians themselves will not reap the fruits of the new elements of society scattered among them by the British bourgeoisie, till in Great Britain itself the now ruling classes shall have been supplanted by the industrial proletariat, or till the Hindoos themselves shall have grown strong enough to throw off the English altogether. . . .

The profound hypocrisy and inherent barbarism of bourgeois civilization lies unveiled before our eyes, turning from its home, where it assumes respectable forms, to the colonies where it goes naked. . . .

When the great social revolution shall have mastered the results of the bourgeois epoch, the market of the world and the modern powers of production, and subjected them to the common control of the most advanced peoples, then only will human progress cease to resemble that hideous pagan idol, who would not drink the nectar but from the skulls of the slain.

—Karl Marx,
The Future Results of British Rule in India (1853)

PREFACE

This is the third in a series of volumes of Victor Kiernan's essays which I have had the honor to edit and introduce. The first, *History, Classes, and Nation-States* (1988), brought together his best articles on early-modern and modern European history, and the second, *Poets, Politics, and the People* (1989), brought together a selection of his most important writings in British historical and literary studies. Beyond the present work there are two additional volumes to be prepared for publication, *Intellectuals in History* and *Britons Old and New*.

As impressive and significant as are his books and articles on specifically British and European subjects, Kiernan's major contributions and fame as a scholar are probably based on his efforts in international and world history, that is, his pioneering work on imperialism and colonialism. As I relate in the introductory remarks which follow, Kiernan's studies of European (and American) expansionism have regularly opened up new areas to investigation and consideration. Moreover, Kiernan's writings are extraordinarily diverse in historical and geographical range and, as a consequence, of the three volumes on which I have worked thus far, the contents of the present one were really the most difficult to determine because the possibilities were so numerous. In the end, I chose to limit the collection to the modern European imperial experience, thereby eliminating pieces on ancient history and on both the United States and Latin America. At the same time, the selection of chapters still registers the thematic range of Kiernan's work, including political-economic, military, social, and cultural studies. Though I am not always in agreement with the arguments presented, I feel strongly that they must be attended to.

Even in the making of edited volumes such as this, there are many people to acknowledge. For allowing us to reprint articles which originally appeared in their publications, I thank the Center for Development Studies at the

University College of Wales in Swansea, Macmillan Press, Cambridge University Press, and the editors of *New Left Review, History of European Ideas,* and *New Edinburgh Review* (the particular references are noted at the outset of each chapter's notes).

Friends and colleagues near and far who in varied (and sometimes unknowing) ways contributed to this project are Christopher Hill, Ron Baba, Craig Lockard, Tony Galt, Lynn Walter, Lisa Barlow, Larry Smith, Ellen Wood, Terry Brotherstone, Frank Furedi, David Jowett, Ron Sexton, Stephanie Cataldo, Heather Kiernan and, at the publishers, Maura Burnett, Claudia Gorelick and Ray Walker.

Especially, I want to acknowledge my incomparable editor and friend at Routledge in New York, Cecelia Cancellaro. Smart and enthusiastic, in an age of corporate priorities she makes publishing not only a valuable and worthwhile professional and intellectual experience but culturally significant *and* great fun.

As ever, my family, Rhiannon and Fiona and especially, my wife, Lorna, make it all come together. It's not just their patience but their participation which is essential; not to mention, while my skills are limited, theirs continue to develop and there would be no books without them.

I have stated before that in working with Victor Kiernan and his writings I feel like a student learning new things and I realize how little I actually knew before our encounter. Thank you, Victor, for assisting in my continuing education. But I also want to thank you and Heather for making my visits to Woodcroft in Stow, Scotland, so enjoyable and for your visits to Wisconsin to talk to my students on diverse topics.

Harvey J. Kaye
University of Wisconsin-Green Bay
April 1994

INTRODUCTION:
IMPERIALISM AND ITS LEGACIES

It is not enough to know the *ensemble* of relations as they exist at any given time
as a given system. They must be known genetically, in the movement of their
formation. For each individual is the synthesis not only of existing relations, but
of the history of these relations. He is a précis of all the past.
—Antonio Gramsci

The Presentness of the Past

The title of a recent American symposium bluntly asked, "Imperialism—
A Useful Category of History Analysis?"[1] And in view of recent international
events and developments, it should not be surprising that models, theories,
and concepts which had been formulated, or reformulated, to comprehend
world history in earlier decades should now be subject once again to reconsid-
eration, revision and, possibly, rejection. Following the Second World War
(1939–45) we saw the ascendance of American political and economic power
in the West, the structuring of a seemingly eternal Cold War between the
United States and the Soviet Union and their respective allies, and the dramatic expansion of the nation-state system as a consequence of decolonization
and the retreat of the great European empires. We are now witness to the
rise of Japanese and German capital to challenge American corporate hegemony; the industrialization and rapid economic development of East Asian
states such as Taiwan and South Korea and the "opening" of the Chinese
economy to international capital and domestic private enterprise; the collapse
of the Soviet Union and its command of the East European nations; and,
thus, the sudden end of the Cold War, leaving the United States the unrivaled,
though economically debilitated, superpower in a world of gross inequalities,
surging national and ethnoreligious fundamentalisms, and aspiring regional
hegemons in possession or pursuit of nuclear armaments. Global restructuring
rightly commands reassessment of the paradigms and language which have
prevailed in the social sciences, particularly in fields such as international
relations and development studies.[2]

At the same time—even if the claim by neoconservative writer Francis
Fukuyama that the triumph of the West represents the "end of history" is
nothing more than a brilliantly timed ideological coup in favor of corporate

capitalism[3]—it is clear that what survives of radical democratic and socialist lefts internationally are staring at seemingly overwhelming and impossible political challenges and that, therefore, at the least, fresh and innovative thinking is demanded. That much is evident. Yet, however "new" and "original" the circumstances and difficulties before us, it is equally essential that they be thought through in *historical* terms. Only in historical perspective can we perceive continuity and change and begin to appreciate the making and unmaking of the crises and problems we confront and of the relations we would hope to reform, undo, or secure more firmly. As the late E. H. Carr wrote at midcentury, we need "to analyze the past in the light of the present and future which is growing out of it, and to cast the beam of the past over the issues which dominate present and future. . . . A historically-minded generation is one which looks back, not indeed for solutions which cannot be found in the past, but for those critical insights which are necessary both to the understanding of its existing situation and to the realization of the values which it holds."[4]

In fact, it is arguable that historical study and thought become all the more imperative in the face of apparently rapid, deep, and extensive changes, for at such times there is a dangerous, though understandable, tendency to assume that contemporary experience is so radically discontinuous from that which preceded it that we are entitled to draw a line across history effectively separating the past from the present. To posit such a "break" is not necessarily wrong—though knowing when we ought to do so still requires knowledge of the past itself, or as C. Wright Mills put it, "we must often study history in order to get rid of it."[5] Nevertheless, even where it might be deemed appropriate, such a line must not be drawn too sharply for it can too easily provide for an artificial and amnesic sense of the originality of the present, suppressing appreciation of our continuing relation to the past *and* recognition of how the past is still determining our experience and bearing.

This is not simply an academic and intellectual problem but, most definitely, a broader cultural and political one, especially regarding the question of imperialism and its legacy, a question inherently bound up with issues of national identity and governance. Contrary to J. H. Plumb's optimistic prognosis, the "past" is not dead and its use and abuse by the powers that be remains a persistent practice.[6] And in an age which celebrates democracy and the self-determination of peoples, at least rhetorically, it should be expected that the governing classes of the "formerly" imperial European nation-states would seek to treat the (relatively recent) experiences of empire and colonialism as *in the past* and, geographically speaking, as having been *external* to national life and culture—even as they selectively recall those very moments as evidence of their respective nation's accomplishments, glories, and contributions to the making of the modern world and civilization. A similar, though—as ever—unique, situation exists in the American case, where the dominant rhetoric has repeatedly denied any imperial and colonial ambitions and pursuits in favor of references to Manifest Destiny, the Monroe Doctrine, hemispheric stability and security, and defense of the free world.[7]

Recently, these points have been made most effectively by the literary scholar and critic Edward Said in his book *Culture and Imperialism*. For example, he observes:

> The asymmetry is striking. In one instance, we assume that the better part of history in colonial territories was a function of the imperial intervention; in the other, there is an equally obstinate assumption that colonial undertakings were marginal and perhaps even eccentric to the cultural activities of the great metropolitan cultures. . . . These elisions and denials are all reproduced . . . in the strident journalistic debates about decolonization, in which imperialism is repeatedly on record as saying, in effect, You are what you are because of us; when we left, you reverted to your deplorable state; know that or you will know nothing, for certainly there is little to be known about imperialism that might help you or us in the present.[8]

Concerned, with good reason, about Western historical amnesia and selective remembrance, Said demands critical reexamination of the imperial and colonial experiences. He insists that historians and cultural analysts renew their investigations into the *manifold* character of modern imperialism and colonialism—the political, economic and, relatively understudied, cultural dimensions—and, furthermore, that we set about revealing the degree to which imperialism was a formative and defining element in the development not only of the Asian, African, and Latin American states and societies but of the "metropolitan" nations and social orders as well.

Said's interest is not merely "historical," that is, he does not urge such work solely as a means of revising our knowledge of the past but also, as Carr emphasized, as a way of effecting changes in our understanding of the world today or, more precisely, to enhance our appreciation of the "presentness of the past." Stated in the most basic of terms: "European imperialism still casts a considerable shadow over our own times. Hardly any North American, African, European, Latin American, Indian, Caribbean, Australian individual—the list is very long—who is alive today has not been touched by the empires of the past."[9] Acknowledging that the postcolonial states and peoples themselves cannot be exempted from criticism, Said explains that the intention is not merely to evoke greater admission of Western responsibility for its imperial degradations—that is, to encourage a "politics of blame"—but to increase awareness among both the colonizer and the colonized of the legacies of imperialism and colonialism *and* how they continue to shape our cultures and social relations and practices at both the national and the international levels.[10] The ends are necessarily political:

> More important than the past itself . . . is its bearing upon cultural attitudes in the present. For reasons that are partly embedded in the imperial experience, the old divisions between colonizer and colonized have reemerged in what is often referred to as the North-South relationship, which has entailed defensiveness, various kinds of rhetorical and ideological combat, and a simmering hostility that is quite likely to trigger devastating wars—in some cases it already has. Are there ways we can reconceive the imperial experience in other than compartmentalized terms, so as to transform our understanding of both the past and the present and our attitude toward the future?[11]

Although Said grants that the kinds of scholarly and intellectual engagements for which he is calling have begun in several quarters, he states that "concern with the issue has not been intense" and that there is much "more to be done." Looking toward the further invigoration and extension of such endeavors, he points to the works of the British historian V. G. Kiernan as being "milestones" and models for them.[12]

V. G. Kiernan, Historian of Imperialism

Victor Kiernan is one of the most remarkable scholars of the twentieth century. Including grand scholarly monographs, masterful synthetic texts, original research articles, insightful reflective essays, and probing reviews and opinion pieces, his studies have ranged historically from the ancient to the modern; globally from Britain and Europe to Asia, Africa, and the Americas; and topically from the arts and letters to armies and wars and back again. And there is more. Along with his voluminous historiography and political and literary essays, he has composed a children's novella, poetry and short stories (and music), and selected memoirs—plus, he has translated into English three volumes of Urdu and Hindi poetry and prose.[13] As his longtime friend the renowned historian Eric Hobsbawm declared, Kiernan's knowledge is "encyclopedic."[14] In an age of increasing intellectual division of labor and scholarly specialization—even as global forces and crises accumulate—Kiernan's energy and reach stand as a model for the rest of us.

Yet it is not only the exuberance and breadth of Kiernan's work which should command our attention. It is also the *critical* perspective and imagination which he brings to it. Kiernan is firmly, and rightly, identified with the British Marxist historical tradition, an outstanding generation of socialist intellectuals including the more senior Maurice Dobb, Dona Torr, and A. L.

Morton, and Kiernan's peers, Rodney Hilton, Christopher Hill, George Rudé, Eric Hobsbawm, John Saville, and Dorothy and E. P. Thompson.[15] His studies have been framed by their shared problematic of the transition from feudalism to capitalism and the making of modern Britain, and, like those of his comrades, they are strongly informed by Marx and Engels's grand hypothesis that "the history of all hitherto existing society is the history of class struggle."[16] Also, if history from below means having "sympathy with the victims of historical processes and skepticism about the claims of the victors," then Kiernan, too, has most definitely been working "from the bottom up."[17]

Still, Kiernan's contributions do stand somewhat apart from those of his fellow British Marxist historians, for in contrast to their pioneering and persistent initiatives to recover the lives and struggles of the common people, the exploited, and the oppressed, "from the enormous condescension of posterity," his have been dedicated more often to revealing the experiences and agencies of those who ruled over them, the wealthy and the powerful. Kiernan, as well, has written of peasants and proletarians, but the greater share of his labors has been concerned with the ambitions of the governing classes, aristocratic and bourgeois, who, as Kiernan regretfully reminds us, are "still in the driver's seat."[18]

Another significant feature of Kiernan's scholarly career which distinguishes it from those of most of his cohorts is his long and sustained interest in world history and international studies, especially the subject of modern European imperialism and colonialism. And, arguably, it is here that Kiernan has made his greatest contributions. Indeed, from the outset in the late 1930s, Kiernan has repeatedly returned, in the light of changing historical circumstances and other researchers, to ask original and critical questions about the origins, operations, and consequences of the imperial and colonial experiences, thereby opening up new areas to historical examination. Significantly, Kiernan understood that imperialism ought never to be reduced to one-dimensionality, for example, as in the field of international history, to diplomatic intrigues, or as so often in Marxist studies, to economic considerations and relations (which, he shows, are themselves far more complex than they appear). Moreover, as Edward Said appreciates, ever sensitive to the dialectical character of social relations and action, Kiernan realized that the making and unmaking of imperial realms entailed at all times both power and resistance and that these have been determining of the lives and cultures of both the colonized and the colonizers. Finally, Kiernan recognized that the histories of modern imperialism and colonialism were marked by tremendous contradictions which continue today to influence postimperial experience and possibilities for good and ill.

Kiernan was born in England near Manchester in 1913.[19] He describes his upbringing as lower middle-class, apolitical but essentially conservative, and actively Congregationalist. Educated at Manchester Grammar School, he entered Cambridge University in 1931 to read history and it was at this time that his intellectual interests and commitments were permanently fused with political concerns (though never subordinated to them!). He was an outstand-ing student and, upon completing his degree in 1934, he was awarded a research scholarship and, later, a Fellowship at Trinity College. Also, in 1934 he joined the Communist Party and became an activist in Cambridge socialist student politics.

These were foreboding times. The onset and persistence of world economic depression and terrible economic and social hardship for the laboring classes, the rise and triumph of Fascism in Central Europe and the Spanish civil war (1936–39) (in which Kiernan's good friend and fellow young communist John Cornford was killed while fighting on the Republican side),[20] and the growing likelihood of a second world war all seemed to offer evidence that the capitalist world was entering upon its final crisis. Thus young British communists believed all the more in the necessity and urgency of their cam-paigns and organizing efforts. Seeing a world characterized by surviving overseas colonial empires, resurgent European imperial aspirations in North Africa and Europe itself, and Japanese expansionism in Asia and the Pacific, Kiernan focused his own research on the historical development of modern colonialism and empire building. In particular, he turned his attention to British activities in Asia, specifically nineteenth-century Anglo-Chinese rela-tions. He also made contact with nationalist Asian students at Cambridge who were attempting to deal with the issues of British and European imperial-ism and colonialism; and thus his major initiative for the Party was to work with an Indian Marxist study group originally organized by his friend Herbert Norman.[21]

Kiernan's Fellowship research at Cambridge resulted in his first major book, *British Diplomacy in China, 1880–1885,* published just before the war in 1939.[22] In one sense it is a traditional work focusing on the agencies and deliberations of diplomats and statesmen to advance their respective national ambitions and interests in late-nineteenth-century China and East Asia. In another sense, however, the work is a serious attempt at innovation, for, as Kiernan explains, he was seeking to unravel the ways in which the politics of diplomacy are linked to, and expressive of, economic forces and, thereby, bring together the two seemingly separate disciplines of diplomatic affairs and economic history. This is smartly accomplished, but the book is still structured by a duality. Within the larger work there is a second, shorter one reflecting Kiernan's larger Marxist-historical concerns, and therein he presents an analysis of China's historic mode of production, of Chinese social structure and its relation to the state, and of Chinese class conflicts. This latter "work" was to be indicative of the direction which much of his postwar and continuing scholarship would take. Although he continued to publish in diplomatic history, he increasingly came to see such matters, insofar as his own scholarship was concerned, as of mostly antiquarian interest.[23]

Instigated by his work with Asian students at Cambridge, Kiernan departed England in 1938 to take up schoolteaching in India, first at the Sikh National College and then at Aitchison College in Lahore (in what is now Pakistan). Spending the Second World War years there, Kiernan continued to pursue the study of British imperialism in Asia, which led him to write another, shorter monograph in diplomatic history, *Metcalfe's Mission to Lahore, 1808–1809*.[24] He also published a children's novel, *The March of Time;* a little collection of his own poetry, *Castanets;* and several stories, two of which appeared in *Longman's Miscellany*.[25] And, improving his knowledge of Urdu and Hindi, he began a series of major literary translations.[26] At the same time, Kiernan continued his political work through the Communist Party of India. In fact, his political engagements began *en voyage*. As he was to write almost fifty years later: "In September 1938 I sailed to India, to see the political scene at closer hand, and with some schemes of historical study. I was the bearer of a lengthy document from the Communist International, which would have been cheering to the British authorities if it had fallen into their hands. Its gist was that Moscow could not campaign at present for legalization of the Indian Party; the reason of course was Soviet eagerness for a collective security agreement with Britain."[27]

In India, Kiernan undertook a variety of jobs for the Party which, with the eventual alliance of Britain and the Soviet Union *and* the threat of an imperial Japanese conquest of the subcontinent, actively supported the Allied war effort as a "patriotic" and "antifascist" crusade. His projects included lecturing and making occasional radio broadcasts, translating and editing pamphlets, and writing letters and other pieces. He also involved himself with the Indian Progressive Writers' Association, which had first been formed in London in 1934.

Unquestionably, Kiernan's experiences in India were tremendously important in shaping his later work and understandings. Existing interests were intensified and expanded: his study of imperialism and colonialism grew to encompass the issue of nationalism and nation-state formation, and he has maintained a lifelong fascination and concern for the politics and culture of the Indian subcontinent. Further, it is likely that this period—living in a colonial society in contact with an intelligentsia aspiring to national independence but divided by political, ethnic, and religious affiliations—contributed greatly to the development of his own perspective on imperialism and colonialism, which, as I have said and as the chapters following attest, has been undeniably critical and yet quite sensitive to the historical contradictions of those experiences.

In 1946 Kiernan returned to England and Cambridge for a further two-year period as a Fellow of Trinity College, following which he secured a lectureship in History at the University of Edinburgh. He was later promoted to Reader and then Professor at Edinburgh before retiring in 1977 as Professor Emeritus. His scholarly accomplishments in these years were numerous and varied and, by all accounts, so too were his teaching responsibilities. Nevertheless, liberated from teaching duties, Kiernan has been able to devote his energies fully to writing, and thus he has produced a flood of books, articles, and reviews on ever diverse subjects while also lecturing widely in Britain, Europe, and North America.[28]

Upon his return to Britain following the war, Kiernan renewed his work with the British Communist Party. He became especially active in the Communist Party Historians' Group—the formative "moment" of the British Marxist historical tradition. Notable here are his comrades' descriptions of Kiernan's critical-intellectual role in the group's debates and deliberations: Eric Hobsbawm refers to him as "our chief doubter" and Christopher Hill recalls that "he kept us on our toes."[29] As a formal enterprise, the Group all but fell apart in 1956–57 when most of its central figures left the Party in protest at the Soviet invasion of Hungary and the failure of the British Party to break with the Soviets and reform itself.[30] Kiernan himself was active in the arguments of the day, but he did not withdraw from the Party until 1959, hoping for changes that did not ensue. Since then he has joined no other political party and has identified himself as an "independent Marxist—with no enemies on the Left."

Again, however many directions his work has taken, Kiernan has continually returned through the course of the past sixty years to the subject of imperialism. During the immediate postwar decades, as the European empires were being dismantled, he authored a number of articles on international and diplomatic history even as he wrote on specifically English subjects, continued his translation of Indian texts, and accomplished the research for an essentially unrelated book project, *The Revolution of 1854 in Spanish History*.[31] Still, in 1969 he published the first of a series of major works on imperialism and colonialism, *The Lords of Human Kind: Black Man, Yellow Man, and White Man in an Age of Empire*.[32] A study in the historical psychology and sociology of race, this book represented not just a dramatic shift in his own concerns but a most innovative work in the social history of the European imperial experience. Set within the process of European expansion overseas, *The Lords of Human Kind* surveys the attitudes of merchants and traders, diplomats and military men, and missionaries and colonial officers (and, to some extent, the women who accompanied them) toward those over whom they sought control and hegemony. Although evidently concerned with the view "from above," Kiernan appreciates that the development of European attitudes cannot be treated in isolation. Thus, in addition to illustrating how Europeans' racial(ist) and ethnocentric perceptions of the "outside world" were conditioned by the particulars of their countries of origin and therein by class, he shows how these views were shaped by the cultures, social structures, and levels of development of the non-European peoples themselves, which were, of course, determinants of those peoples' capacities to resist or, possibly, thwart (as did the Japanese) European advances, encroachments, and conquests.

The Lords of Human Kind is complemented by Kiernan's 1982 book *European Empires from Conquest to Collapse, 1815–1960*. Whereas the former work treats the cultural dimension of imperial expansion, the latter is a historical sociology of Europe's imperial and colonial wars.[33] *European Empires* looks at Europe's armies and technologies of death and their applications to killing in Africa, Asia, and the Pacific, together with considerations of the ideologies and doctrines of colonialism and colonial warfare, the publicity and political consequences at home, and the resistance and rebellions offered by colonial peoples. Reading this book should cure one of any nostalgia for Europe's colonial past.

Indeed, both *The Lords of Human Kind* and *European Empires* were motivated as much by political as by historiographical concerns. The first book was intended to provide a historical mirror in which Britons might reflect on their attitudes and actions toward non-European peoples, which Kiernan recognizes as becoming all the more urgent:

> Its purpose was to assist in a small way towards the better understanding among the different branches of the human family that is incessantly talked of today, less often sought for with any great realism. . . . We in this country need to know more about the European neighbors with whom our governors have decided to amalgamate us, and one way to study them, and ourselves by comparison with them, is to observe how they and we behaved far away from Europe, where national characters displayed themselves more uninhibitedly. At home we need to remind ourselves of the pitfalls that surrounded our forefathers, because we have a racial situation now in Great Britain capable of engineering many of the same prejudices and resentments that the British Empire used to harbor.[34]

European Empires was also for the purpose of historical reflection *and* to highlight the persistence and continuity of the past in the present: "There are, after all, good reasons for prying into the past with the historian's telescope and trying to see more clearly what happened instead of being content with legend or fantasy. Of all the reasons for an interest in the colonial wars of modern times the best is that they are still going on, openly or disguised."[35] The necessity of critical history is compounded by European eagerness to avoid reckoning with, or even properly remembering, its imperial "past":

"Europe today may feel mainly concerned with itself, but there are many discords between it and other regions still to be harmonized; and since its political and economic relations with them are now often subterranean, they call for more, not less vigilant scrutiny by the public. Europe cannot, moreover, discard its memories of life in the world as easily as the frontiers it drew there; they remain part of its being."[36]

Kiernan has also explored American history in his book *America: The New Imperialism,* published in 1978. In it he provides an interpretation of United States history in which expansion and imperialism are conceived as central to its development. Though not offering an original thesis as to the causes of American imperialism, the book is effectively written, connecting the historically particular modes of the United States' "march westward" and hegemonic advances globally to the changing complex of its regional and class forces and conflicts. Kiernan's observations on American history and politics, in the book and related articles,[37] are often acerbic, yet in the very same texts he exhibits and expresses a sensitivity to, and appreciation of, the tensions and contradictions which have characterized American growth and development. At the beginning of the book he writes:

> America's early settlers left an England astir with progressive impulses, and might have seemed to be building in the wilderness the better society that the Levellers tried in vain to build in England. But there was always in this new land a duality, a division of the soul as deep as the racial cleavage between black and white. Aspiration towards a new life was never to succumb entirely to what our ancestors called "the world, the flesh and the devil." Yet these latter temptations remained potent, and imperialist hankerings—running all through America's history and at last becoming its most obtrusive feature—have been one consequence.[38]

Published in the wake of the Vietnam War, *America: The New Imperialism* joined those studies which have sought to demolish that powerful historical myth of Americans which holds that the United States has never been a "colonial" power: but it is also made quite clear in the course of the historical narrative, as well as in an earlier article, "Imperialism, American and European," how the development of American imperialism has contrasted historically with that of Europe: "It lost interest overnight in its first flutter with colonialism, in a volatile fashion impossible to a Europe rancid with hereditary ambitions and vendettas." Nevertheless, foregoing direct colonialism, American empire building led the way toward *neo*colonialism.[39]

Kiernan's studies of imperialism and colonialism (and neocolonialism) have never been pursued in order to elaborate a formal theory of "causes." It is not that Kiernan has been uninterested in theory—though he has sought injunctions against philosophers and social theorists talking only to themselves!—but, rather, that he has seen his task to be that of bringing theory to the bar of historical experience. That is, he brings theory face to face with history, his purpose being to separate out "what may be of permanent value in it from what was ephemeral, or has been discounted by later history."[40] Thus in his 1974 collection of essays *Marxism and Imperialism,* Kiernan commences with a critical-historical survey of classical Marxian thinking on imperialism. He remarks that the strength of Marxist and Leninist thought has been in economic analysis and that "in this preoccupation Marxism continued Marx's own turning away . . . from a many-sided approach to history and society towards a narrower concentration on economic structure." This he finds inadequate, leaving Marxist work on imperialism "most vulnerable to criticism through its comparative neglect of other motive forces, political or psychological." In short, Marxism had been reduced and was now being equated too much with economics and economic determinism. In this respect, *The Lords of Human Kind, European Empires,* and *America: The New Imperialism* can be read as efforts to round out Marxist study.

Kiernan is especially critical of Lenin, whose essay *Imperialism* (1916) was elevated to "canonical status" upon the triumph of the Bolshevik revolution. As a consequence, other significant works were marginalized and research agendas were narrowed, with serious political consequences. Lenin, Kiernan states, was a "systematizer," not an original thinker. Less interested in history than Marx and Engels, Lenin overemphasized economic factors and invested capitalism with "too universal and omnipotent a direction of events." For example, Lenin's monistic approach prevented him from understanding the "passions of nationalism." Continuing, Kiernan shows by way of comparative European references that Lenin's theory of the "labor aristocracy" in which it is contended that the upper strata of the British working class are bought off by capital with imperial profits is historically inaccurate and theoretically problematic; and he also points out that although Lenin recognized that imperialism develops capitalism and creates its own contradiction, he did not comprehend that it would be "pre-capitalist forces—intellectuals and peasants—rejuvenated by modern ideas [who] would provide most of the recruits to the cause of colonial revolt."[41]

Kiernan is not unappreciative of Lenin's contribution: "[His] theory developed into a penetrating commentary on capitalism in our century, its reckless pursuit of profit, its perilous ascendancy over governments and armies and men's minds." However, attending in part to the work of the non-Marxist economist Joseph Schumpeter, who argued that imperialism and war were products of aristocratic ambitions, not of businessmen and capitalism, Kiernan offers a historical criticism: "the imperialism of that day may seem the outcome less of capitalism's own inner structure, as it was then, than of a peculiar, unique amalgam in Europe and Japan of feudal-monarchical elements still strong and industrial capitalism young and ambitious but still unsure of itself, because only in two countries had its coming to power been inaugurated by the overthrow of an older regime."[42] Ever attentive to class conflict and experience in its totality *and* to the presentness of the past, Kiernan concludes his theoretical survey thus: "Modern imperialism has been an accretion of elements, not all of equal weight, that can be traced back through every epoch of history. Perhaps its ultimate causes, with those of war, are to be found less in tangible material wants than in the uneasy tensions of societies distorted by class division, with their reflection in distorted ideas in men's minds. Capitalism is at bottom a relationship among human beings, and no human relationship, or its consequences, can have the logic of geometry."[43]

According to Kiernan, Marxism needed to "broaden its perceptions by taking stock more fully of the diverse forces at work." Here, on the subject of imperialism, as on other historical questions, Kiernan contends that the arguments and ideas of the Italian Marxist Antonio Gramsci have most to offer to the reinvigoration of Marxian study and thought. He writes in "Antonio Gramsci and the Other Continents" (Chapter 7 of the present volume) that although Gramsci's "scattered commentaries do not point toward any distinct innovation in the theory of imperialism, . . . they contain ideas which could be made use of to enrich the Leninist thesis, clothing its bare economic bones with the flesh and blood of social activity, human thoughts and feelings."[44]

Perhaps because the site of his own intellectual career shifted from England out to India then back to England and up to Scotland, Kiernan appreciates the development of Gramsci's perspective not just as that of an Italian rather than a northwestern European but as that of a Sardinian rather than a northern Italian, which made him all the more concerned with both the "fact of domination [and] with the birth and growth of resistance to it." Moreover, although Gramsci believed "European civilization and culture superior to that of other peoples" (as does Kiernan—though Kiernan is quick to note that Gramsci's argument was historically specific to recent centuries and that he saw Europe's lead coming to an end in the not too distant future), the Sardinian-born Italian was equally convinced that all peoples have pasts worth studying, and he was vocally hostile to all theorizing about races and national destinies, believing such efforts to be absurd and dangerous. Kiernan goes on to consider how Gramsci's persistent concern about the unification of the agrarian south and industrial north of Italy in a semicolonial relationship compelled an interest in international studies and, in turn, makes Gramsci's writings worthy of attention by historians and social scientists today.[45]

In the past several years, Kiernan has often been invited to consider and address the *consequences* of imperialism and colonialism both for Europeans and for Africans and Asians—which has led him to say, as in "Europe and the World" (Chapter 4 in the present volume): "It may be reckoned to [Europeans] as a sign of grace that they have learned to be capable in some degree of self-criticism over their conduct; it is unlikely that Roman intruders, Chinese, Arabs, or Turks ever acquired this capacity, except over some odd particular outrage. But far louder today than any self-reproaches of Europe are recriminations from the countries that it annexed or meddled with." Kiernan's own assessments remain critically objective and his observations offer little comfort to either party. In *The Lords of Human Kind* he observes that "at some earlier points the meeting of Europe with other civilizations had been friendly and promising. . . . But for many reasons the meeting of minds between East and West was broken off, or petered out. [Aside from missionaries, who were regularly in close league with hostile European governments,] [m]ost other Westerners had no ideas to offer, and few goods that the East wanted, so that they were always tempted to take what they could by force."[46]

Yet he also observes that "it cannot be too surprising if Europeans sometimes felt that nothing they did to them could be worse than what these 'natives' did to one another." For example, however much his own writings attest to the brutality of conquest and the oppressiveness of colonialism, Kiernan feels compelled to state in the conclusion to *European Empires* that "even with the aid of machine-guns and high explosives, the total of deaths inflicted on Afro-Asia by Europe must have been trifling compared with the number inflicted on it by its own rulers. In Africa chiefly through wars, in Asia chiefly through crushing revolts."[47] Indeed, since Kiernan has consistently been attentive to the preexisting modes of class domination among *both* the colonizers and the colonized, he has necessarily recognized that "so many lands were under alien or semi-alien rule that the overthrow of thrones might be welcomed as the deliverance which Europeans professed to be bringing."[48] (It need hardly be said that remarks such as these are not intended to absolve Europeans of their colonial histories and atrocities.)

What about the longer-term, the so-called developmental consequences of European imperialism and colonialism? This is a question Kiernan himself asks, noting that "Western thinking has usually favoured the view that colonialism, despite much that is shameful in its record, rescued backward or stagnating societies by giving them better government, and transformed them by drawing them out of isolation into the currents of the world market and a world civilisation"; but, of course, as he is fully aware: "Each nation— feeling itself the strongest—has sought to impose its will on others, but to think of itself as their warden or rescuer."[49] His own answer is historical. First, he distinguishes between the early colonialism of Spain and Portugal— when Europe was still too little developed to have much to bestow—and the later northwestern European imperialisms following on the Industrial and American and French Revolutions. Then he considers the differing effects of these latter imperialisms on various Asian and African peoples, for clearly the impact of European expansion on, for example, India, China, and Japan was dramatically different from the earlier cases, and from country to country.[50] Nevertheless, allowing for significant historical and moral reservations, it appears that Kiernan does comprehend European imperialism and colonialism as having been "progressive," at least initially, in the "development" sense.

It is here that we encounter most directly a central characteristic of Kiernan's conception of history, one that links him closely with Marx and Engels. I am referring specifically to his sense of history as *tragedy*. He aims us toward it himself with reference to imperialism when he writes: "Conquest and occupation were grievous experiences; whatever beneficial results might ensue, the cure was at best a harsh one, like old-style surgery without anesthetics. Only in the light of their tragic vision of history could Marx and Engels contemplate conquest as sometimes a chapter of human progress." On another occasion, he asserts that there is a "somber contradiction at the heart of imperialism."[51] That is, if we subscribe to the assumption that economic development—or "modernization"—is preferable to the persistence of "preindustrial" social orders, then we are drawn inevitably to the historically "realistic" position that northwestern Europe's intrusions overseas were a required catalyst for change and development because it was the only region dynamic enough to accomplish it. In an essay entitled "Empires of Marx's Day," Kiernan further explains: "European expansion of their own time, [Marx and Engels] viewed in much the same light as they did capitalism inside Europe. Both were brutish and detestable, but necessary goads to progress for those who suffered them."[52] This was Marx and Engels's view, and thus they welcomed capitalism's revolutionary momentum; this is also Kiernan's view— up to a point. As he reminds us, though Marx and Engels had a tragic vision of the past, they were optimistic about the future and, indeed, too ready to separate the two, crediting capitalism with too much revolutionary determination; as a result, they failed to recognize the way in which it would compromise and incorporate precapitalist forces to accomplish its ends.

Kiernan, too, sees European imperialism as having been necessary to instigate change and, potentially, development, and yet, advantaged by history, he also recognizes—more so than Marx and Engels—how the tragedy was compounded. Not only did imperialism have the effect of reinforcing class power at home and abroad—this fact Marx and Engels had sadly realized— but, as Kiernan shows, it often helped to bring about the coalescence of bourgeois and aristocrat in Europe (thereby making a fatally important contribution to war and Fascism in the twentieth century) and the buttressing or calling into being of "parasitic ruling groups" in the colonies. Thus at the same time that Kiernan sees imperialism as having been progressive—at least to some extent—he also indicates how, in time, it was inevitably "deforming" to both colonizers and colonized. In the end he declares that the real contribution of European imperialism "was made less by imposing its rule on others than by teaching others how to resist it,"[53] referring both to the capitalist modernization from above of Japan and the ideologies and forces of nationalism and socialism in Asia and Africa, which, I would add, have generated their own dialectics of hope and tragedy.

An Outline of the Present Work

The chapters which follow these introductory remarks have been selected from a lengthy bibliography of Victor Kiernan's writings in international studies and world history treating modern imperialism and colonialism. The intention guiding their selection was to create a volume which was coherent in its problematic and, at the same time, fully revealing of Kiernan's diverse researches and reflections.[54] The articles chosen extend historically from the origins to the aftermath of Europe's overseas empires and thematically from political economy and development to culture and ideas; respectively and together they address past and persistent consequences of the imperial experience both for Europeans and for those they endeavored to conquer and to rule. These essays well attest to Kiernan's commitment to critical historical study and assessment. Ever conscious of the tragic, ironic, and paradoxical character of human history, and ever insistent that history command theory and polemics, Kiernan is undeniably Eurocentric—to be otherwise, he would rightly contend, is to foolishly deny Europe's pivotal role in the making of *world* history—but his arguments provide little succor to either Eurocentrists or Third Worldists.

These essays also attest to Kiernan's exceptional skills as a historical essayist, skills enhanced by his extensive reading in European and world history and literature and his long critical engagement with Marxian historical theory. Indeed, at a time when historians and their colleagues in the humanities and social sciences are anxious about their ability to speak to extraacademic audiences as public intellectuals, we would do well to attend as much to the form and style of Kernan's writings as to their content.

In Chapter 1, "Modern Capitalism and Its Shepherds," Kiernan provides a historical narrative of the development of world capitalism by way of the respective national capitalisms which have composed and recomposed it since it began to take shape in the sixteenth and seventeenth centuries in northwestern Europe. This essay joins together the British Marxist historians' problematic of the transition to capitalism and Kiernan's own respective interests in European nationalism, state formation, and imperialism. In contrast to conservatives who celebrate the "rise of the West" without reference to the dark side of that experience, but also in contrast to Third Worldists who see the making of the modern world in terms only of Europe vs. Africa, Asia, and the Americas, Kiernan's survey reminds us that the making of "Europe" itself entailed a process of class conflict and domination, militarism and war, conquest and multinational imperial states.[55]

Indeed, Kiernan shows, European imperialism(s) took shape *in Europe,* and Europeans brutalized—and were to continue to brutalize—each other at least as much as they were to brutalize others beyond their continent's frontiers. Moreover, contra the many myths of the national and popular origins of the modern polity, Kiernan's historical sociology records how "the 'nation-state' was built much more by the state than by the nation or people, and to a great extent the same is true of the economy." Thus, focusing on the historically specific *class* politics and structuration of the respective but connected processes of nation-state creation and economic and industrial transformation, Kiernan presents us with a parade of emergent and rising national capitalisms: English/British, French, German, Russian, American, Japanese. . . . And, in truly Kiernanesque fashion, the chapter closes not with answers or visions or with a new theory of imperialism but, in the face of the collapse of communism, the end of the Cold War, *and* a triumphant but crisis-torn capitalist world economy, with sober and pressing questions regarding the possibility of historical alternatives.

In Chapter 2, "Development, Imperialism, and Some Misconceptions," Kiernan takes up the issue of the relationship between imperialism and "Third World" economic development. In a certain way it represents Kiernan at his best, that is, regarding his insistence that history not defer to theory or politics, specifically, in this instance, to the radical intellectual politics of dependency theory as originally formulated by the economist Andre Gunder Frank (and later reformulated by Immanuel Wallerstein in the world-system model). In response to the claims of dependency theorists that European *development* and Third World *underdevelopment* are the two poles and consequences of a simple relationship and process of imperial exploitation, Kiernan considers three fundamental problems: the emergence of capitalism in northwestern Europe and not elsewhere, the Industrial Revolution in Britain and the significance of Empire profits, and the failure of other regions in the nineteenth century—except Japan—to develop.

On the making of capitalism, Kiernan fully accepts that it required an accumulation and concentration of resources but, distinguishing between Iberian overseas expansion and later northwestern European imperialism and, crucially, between mercantile and industrial capitalisms, he demonstrates how that fundamental accumulation began not in colonial transfers but in transfers from poor to rich in Europe itself and was put to developmental and transformative purposes not by Spanish and Portuguese seigneurs but by determined middle classes in England and the northwestern part of the Continent. (He warns, following Max Weber, that Marxists themselves must not discount culture, religion, and values.) He also reviews the possibilities of autonomous capitalist development in China, India, and Turkey and finds them lacking.

Kiernan then proceeds to the question of the role of imperial profits in the Industrial Revolution, pointing out that British industrial development was built on small capital investments, not imperial loot, though he adds that India was an important market for the production of British mills. Especially interesting is his observation that imperial India not only laid the basis for Indian nationhood, it also advanced British cohesion and national identity by unifying the northern millocracy and southern financiers and mercantilists. Nevertheless, Kiernan states, British imperialism eventually deterred Britain's own economic development and clearly inhibited Indian industrialization. Furthermore, whatever progress British rule brought, in time it deformed Indian social structure—a "parasitic empire . . . attracted to itself . . . [and strengthened] parasitic elements in colonial society." Indeed, Kiernan argues, as much as Asia needed "a shaking up" in order to develop, the problem of colonial rule is that it was "too long protracted."

Chapter 3, "Colonial Africa and Its Armies," is a study of a specific imperial practice, the recruitment of native African troops to serve in colonial forces. As Kiernan put it in *European Empires:* Why study colonial wars? Because they are still essentially taking place! Here, he surveys the manifold ways in which African troops were deployed in their own lands, in other colonies, *and* in Europe for the first but not the last time during World War I. Of course, as Kiernan notes, there was nothing historically original in this practice: "One of the prizes of empire has always been a supply of colonial soldiery, for use on the spot or elsewhere"—not to mention the centuries-long European tradition of hiring mercenary armies, which only really gave way to national conscription in the nineteenth century.[56]

An important factor enabling Europeans to initiate the recruitment of African soldiers was intertribal hostility, the impact of which on those hostilities was variable and mixed. The establishment of colonial armies significantly contributed to the breakup of "traditional life," for the men who were brought together and sent "abroad," like their European counterparts, returned with altered ideas about themselves and their world. At the same time, it is unclear if it intensified or reduced tribalism; though, as Kiernan indicates, it probably contributed to emerging nationalisms and aspirations for independence, that is, it likely instigated an awareness that "if we're good enough to fight, we're good enough to govern!" Still, Kiernan concludes, the armies Europeans "bequeathed to the new Africa . . . have been . . . more of a nuisance than an asset."

Chapter 4, "Europe and the World," and Chapter 5, "Imperialism and Revolution," address the balance sheet of imperialism and colonialism most directly. The dominant Western view has been that European colonialism liberated, modernized, and revolutionized Africa and Asia; the view of the former colonial peoples is that imperialism oppressed and exploited the colonized, creating "backwardness" and formidable barriers to progress. Therefore, while the former have been willing to grant "aid," the latter demand "restitution." Although Kiernan is unwilling to pursue a detailed accounting, he readily acknowledges that the balance sheet is heavily weighted against the former colonizers, but, he necessarily adds, not totally so. Here again, he states for the record that Europeans treated each other at least as badly as they did colonial peoples and, moreover, that African and Asian peoples were similarly antagonistic and violent toward their fellow continentals. Further, only a few Europeans were capable of transforming themselves—in processes which were neither easy nor kind!—and, all the more so in the African and Asian cases, "vested interests and conservative instincts . . . grew to be strong and immobilizing." As he observes, Western Europeans revolutionized themselves, Eastern Europeans were revolutionized from above by Westernizing rulers, and Africa and Asia were revolutionized "still more, from outside."

As Kiernan makes plain, however, the "civilizing mission" which Europeans proclaimed for themselves was marked by a most uneven record. Colonialism was undeniably parasitic and predatory (though, as he is quick to append, the benefits of imperialism to Europeans themselves were most unequally distributed by region and class). Moreover, its ugliest features were not restricted to Europeans' overseas colonial endeavors. The racism and violence of imperialism and colonialism "recoiled" and "barbarized" European life as well. Finally, regarding the issue of restitution, Kiernan wonders "how far back" such an accounting should go. . . . The point is, he explains, that the industrial capitalist powers no longer need to "squeeze" the Third World and thus that what is most urgently called for are changes to eliminate the "factors making for exploitation of other peoples."

Against the grain of the dominant historiography, Kiernan informs us that "a clear-cut antithesis of Europe and its neighbors has only emerged in recent times." In this vein, Chapter 6, "Europe in the Colonial Mirror," considers the problem of "European" identity and how it was shaped by the imperial and colonial experience. That is, how much did European expansion stimulate the long-present but, until recently, limited sense of a European "civilization"? Kiernan carefully observes that Europe has never been homogeneous but always driven by social and cultural contradictions and conflicts; indeed, he writes, "No civilization has been more deeply divided and self-contradictory than the one which invented democracy and fascism, parliament house and gas chamber." Nevertheless, commencing in the sixteenth century, a sense of European identity did begin to emerge out of the conquests of the Americas, for it was recognized that Europeans—however diverse and even antagonistic in relation to each other they were—did share customs and institutions. An especially interesting aspect of Kiernan's discussion of the connection between the imperial experience and European culture is his discussion of the development of the humanities and social science disciplines. He also discusses further the relationship between the Europeans "civilizing mission" and their religious commitments and how the former reinforced the latter back home in Europe. (Referring to Japan, Kiernan does not fail to note that imperialist "civilizing missions" were not unique to Europeans.)

In Chapter 7, "Antonio Gramsci and the Other Continents," Kiernan surveys the Italian Marxist's writings and outlines the contributions which Gramsci's ideas might make to Marxist studies of imperialism (see above). Finally, Chapter 8, "After Empire," stands somewhat apart from the previous chapters. In contrast to the other, far more scholarly, pieces in this volume, this essay is a work of social and cultural criticism in which a historian of imperialism with experience in Asia working with Indian radicals, and now long resident in Scotland, thinks aloud and honestly about Britain in the post-empire era. It is admittedly cranky in tone, but it asks important questions about the challenges of diversity and multiculturalism and it is equally critical and demanding of Britons and immigrants alike. Readers will be reminded by its apparent cultural elitism of Ortega y Gasset's *Rebellion of the Masses* (1929); however, in decided contrast to those of the Spanish philosopher, Kiernan's disparagement of mass culture and his aspirations for change are not conservative but revolutionary and radical-democratic.

Notes

1. The 1992 symposium organized by MARHO, the Radical Historians' Organization, is reproduced in the *Radical History Review*, no. 57 (Fall 1993): 4–97. On the Marxist theory of imperialism, see Anthony Brewer, *Marxist Theories of Imperialism: A Critical Survey* (London, 1990), and Charles A. Barone, *Marxist Thought on Imperialism: Survey and Critique* (New York, 1985).

2. Regarding the issue of reconsidering historical and social science models in international studies, see Nigel Harris, *The End of the Third World* (London, 1986) and *National Liberation* (London, 1990), and F. Cooper et al., *Confronting Historical Paradigms: Peasants, Labor, and the Capitalist World-System in Africa and Latin America* (Madison, Wis., 1993).

3. F. Fukuyama, *The End of History and the Last Man* (New York, 1992).

4. E. H. Carr, *The New Society* (London, 1951), 17–18.

5. C. Wright Mills, *The Sociological Imagination* (New York, 1959), 154.

6. J. H. Plumb, *The Death of the Past* (London, 1969); on the use and abuse of the past by the New Right, see Harvey J. Kaye, *The Powers of the Past* (London and Minneapolis, 1991). See also the special issue of the *New Internationalist*, no. 247 (September 1993), entitled "Myth and Memory: The Uses and Abuses of History."

7. For a recent example of such in the United States, see Jeane J. Kirkpatrick, *Dictatorships and Double Standards* (New York, 1982).

8. Edward W. Said, *Culture and Imperialism* (New York, 1993), 35.

9. Said, *Culture and Imperialism*, 5.

10. Said, *Culture and Imperialism*, xxiv, and E. W. Said "Intellectuals in the Post-Colonial World," *Salmagundi*, nos. 70–71 (Spring–Summer 1986): 45. But I should also note here two works which are critical of Said's intellectual politics: Aijaz Ahmad, *In Theory: Classes, Nations, Literatures* (London, 1992), esp. 159–220 (Chapter 5), and Kanan Makiya, *Cruelty and Silence: War, Tyranny, Uprising, and the Arab World* (New York, 1993), esp. 278–80, 317–20.

11. Said, *Culture and Imperialism*, 17.

12. Said, *Culture and Imperialism*, 60. For V. G. Kiernan's critical response to Said's provocative and pathbreaking work *Orientalism* (New York and London, 1977), see his review in the *Journal of Contemporary Asia* 9 (1979): 345–51. For examples of work on imperialism and British and American culture, respectively, see John M. Mackenzie, ed., *Imperialism and Popular Culture* (Manchester, 1986), and Amy Kaplan and Donald E. Pease, eds., *Cultures of United States Imperialism* (Durham, N.C., 1994). Also, in South Asian studies, see Ranajit Guha and Gayatri Chakravorty Spivak, eds., with a foreword by Edward Said, *Selected Subaltern Studies* (New York, 1988).

13. For a complete bibliography of Kiernan's writings to 1977, see the special issue of *New Edinburgh Review*, "History and Humanism," prepared in his honor, vol. 3809 (Summer–Autumn 1977): 77–79. Additionally, see the bibliographic references in my chapter "V. G. Kiernan, Seeing Things Historically," in H. J. Kaye, *The Education of Desire: Marxists and the Writing of History* (New York and London, 1992), 65–97. For a fuller sense of the diversity of Kiernan's work, see the two collections preceding the present volume: H. J. Kaye, ed., *History, Classes, and Nation-States: Selected Writings of V. G. Kiernan* (Oxford and New York, 1988) and *Poets, Politics, and the People: Essays by V. G. Kiernan* (London and New York, 1989).

14. E. J. Hobsbawm, "The Historians' Group of the Communist Party," in *Rebels and Their Causes*, ed. M. Cornforth (London, 1978), 24.

15. On this British socialist tradition and its members and practitioners, see Harvey J. Kaye, *The British Marxist Historians* (Oxford and New York, 1984) and *The Education of Desire*.

16. On the transition question, see M. Dobb, *Studies in the Development of Capitalism* (London, 1947); R. H. Hilton, ed., *The Transition from Feudalism to Capitalism* (London, 1976); and T. H. Aston and C. H. E. Philpin, eds., *The Brenner Debate* (Cambridge, 1985).

17. Barrington Moore, *Social Origins of Dictatorship and Democracy* (Boston, 1966), 522–23.

18. E. P. Thompson, *The Making of the English Working Class* (London, 1963), 12, and V. G. Kiernan, in a letter to H. J. Kaye, June 1988.

19. The biographical and historiographical discussions which follow are a revised and enlarged version of the first part of Chapter 3 of *The Education of Desire*, "V. G. Kiernan, Seeing Things Historically."

20. On Cornford, see Kiernan's "Recollections," in *John Cornford: A Memoir*, ed. P. Sloan (London, 1938), 116–24, and Peter Stansky and William Abrahams, *Journey to the Frontier: Two Roads to the Spanish Civil War* (1966; reprint, Stanford, 1994).

21. See Kiernan's essay "Herbert Norman's Cambridge," in *E. H. Norman: His Life and Scholarship*, ed. R. W. Bowen (Toronto, 1984), 25–45.

22. V. G. Kiernan, *British Diplomacy in China, 1880–1885* (Cambridge, 1939; reprinted with a new foreword, New York, 1970).

23. Ibid., "Foreword to the 1970 Edition." Among the later diplomatic history pieces he most enjoyed writing is "Diplomats in Exile," in *Studies in Diplomatic History*, ed. R. Hatton and M. S. Anderson (London, 1970).

24. V. G. Kiernan, *Metcalfe's Mission to Lahore, 1808–1809* (Lahore, 1943).

25. V. G. Kiernan, *The March of Time* (Lahore, 1946); *Castanets* (Lahore, 1941); and "Brockle" and "The Señorita," in *Longman's Miscellany* (Calcutta), nos. 3, 4 (1945 and 1946).

26. V. G. Kiernan, trans. and ed., *Poems from Iqbal* (Bombay, 1947; rev. ed., London, 1955), *Poems by Faiz* (New Delhi, 1958; rev. ed., London, 1971), and *From Volga to Ganga* (Bombay, 1947).

27. V. G. Kiernan, "The Communist Party and the Second World War—Some Reminiscences," in *South Asia* 10, no. 2 (December 1987): 61–73.

28. In addition to the writings on imperialism to be discussed below, I cannot fail to note Kiernan's books *The Duel in European History* (Oxford, 1989); *Tobacco: A History* (London, 1991), which he wrote in the wake of quitting smoking; and *Shakespeare, Poet and Citizen* (London, 1993), the first of two volumes on the great English playwright.

29. Hobsbawm, "The Historians' Group," 31, and Christopher Hill in conversation with H. J. Kaye in January 1987.

30. The British Marxist historians continued to work together on the independent journal that several of them had founded in 1952, *Past and Present*. The Historians' Group itself survived in severely scaled-down form until recently when it was reorganized as the Socialist History Society.

31. V. G. Kiernan, *The Revolution of 1854 in Spanish History* (Oxford, 1966).

32. V. G. Kiernan, *The Lords of Human Kind: Black Man, Yellow Man, and White Man in an Age of Empire* (1969; reprint, New York, 1986).

33. V. G. Kiernan, *European Empires from Conquest to Collapse, 1815–1960* (New York, 1982).

34. V. G. Kiernan, preface to *The Lords of Human Kind* (Harmondsworth, Penguin ed., 1971), xv.

35. Kiernan, *European Empires*, 52.

36. Kiernan, preface to *The Lords of Human Kind*, xxxix.

37. For examples of related articles, see V. G. Kiernan, "American Hegemony under Revision," in *The Socialist Register, 1974*, ed. R. Miliband and J. Saville (London,

1974), 302–30, and "Sunrise in the West: American Independence and Europe," *New Edinburgh Review* (1976): 25–37.

38. V. G. Kiernan, *America: The New Imperialism* (London, 1978; new preface, 1980), 1.

39. V. G. Kiernan, "Imperialism, American and European," in his *Marxism and Imperialism* (London, 1974), 130.

40. Kiernan, *Marxism and Imperialism*, viii.

41. Ibid., 38–54.

42. Ibid., 61. See also Joseph Schumpeter, *Imperialism and Social Classes* (1919 and 1927; English trans., New York, 1951).

43. Kiernan, *Marxism and Imperialism*, 67.

44. For Kiernan on Gramsci, see also his "Gramsci and Marxism," in Kaye, *History, Classes, and Nation-States*, 66–101, and "The Socialism of Antonio Gramsci," in *Essays on Socialist Humanism*, ed. K. Coates (Nottingham, 1972), 63–86.

45. On Gramsci and the Italian "southern question," see John A. Davis, ed., *Gramsci and Italy's Passive Revolution* (London, 1979). For discussions of applying "Gramsci" to the study of international relations, see Stephen Gill, ed., *Gramsci, Historical Materialism, and International Relations* (Cambridge, 1993).

46. Kiernan, *The Lords of Human Kind*, 17.

47. Kiernan, *European Empires*, 227.

48. V. G. Kiernan, "Imperialism and Revolution," Chapter 5 in the present volume.

49. V. G. Kiernan, "Tennyson, King Arthur, and Imperialism," in Kaye, *Poets, Politics, and the People*, 129–51.

50. V. G. Kiernan, "Development, Imperialism, and Some Misconceptions," Chapter 2 in the present volume.

51. V. G. Kiernan, "Europe and the World," Chapter 4 in the present volume.

52. V. G. Kiernan, "Empires of Marx's Day," in *A Dictionary of Marxist Thought*, ed. T. B. Bottomore (Oxford and Cambridge, Mass., 1983), 147–49.

53. V. G. Kiernan, "Imperialism and Revolution." See also A. Ahmad, "Marx on India—a Clarification," in his *In Theory*, Chapter 6, 221–41.

54. Note should be made of Kiernan's recent article "Languages and Conquerors," in *Language, Self, and Society*, ed. P. Burke and R. Porter (Oxford, 1991), 191–210.

55. See also V. G. Kiernan, "Why Was Early Modern Europe Always at War?" in *Violence and the Absolutist State*, ed. S. T. Christensen (Copenhagen, 1990), 17–46.

56. See Chapters 4, "Foreign Mercenaries and Absolute Monarchy," and 6, "Conscription and Society in Europe before the War of 1914–1918," in Kaye, *History, Classes, and Nation-States*.

1

MODERN CAPITALISM AND ITS SHEPHERDS

Merchant capital and usurer capital have been ubiquitous, but they have not by themselves brought about any decisive alteration of the world. It is industrial capital that has led to revolutionary change and been the highroad to a scientific technology that has transformed agriculture as well as industry, society as well as economy. Industrial capitalism peeped out here and there before the nineteenth century, but on any considerable scale it seems to have been rejected like an alien graft, as something too unnatural to spread far. It has been a strange aberration on the human path, an abrupt mutation. Forces outside economic life were needed to establish it; only very complex, exceptional conditions could engender, or keep alive, the entrepreneurial spirit. There have always been much easier ways of making money than long-term industrial investment, the hard grind of running a factory. J. P. Morgan preferred to sit in a back parlor on Wall Street smoking cigars and playing solitaire, while money flowed toward him. The English, first to discover the industrial high road, were soon deserting it for similar parlors in the City, or looking for byways, short cuts, and colonial Eldorados.

Wide variations within modern capitalism go with the fact that however much a novelty, it could only develop within molds shaped by the past. A very important one was feudalism, of the exceptional west-European kind, whose nearest relative was Japanese. Capitalism and feudalism were not mutually exclusive in their modes of thinking or feeling. A dominant class's ideology spreads downward, as Marx and Engels saw early; and the instincts of any class may be, like its religion, surprisingly flexible and adaptable. Laura Stevenson shows how Londoners of Shakespeare's day could look back on their city's great figures not so much as great businessmen but as merchant-princes, animated by the same nobility of character as any feudal magnates of their time.[1] Three centuries later American workmen took the proud title "Knights of Labour."

In most cases the "nation-state" was built much more by the state than by the nation or people, and to a great extent the same is true of its economy. It has been recognized that mercantilism was largely a translation into economic terms of the bureaucratic machinery set up by the "absolute monarchies." There must always have been mutual exchanges between the methods and techniques of the countinghouse or factory and those of officialdom. When full-grown, businessmen plumed themselves on their rugged independence and were all for laissez-faire, as they still are in America; but this only meant that they wanted no interference from government, while they did want government to come to their help whenever there was occasion. Manchester wanted cotton-textile production in British India curtailed, in order to restrict competition. Free enterprise has always been ready to accept gifts, and not quite in the spirit of Pooh-Bah pocketing bribes in order to mortify his excessive family pride. Much more reluctantly, businessmen had to learn to submit at times to a degree of regulation by the state for the sake of social peace.

From Agrarian to Industrial Capitalism

After several false starts, chiefly in Italy and the Netherlands, it was in England that the new mode of production eventually got going, and then by the roundabout route of agrarian capitalism, nowhere else adopted over a whole country. It was capitalism of a very bastard sort, working within a framework nearly as "feudal" as the serf-worked estates of eastern Europe. As there, state power was essential to get it going and police it, mainly in the period when a peasantry felt by its masters to have grown too independent, or *uppity,* was being degraded into a landless labor force available for hire. At that stage foreign mercenary troops might have to be brought in to crush resistance—a sidelight on the patriotism that Tudor Englishmen are always credited with. The system could then be comfortably run by the landlord, who rented his land to farmers, petty capitalists, and controlled the laborers on their behalf by his authority as justice of the peace or seigneur with a government licence. "His decree," a writer could still complain in the nine-teenth century, "so far as his labourers and cottage tenants are concerned, is as good as law."[2] In other countries by then, governments were coming forward to help in setting up industry; in Britain this was less necessary because centuries of capitalist agriculture had familiarized the use of wage labor and inured the masses to discipline. At the same time, however, they had consolidated the power and influence of the landed aristocracy to a point that would make it a heavy clog on later industrial development.

Inseparable from the rise of modern states were their standing armies and navies. While warfare was terribly destructive (but least so for England, which learned to fight all but its civil wars abroad), it could provide profitable opportunities for a good many. Northampton's staple trade of shoemaking got its start through orders for footwear for the parliamentary army in the civil war, and all hostilities for the next two centuries gave it a further fillip. Less of a mixed blessing than war was Europe's perpetual preparation for war. Armies generated ancillary activities from the building of forts to the sewing of uniforms. All these cost money, and the chief concern of the English political arena was deciding who should foot the bill. For a while, landowners found themselves paying more than they liked, but as statesmanship matured, things were better managed and most of the paying was transferred to the lower classes—an arrangement doing credit to the Age of Reason (and admirably described by John Brewer).[3]

Many parallels can be seen, moreover, between the running of a regiment and that of a factory, each on hierarchical lines and each with an often dehumanizing tendency to reduce the human being to one machine among others. Armies set an example which could encourage the transition from scattered "cottage industry" or "putting out," to labor gathered under the factory roof. Popular phrases like "captains of industry"—attributed to Thomas Carlyle—or "Napoleon of finance" show how analogies between military and capitalist organization caught men's eyes. Their standard routines, their practice of living by timetables, their need of concerted effort, might qualify an individual to be either a useful officer or a useful manager, a sergeant or a foreman.

It may be a mistake to suppose that economic advances of any dramatic kind have been favored by peaceful, humdrum conditions. In quiet times men collectively as well as individually have been prone to sink into dull repetition. Political upheavals, even disasters, have compelled them to improvise, to look for new ways. Modern wars have stimulated innovation, not so much through immediate military wants as by fostering an atmosphere of change and expectation.

Acceptance of industrialism required great shocks to the old order, disruptions painful to all societies in flux. What above all supplied Europe with the necessary earthquake was the span of years from 1789 to 1815, when a great revolution ushered in two decades of war. Neither political revolt nor battle by itself, but the two things working together, transformed Europe, or prepared its people's minds for the grand transformation.

The English State cannot be credited in any straightforward way with setting the Industrial Revolution in motion. On the contrary, mechanized industry once born could grow only slowly, partly at least because, as Ernest Gellner has observed, a rapid growth would have alarmed the reigning landlords.[4] In indirect ways, and in partnership with the mercantile interests, they had been creating many of the necessary conditions. This applies especially to the obsessive contest with France for West Indian islands and slave plantations. Most of the colonial products coming in were semiluxury items for mass consumption: coffee, tea, sugar, tobacco—all bad for health but good for business. A proportion could be sold on the Continent and bring wealth into Britain, part of which might find its way into investment; but the chief service these goods rendered to industry must have been to induce labor to work harder and more regularly in order to be able to buy them, and to suffer hardships more patiently because such tranquilizers were available. When Napoleon tried to close the Continent to colonial goods, because Britain had got control of all the sources of supply, he was flouting one of the strongest appetites of the age. Consolations from the New World had more appeal than those, also on offer, in the next world.

Discipline and Docility

Industrial revolution, the harnessing of machine power, was needed, above all perhaps, to teach the workman docility. In the opinion of many, English craftsmen had become in the eighteenth century too comfortably off, too expensive. It was assumed that Dutch exports prospered because Dutch labor was cheap. A pamphleteer of 1713 made the same complaint about France. "The *French* did always out-do us in Price of Labour: Their common People live upon Roots, Cabbage, and other Herbage; four of their large Provinces subsist entirely upon Chestnuts."[5] Ideal workers indeed, whom employers might hope to train to live entirely on cold water and fresh air. Traveling through France and Italy in 1766, Tobias Smollett contrasted the high living standard and high cost of English labor with foreign cheapness.[6] He saw no birds in southern France: they were all eaten. There is a convincing ring in the dictum of Andrew Ure, the philosopher of industry, that steam had to be called in to subdue the rebellious hand of labor. Some improvements in machinery were avowedly designed to overcome resistance to wage reductions. Like the peasants before them, the workers had to be brought to heel.

Confrontation meant that mill owners would often have to look to the authorities for active support. This was forthcoming, on the general principle that "the men are always wrong"; but a landlord government could not feel overeager to oblige the new millowning class which was drawing workers together in such multitudes. With no real police force on call before the 1830s, control might not be easy. Millowners were seldom men of a stamp that fox-hunting squires could find congenial. Industry was making its home in remote valleys in the north of England and southern Scotland; the resulting division of Britain has become permanent. A good part of the work force was still more alien. Labor was not very mobile, at least before the railways; most mill recruits moved only short distances. There was, however, a great exception: the reservoir of cheap labor represented by the Celtic regions of the British Isles—the same that supplied a large part of the manpower for the army which was building the empire. Poverty-stricken Irish peasants had learned to come to Britain for seasonal jobs on the land; to settle in the manufacturing towns was only another step. Their destitution was another sideways contribution to industrialization by the ruling class; rack-renting by Anglo-Irish landlords and the bloody reconquest of a rebel Ireland in the late 1790s were indeed indispensable components of the whole complex process. Lancashire was geographically well placed to draw labor from both Ireland and Wales; and the Glasgow area, similarly, from Ireland and the Highlands, crushed and disarmed after the "forty-five," and always poor, overcrowded, and landlord-ridden. But for England's possession of all these colonial regions within the British Isles, industry might have spread still more slowly, but also more evenly.

Between a stand-offish ruling class and a hostile working class, the pioneers of industry were uncomfortably situated. In the long run the relative failure of British industry to maintain its momentum must be ascribed in part at least, to a lack of energetic pushing and prodding by the state. Capitalism has never been a fully self-acting, self-propelling force. Its greatest windfall during the early stages was the long-drawn period of war, from 1793 to 1815, against first Revolutionary and then Napoleonic France. This brought the older and newer propertied classes closer together in the face of common enemies both abroad and at home. Patriotism could be invoked against opposition of any sort; labor unrest and political sedition could be bracketed, all the more because the struggle against Napoleon was economic as well as military, and industrial exports to new markets like South America had a vital part to play. With half a million men mobilized for the army and navy, there was armed force in plenty for repression. Men of all respectable classes were putting on uniform, joining the Yeomanry Corps that were forming everywhere. They were preparing to deal with Bonaparte if he made his threatened appearance, but standing ready also to put down "Riots and Tumults"—as the "Articles of Enrolment" of a corps raised at Doncaster pledged its members to do.

Capital accumulation was greatly speeded by the war profiteering of those years, even if only a minor part of the gains went into industry; they had an index in the ballooning of the National Debt—the indebtedness, that is, of taxpayers to those with plenty of money to lend the government. Even labor conditions must have felt some relief from the removal of so much manpower from the market, though rising prices had an opposite effect. It might be possible to trace the Luddite or machine-wrecking outbreaks toward the end of the era to improvements in machinery intended to make up for a shortage of hands. Analogies can be seen between this period and the "Eighty Years War" of Dutch independence from Spain, when Holland was being turned into a capitalist republic, with an influx of refugees from the southern Netherlands as a key factor.

After the return of peace, frictions developed between the two wings of property: mill owners were strong enough now to take the lead in a movement of the commercial middle classes at large against the power and privileges of the old order. They were demanding constitutional changes from which Toryism had been sheltered by its patriotic pose during the war. Both sides were satisfied by the compromise of 1832: parliamentary reform with the masses left out. On the economic front, Richard Cobden and his fellow mill owners led the agitation against the Corn Laws which impeded food imports and kept landlord rents and costs of living high. They were not done away with until 1846.

Meanwhile a stream of official inquiries and reports on factory conditions—much admired by Marx—and legislation arising from them, were viewed by mill owners as a reprisal for their attacks on the ruling class. In part they may have been so, and certainly they imposed restraints on factory owners such as landowners did not dream of imposing on themselves. All the same, they were helpful, not harmful, to industrial peace and progress. Without some paternalistic regulation the work force might have revolted, or withered away. With it, public opinion could come round to a more favorable view of industrial growth and the jobs it provided, as an antidote to social discontent instead of an irritant. In 1848 the first volume of Macaulay's *History* could draw a heartwarming picture of national prosperity.

The Rise of Modern Nationalism

As in other countries later, railway building and the rush to invest in it signaled the first full involvement of the propertied classes in industrial expansion; but the collapse late in 1845 of the "railway mania" showed what lack of central planning could lead to. It might have been expected that the government would take more interest, if only from a strategic point of view. All railways were "strategic" in the sense of being a potential addition to the forces of law and order. An engraving of 1835 shows a train on the newly opened Birmingham-Liverpool line, two of its wagons full of soldiers.[7] Wellington, however, the panjandrum of Tory wisdom, was too far behind the times to care about the iron horse; construction was left to private planning, and was consequently ill-planned and wasteful. Later in the century, ownership and control were drifting away from the industrial bourgeoisie into the hands of City men.

When Chartism faded away after 1848 the "millocracy" enjoyed a thirty-year spell of complacent confidence, summed up in the adage "What Manchester thinks today, England will think tomorrow." Steam would solve all problems—all that was necessary was for its ministers, the manufacturers, to be given a free hand. So far were laissez-faire attitudes pushed that they almost implied a withering away of the state, like the one Marx preached from his different pulpit. It may be that every class that is conscious of marching in the vanguard of progress has a feeling that government has become irrelevant: it needs no artificial prop and is sure that everyone must admire it and trust to its leadership. Even so, this was not the full, authentic bourgeois philosophy expounded by John Bright and Cobden; it could not be, because capital and labor were too far apart, capital too isolated. Patriotic drumbanging was the easiest way to bring them together now and then, and in 1854–56 mill owners and workers joined hands, to the disgust of Bright and Cobden, in applauding the Crimean War, although what it was being fought for nobody could tell. In the next year, the Indian Mutiny set off an even louder outburst of hysteria. Whitehall policies were succeeding in drawing the country together, at the cost of denaturing both sides of the industrial society.

In another way, too, the imperialist strategies of the past and present, by creating colonies around the globe, and the old colonies now the United States, made it easy—and steamships made it easier—for disgruntled or ambitious workers to emigrate to better homes. Britain was losing men and women of varied talents and skills, whose energy might have helped to keep its industry moving. Still more, it was losing much of the dynamic of struggle between labor and capital, which might have compelled the government to take a more active and stimulating hand in the economy.

Scots, further removed from the blighting air of Lombard Street, showed more readiness than Englishmen for the advance from light to heavy industry. Steamship building gave plenty of opportunity; a new ironclad navy had to be built; there was a lucrative world market for warships and armaments. But from the 1880s, there was stiffening competition from the newly industrializing countries, and Britain, in default of wholesome guidance from the state, proved unequal to the effort of modernizing its methods and holding on to its technological lead. Instead it chose the easier path of trailing behind the aristocracy—of the shires and the share-jobbers—whose eyes were increasingly fixed on the empire and its allied lures. More and more capital was being exported. British banks, unlike German banks, had little inclination to invest in manufacturing: for one reason, because so many merchant bankers were foreign immigrants with hardly any connection with Britain outside the square mile of the City. When Gladstone proposed Home Rule for Ireland in 1886 and most of the wealthier Liberals left the Party and joined the Tories, it was not only a political shift taking place but an accompaniment of the social-economic shift from manufacture to finance.

Everywhere, industry brought fresh social tensions. To conservatives the factory proletariat looked outlandish and fearsome, a Caliban monster, or (as was often said) like the barbarian invaders of Rome coming back to destroy civilization again. Yet it could not fail to be noticed that Britain, with more factories than any other countries, survived the fateful year 1848 with less disturbance than nearly all of them. The rebel workers of June in Paris were mostly artisans, flocking to the barricades from small workshops, not big mills. One cause of unrest in many regions was unemployment, and industrial expansion could be looked to as a means of lessening this.

Moreover, the French Revolution and Napoleon between them had set modern nationalism ablaze. There had been older forms of patriotism, not in Europe alone; but it may be true, as orthodox Marxism has said, that neither the modern version nor industrial capitalism could blossom without each entwining itself round the other. To be kept at the proper temperature, nationalism needed occasional wars, and nothing less could suffice to divert the fevers of 1848 into a more commendable channel. Louis Bonaparte's coup of December 1858, wrote Engels, looking back on it long after, "secured for Europe the assurance of domestic tranquillity, in order to give it the blessing of a new era of wars."[8] Sure enough, a series of European conflicts followed, with Bonaparte (now Napoleon III) leading the way, and Bismarck coming out on top. Their scrimmages made it very clear that without a modern industry no country could now be well prepared for fighting; it behooved governments therefore to make sure that industry flourished.

Quite apart from this, there was a feeling among the educated classes everywhere that without the up-to-date furnishings and style of living made possible by manufactures and advertised by the Crystal Palace, a country must be regarded as backward. Spain was looked down on by foreigners, and by traveled Spaniards, and sometimes dubbed "the China of Europe." This was not for want of "strong government." There was a conscript army quite big enough to keep the working class in what was called "order," and there was no shortage of dictators, all of them from the army. There was also tariff protection, not entirely nullified by British possession of that grand smuggling depot, Gibraltar. But assets like these have never been enough by themselves. What was lacking was a government and civil service with some intelligent training and a bourgeoisie eager to show what it could do. Liberal governments debauched their supporters, the moneyed middle classes, by selling off public lands at knockdown prices; the most energetic businessmen were foreigners, like the Britons who set up the first factory at Malaga.

Liberalism, the creed of the European bourgeoisie, was always full of inconsistencies and often unstable under trial. To a great extent it was displaced by nationalism, at a time, too, when the latter was taking on a more aggressive character, and industry in most countries was closely tied to the state by tariffs, subsidies, government orders. In Britain the shift could be seen in the schism over Ireland, when so many Liberals became "Liberal Unionists." In Germany after the unification, most Liberals turned into "National Liberals." Except among peoples still struggling for independence, patriotism was quickly preempted by right-wing parties and interests; but changes in class attitudes were not all on one side. In Germany the bourgeoisie might undergo "a certain process of feudalization,"[9] but blue blood was more than ready to take a share of the profits piled up by "chimney barons."

Militarism and Order

Underlying their newfound fraternity was the perennial need to keep the working class, badly infected now with socialism, under control, and for this purpose no one could be better relied upon than Bismarck and his victorious generals. The sword had become inseparable from bourgeois society, Karl Liebknecht, the German socialist, wrote. "Capitalism and its mighty servant militarism by no means love each other," but each accepted the necessity of the other.[10] Liebknecht's book on the European military plague, which got him into prison in 1907 on a treason charge, showed very clearly how the armies and their propaganda served to bolster industrialism and see it safely through its difficult opening decades, by combatting socialism, helping to break strikes, and so on, even though none of them overtly held political power in that epoch. One special need for their services was that industry was sometimes growing most quickly in national-minority regions, like Catalonia and Russian Poland, where labor discontent was compounded by nationalist feeling. Another was that capital and technology often had to be solicited from abroad; and foreign investors required, as they did in their colonies, firm maintenance of "order."

Between constitutional and economic progress, it has been pointed out, there might be very little correspondence. Tom Nairn observes that from 1870 to 1914 the Hapsburg empire had a much better growth rate than Britain.[11] Francis Joseph, its ruler for more than half a century, never showed himself in public except in uniform, as though to emphasize that this was an empire founded on conquest, and that its cosmopolitan regiments were the army of the Hapsburg dynasty. His ally William II, meeting the American special envoy Colonel House in 1914, on the brink of the war, was indignant at any thought of Germany's sacred *Militarismus* being tampered with. His middle-class subjects acquiesced, often with nervous qualms, in the archaic government they lived under, out of fear of socialism. Two crushing defeats in war were to be the penalty for kowtowing to Kaiser and Fuehrer.

The crucial part was played on the Continent by conscription. Formerly, liability to service had been selective; in the years before 1914 it became, in principle if not entirely in fact, universal. Army discipline, drilling, bullying, indoctrination, could be counted on to turn out not only obedient soldiers but docile workers; employers in Germany showed a distinct preference for men who had been through their spell of service. Conscription helped them to defy the menace of socialism. In France it was often made use of to end strikes, since workmen could at any time be declared soldiers, and brought under martial law. Altogether, industrial capitalism was developing oppositely from what the "Manchester School" had hoped for and taking on a dangerous slant toward authoritarian and sabre-rattling habits.

In France under the old monarchy the bourgeoisie had been accustomed to paternalistic treatment. The revolution it was jostled into—rather than leading—in 1789 left it floundering, fearful of the mass excitements that had been unchained, and ready to let Napoleon take charge. He took a firm line with the workers and was never so popular with them as with the middle classes and the better-off peasants. He claimed (he was not a man to trouble himself about exact truth) to be the creator of French industry. He did foster it, with subsidies and prizes for manufacturers, whom he provided with a spacious European market under French occupation and free of British competition. Desire to overcome Britain by economic means intensified his ambition to dominate all Europe. Marx sometimes thought of Napoleon, with his excessive addiction to war, as the evil genius, not the good angel, of French industry. He left it in 1815 in a mood of depression, and for a quite long period growth was sluggish. Fear of the working class must have been one reason. Memories of recent revolution made the labor movement more political, and its revolts more violent, than in Britain, above all in 1848 and 1871.

The 1830 revolution ushered in the reign of a narrow financial oligarchy; 1848 brought the industrial bourgeoisie to the front, but in a very nervous mood after the workers' revolt in June. Napoleon III came to power by guaranteeing not only to protect property but to bring about social peace through economic expansion, as promised in the *Idées napoléoniennes,* written in exile. He was a ruler of a new species, one who had seen the world and hobnobbed with men of ideas. "Industry and trade," Marx wrote not long after the coup d'état, "hence the business affairs of the middle class, are to prosper in hothouse fashion under the strong government."[12] Like his uncle, Napoleon did give industry a push forward, this time with railway building in the lead. Corruption was rampant, but bribery under some name or other has nearly always shown itself useful for lubricating relations between politics and economics. More serious, he had to balance and maneuver among contradictory pressures, his fumbling foreign policies led to one war after another— he could not be a Napoleon without proving that he could win battles—and the industrial boom ran down.

Defeat by Germany in 1870 brought to light a class antagonism still more extreme than in 1848. A massacre of Paris workers inaugurated the Third Republic, and its interventions in favor of capital were often highly arbitrary. Bourgeois power and capitalist profits were cushioned by national hatred of Germany; many workers rejected socialism as a German idea. Politicians preached a war of revenge, and it was obvious now, as it had not been after 1815, that for France to reestablish its position in Europe industrial strength was a necessity, especially with German production so expansive. Manufacturers wanting tariff protection had a simple case to argue. Beyond the Rhine the argument was readily duplicated.

Germany's National Capitalism

Germany, despite the lateness of its national unification, had a background of orderly, regular life, a model of bureaucratic administration known as cameralism, pedantic but thorough and conscientious, very unlike the loafing amateurism of Whitehall. An old German principality was very much like a big landlord's estate; in Brandenburg, the original Hohenzollern territory, a considerable part of the land was the reigning family's property. In Brandenburg-Prussia the army and its separate treasury had been the nucleus of the state and of something like a planned economy. Frederick the Great (1740–86) gave it a further dimension by fostering a commercial class; immigrants were invited to settle, and Huguenots flocking to Berlin made it for a time a town more French than German.

In 1815 the Rhineland provinces annexed by Revolutionary France were handed over to Prussia. They did not relish this; and some part of the industrial energy they displayed in the following years may be seen as an attempt to strike out on a line of their own, since under Prussian sway they could have no political life. All over Germany middle-class liberals wanted national unification, but not in the way it came about in the 1860s, through Prussian conquest. They then had to make the best of the Bismarckian dispensation. Capitalism here, by contrast with free-trade England, was *national* capitalism (at one time it would be known as "National Socialism"). A late starter, with resentful neighbors, Germany had to industrialize without delay. Powerful cartels strengthened competitiveness in foreign markets; they could also augment business influence over a non bourgeois government. There had been no call for this in laissez-faire Britain, where industry remained small-scale and decentralized.

German business might have to fawn on the "All-Highest" state and its Hohenzollern embodiment; in return the government well understood its duties toward capitalism, and more readily because, like other royalties, the Hohenzollerns had very large private investments of their own. Bismarck's alliance with Austria against Russia was a diplomatic revolution, but a more prophetic one was his training of the diplomatic service to push German sales in markets all over the world. Aristocratic English ambassadors thought this undignified; they, like others, had to follow suit, but they did so grudgingly. Class influences in Germany ran in both directions. Industrialists may have owed some of their energy, initiative, ruthlessness to the same qualities in the Prussian military caste which they were learning to admire; and the latter's ambition of dominating Europe must have fed thoughts of a parallel economic sovereignty. All economic trends are conditioned by prevailing collective moods, and the surging tide of German production was the outcome, as well as part of the cause, of a post-1870 atmosphere of triumphant self-assertion.

Capitalist as well as philosopher or soldier could feel the glow of the Nietz-schean Will-to-Power.

Prevailing moods could affect the working class as well. Industrialization created strains and imposed sacrifices, which could be muffled by the rhetoric of duty to the Fatherland. But there were some benefits too for the workers. As Marx and Engels saw, hitherto imports from Britain, undercutting handicraft products, had been spawning a "latent proletariat."[13] Now there were jobs, ill-paid as they might be, for millions who had had little choice but to go hungry or to emigrate. Bismarck, moreover, followed Napoleon III in appreciating the value of conciliation, and his program of social insurance, meager as it was (like Lloyd George's later imitation), could do something to blunt the socialist attack.

More insidiously, notions formed in the long feudal-absolutist era could find entry into working-class as well as middle-class minds. Industrial revolution was coming suddenly and swiftly, and men's thinking could not alter at the same pace. Habits of fidelity to a prince, looking up to a landowner, could make loyalty to an employer or an emperor a sort of instinct. (It seems that many Germans from a working class exposed to socialist or communist teaching for two generations took quite seriously their compulsory army oath of loyalty to Hitler and felt bound by it.) Before 1914 Liebknecht was convinced that military men were planning for the great day when the workers would revolt and the army could shoot them down, and they were hoping it would come soon, before socialism grew too strong.[14] But he pointed out that direct army meddling in industrial disputes was less frequent in Germany than in almost any other country.[15] It was not needed; their handling could be left to the police.

Russia, the United States, and Japan

In Russia, czarist rule had begun in close association with the rich mer-chantry of Moscow; in the eighteenth century, mining and iron working were state enterprises, often making use of serf labor. Nascent private industry received official encouragement. One cause of the breach between Alexander I and Napoleon in 1812 was the cotton mills wanting freedom to import their raw material, in defiance of the Continental System and its ban on colonial imports. In the modernizing era after the disasters of the Crimean War, when serfs were set free and the army was remodeled, the importance of railways and industry was obvious. They could not be developed without massive state support; it was often government that raised loans abroad and funneled capital into industrial enterprises. In that country, always simmering with discontents, where peasants left their villages to work in factories with their minds already infected, army and police vigilance was as necessary as capital to keep the wheels turning. But it could not make up for a social disharmony so extreme. Isaac Deutscher was one of those who have doubted whether industry could really have got going, on the lines it was following before 1914.[16] Management of foreign policy by Nicholas II was even more irresponsible than by his cousin William II. His private interest in a timber speculation on the Korean border was a contributory cause of the war of 1904–5 with Japan, leading to defeat and revolution.

The USA began life with a ready-made bourgeoisie and energetic money-making habits, no aristocracy to hide behind, and no need of government tutelage. Businessmen and politicians had close links, but different from the kind that existed in Europe. There was no social gulf between them, no incompatibility of values. Distance from Europe made diplomatic or military affairs as a rule very secondary; this and a federal constitution allowed the central government to remain in the background. Much official routine was left to the states, with whose pliable legislatures an enterprising man with dollars could usually reach agreement. Approaches to Washington were little required except for such purposes as obtaining tariff protection, or grants of public lands to railways and other undertakings, and for occasional adventures like the wars with Mexico in 1845 and Spain in 1898.

Southern slavery and cheap cotton lent aid to capitalist development from outside its own sphere. When the South wanted independence, the North, rather than lose its resources, embarked on the most serious armed conflict in American history: the Civil War of 1861–65. It gave a great stimulus to industrial growth and profits, and from then on the USA was launched on the pursuit of economic supremacy. This could be an object of national pride, as well as a promise of prosperity for all, and, like the plunge into imperialism in 1898, do something to reunite the war-torn country. An enormous territory awaiting occupation and development, or plundering, meant that industry did not need big orders for armaments. Nor was any heavy coercive apparatus needed to bridle the work force. Acute discontent would not easily gather, because Americans, like Europeans, were free to emigrate westward. When an industrial proletariat appeared, much of it was foreign-born and fairly simply controlled by the expedient—adopted, for instance, at Buffalo—of putting police officers from one ethnic group in charge of districts where other communities lived. Often the task could be left to private enterprise, in the shape of Pinkerton men, a mercenary force armed with rifles and revolvers. In reserve was the national guard of each state, the middle classes in arms, ready at need to enforce a dictatorship of the bourgeoisie. Instead of the welfare strategy toward which Europe was taking tentative steps, America was moving toward the high-wage policy pioneered by Henry Ford; it broadened the home market and allowed it to absorb some of the surplus production that was causing uneasiness after 1900.

It is a tribute to the protean versatility of capitalism that in the decade when America after the Civil War was starting its dizzy flight, Japan, its antithesis, was beginning to look in the same direction. Japan was to be the only grand success in the field outside Europe, and one on completely different lines. Marx speculated about whether Russia might make a leap from the "primitive communism" of the village *mir* to modern socialism; Japan proved that there could be a jump from feudalism to capitalism. No doubt merchant capital and town life had matured considerably during the two and a half centuries of the Shogunate, the hegemony of the Tokugawa clan lords; so much so that by the middle of the nineteenth century Japan's insistence on strict isolation was coming under question.

Gradual awakening from medieval dreams was suddenly hastened by the danger of the country being reduced to a colony of one of the Western empires. Whether it was a good thing for itself or the world that Japan was able to avoid this fate is a question that does not easily answer itself. What happened was the termination of the old feudal order, not in a revolutionary way but by a merging of elements ready for change within aristocracy and merchantry and their adoption of a program of equipping the country with modern technology, first and foremost for military purposes. Light industry could be left to merchants; heavy industry was initiated by the state and then entrusted to private hands, which may have been, as alleged, more competent.

So arduous an endeavor could not but impose painful ordeals and sacrifices. To mobilize national energies behind an autocratic, though populist, leadership, the old imperial dynasty, pushed into obscurity by the Shoguns, was brought out and brushed up. An artificial cult of Mikado-worship was grafted on to the old native Shinto religion, and everything the new regime did could be presented as the will of a divine emperor. Along with it, the Bushido code of samurai chivalry was broadened into a national creed, just when the samurai were being dispersed and, as a class, disappearing. Even in older times it could make a strong impression on plebeians, like the gentry code of honor in Europe. In the eighteenth-century play *Chushingura* (very popular ever since it was written) about a band of retainers pledged to revenge their dead lord, the heroes are fitted out with arms by a well-to-do businessman who admires their knightly dedication.[17] Now all Japanese could share it and fancy themselves paladins. There were many in Europe too (Fabian socialists among them) in the years before 1914 who thought highly of Bushido as a wholesome diet for a virile people. Obsessive veneration for the past found another expression in the institution of the Genro, or council of Elder Statesmen, repositories of the nation's deepest wisdom.

Thus Japan was setting out on the road to material progress with a mentality far more atavistic than any in the West and with a heavy-handed police to safeguard the public against any germs of "dangerous thoughts." Progress and retrogression went together; Japan's economic success, combined (down to 1945) with abysmal moral failure, may suggest that the ability to mass-produce commodities and sell them does not rank among mankind's higher attributes, any more than does the capacity for mass destruction. Rationality could not be allowed to open its eyes among the masses, for whom a better life could be only a distant hope. Conscription was a new burden added to older ones. Peasants and factory workers, a good proportion of them women shut up in barracks, were under stern discipline, though with an admixture of feudal paternalism. Emigration, the European worker's escape route, was scarcely possible here. Imperialism, seizure of colonies, was an alternative to be taken up all the more urgently, along with cultivation of extreme militarism and racialism.

The Arms Race

As 1914 approached, the capitalist world—Europe loudest—resounded with clamor about wicked foreigners. The workman had to be convinced that his real foe was not his employer but the enemy outside who was trying to ruin the country by unfair competition and in the end by armed force. Britain would use its navy to blockade Germany; Germany would use its army to seize French and Belgian ports; and so on. Politicians, journalists, economists, bishops, swelled the chorus. Norman Angell wrote his famous book *The Great Illusion* in 1910 in an attempt to dispel this hysteria, but in vain. In some ways it was he himself who suffered from illusions. He was at bottom an old-fashioned Cobdenite, good at exposing economic fallacies, but taking capitalism for granted as the norm of human existence, and astonished—as Cobden and Bright had been—that it could not behave more rationally.

Apart from political motives, capitalism had discovered by now that the quickest way to the biggest profits was making and selling armaments, a more and more important sector of the European economy and the one where bribery could be most useful. Sir Bazil Zaharoff's career was only one lurid illustration of this. The arms race had some dividends for workers too. No more devoted work force could be found than at the Krupps factory, where the Kaiser was fond of delivering histrionic speeches. Business and politics were converging realms. Any explosion like the delirium of 1914 would be caused not by either of them independently but by the two combustibles getting too close.

In 1885 Engels predicted that when the next European upheaval came "the saviour of society from the communist worker" would be the party of "petty-bourgeois democracy."[18] He might have been prophesying Nazism. In Italy and Germany after 1918 capitalism was in peril because the Italian army had been discredited, the German defeated and its monarchy swept away—and ten years later German industry was paralyzed by the Slump. Mussolini and Hitler came to the rescue by organizing paramilitary movements of the lower middle classes and putting them at the service of the state, which was thus enabled to continue its old role as an institution standing ostensibly—and in part really—outside the economic sphere. In France during the Slump years the right wing lacked sufficient unity and strength for a similar solution to be feasible; it found a substitute by welcoming Nazi occupation. Only a few turns of the screw were needed for the Japanese officer corps and ultranationalist societies to erect a native version of fascism and set about the conquest of China. By such reckless adventurism—akin to what was always the crying fault of their predecessors, the absolute monarchs—the dictators brought capitalism to the verge of another and final collapse. But by then another preserver was at hand, the USA.

With the American eagle spreading its wings over an exhausted brood in Europe and Japan, each of these tried one method or another of helping itself back to economic health and social conservatism. France had striking success with a form of *économie dirigée*, presided over by the government's technical experts. Britain's civil service has no equivalents, and a half-hearted experiment in state capitalism has given way to public properties of all sorts being sold off cheap and a return to an antiquated kind of free enterprise. Enterprise has been shown chiefly in takeover bids and asset stripping; a good part of manufacturing industry has used its freedom to lie down and die. There is a symbolic touch in the fact that "undertaker," which formerly meant an entrepreneur, now in Britain means only what Americans call a mortician. As of old, the country is exporting capital instead of investing it at home. Lately Italy, once limping far behind in the industrial race, has claimed to have overtaken Britain. It seemed to Gramsci that fascism might at least do Italy some good by galvanizing the lagging economy, that it might turn out indeed to be a distorted form of bourgeois revolution.[19] At any rate Italy shared the experience of fascism with Germany and Japan, today the two most flourishing of all economies—before 1945 the two most thoroughly militarized and disciplined—in not much earlier days among the most rootedly feudal.

Postwar Recovery

Neither Germany nor Japan, by contrast, has based its recovery on arms production, as France and Britain, following the baleful example of their patron, America, have to a great extent been trying to do. Here is a strange reversal of beliefs held until not many years before the Second World War—by Neville Chamberlain, for example, in spite of his Birmingham background—according to which armaments were an economic burden and too many of them would mean inflation and unrest.[20] Today part of the game is to sell as many guns as possible abroad, with the welcome help of the quarrels that plague so much of the world. Nazi rearmament, coinciding with, if not causing, Germany's economic recovery in the 1930s, may have changed many minds; still more, the spectacle of the unbounded profiteering that American arms manufacturers have been licensed to indulge in. A prisoner of its own Cold War propaganda, the Pentagon was a captive customer. Easy profits for some may be enfeebling for the rest of an economy; realization has been dawning that preoccupation with weapons and their secrecies is liable to sterilize a good deal of technical inventiveness as well as other resources. This and the concomitant strategy of worldwide bases and garrisons, and lavish aid to allies or puppets, have overstrained the giant and wiped out an enormous surplus of American investment abroad. Everyone has of course long since forgotten the recommendation of the Peace Conference of 1919—one of its few wise thoughts—that there should be no private manufacture of arms.

Japan's success since 1945 has been phenomenal: American economists agree with most others that somehow Japanese capitalism has devised a structure and conjured up a mentality that have lifted it above the American level, just as America and Germany reached a higher level than the British. This has been achieved without military rule, and without heavy reliance on arms production, but not without a good deal of *dirigisme*, state planning and guiding: Japan has not shared the delusive Anglo-American faith in the private enterprise of multinational corporations. At the outset, there was an American army of occupation to rule out any challenge from the Left; and Cold War exigencies have compelled the USA and its clients to admit a one-way flood of Japanese exports, to the undermining of their own manufactures.

Japan may have renounced war, under the shock of the 1945 bombs, but the emotional patterning of a warlike past has left deep traces. A company has a permanent following of employees, a substitute for the old feudal clan, who meet daily to sing a hymn in its praise. Young executives have been sent to army training schools for brief intensive courses in whatever can inculcate "total submission to the group," "mindless harmony of working life."[21] There are civil schools too, where budding managers are tuned up to a proper pitch of resolution by gymnastics or contortions and wild chanting.[22] They may look like tribesmen performing war dances, but—presumably because their profession is at bottom a primitive affair—the self-hypnotizing works. How long it would take to turn these young men back into soldiers like their fathers may be another question. Clearly there is no longer need of policemen to curb deviant thinking. Former thought control has been internalized: uniformity of belief is sucked in with every breath. Something of the same kind has been visible in the USA too; it may be called the capitalist conception of freedom. In a way it may be more mind-crippling than what went before in Japan. "There will be freedom while there is life," a novelist wrote in his wartime diary; the authorities silenced people, but did not compel them to speak.[23]

In Europe bourgeois revolution petered out in failure, but the bourgeoisie was set at liberty to fulfill its material ambitions, under the aegis of an ancien régime whose fear of socialism is shared. In somewhat the same fashion, decolonization after 1945 meant that Third World countries often failed to win complete independence but could achieve progress, if lopsidedly, through community of interests between their dominant groups and Western capital eager both to profit from cheap labor and to prevent any drifting into the Communist camp. This has been strikingly the case in Far Eastern areas where the World War left America's forces in occupation. America's preference, already formed by trial and error in the Philippines, was for indirect control, instead of annexation, through local "leaders" and armies and police forces with American equipment and training.

Free Enterprise and Dictatorship

What may be called "military capitalism" had always played a part in the industrial evolution of Europe and was now to show itself fully fledged in the most buoyant Third World economies, headed by South Korea. As in Japan under American occupation, in Korea and Taiwan there was a measure of agrarian reform, or social modernization, to clear the way for effective deployment of Western capital and technology. Their peoples had always had lively commercial traditions. Both had been Japanese colonies, habituated to the sternest discipline, sternest of all during the Second World War when some Koreans had been zealous collaborators. In Hong Kong and Singapore, business aptitudes frustrated in their native China were free to blossom in emigration. Korea had also, like Vietnam and unlike most Asian (especially Muslim) countries, a very old national consciousness, which could be harnessed now to economic development. For political reasons too, South Korea's rulers and their American backers had to keep ahead of North Korea and those of Taiwan to compete with Communist China. The outcome proves that men and women can be got to work usefully under police rule, a fact that may have some relevance to debates about the productivity of serf labor in eastern Europe or slave labor in the Americas, both sometimes made use of in industry and both lasting into the nineteenth century. Rousseau was not romancing when he wrote, "Man is born free, and everywhere he is in chains."

In South Korea power was seized in 1961 by Major General Park. As S. E. Finer points out, he "represented" no more than 3,600 soldiers, out of an army of 600,000, and the local American commander briefly declined to recognize him;[24] but Washington had only the blandest smiles, and he was free to play the despot until his murder in 1979. An understudy carried on; not until 1989 could mass protests, with a student vanguard and workers joining in, bring about some change. Away from the Far East too, and in Europe as well as other continents, America has been hand in glove with dictators, mostly military men. Among them have been some of the most vicious brutes known to history, from General Franco to General Pinochet. Britons love a lord, it used to be said, and American politicians love a dictator, so long as he has sound views on free enterprise. A uniform, with epaulettes and metals, lends him a reassuringly familiar look, whatever the color of his skin. Armies have always felt like a separate estate of the realm, as in Germany before 1918 or Japan before 1945 they actually were. In Latin America, with the church no longer sound, and a medley of races and social strata only imperfectly transformed into modern classes, and often no identifiable leading class, it has come naturally to armies to usurp this position, and for property and Washington to rally around them.

Autocrats with any up-to-date pretensions have felt it incumbent on them to show themselves on the side of economic progress. In Pakistan, General Ayub made some headway, but one thing lacking was genuine agrarian reform, or defeudalizing of the countryside; another was a genuine bourgeoisie, most of the capitalists being unpopular newcomers clustered in Karachi. In Bolivia in the early 1970s Colonel Banzer's regime was "hellbent on economic growth whatever the social cost," with policies designed "primarily and almost exclusively to satisfy the needs and desires of private enterprise."[25] Pinochet's coup was applauded by the Chilean middle classes, but he had to ensure American support and arms supplies by aligning himself with the monopolists, the interests closest to Washington and world capitalism. Military timetables were running ahead of local standard time. Brazil has been another demonstration that strongarm rule and murder squads cannot by themselves guarantee progress. Its economic miracle consisted too much of grandiose public works; a high proportion of the bigger companies were state controlled; a native capitalist class was not forming because talented individuals were snapped up by the multinationals; a vast foreign debt was accumulating. The end came with inflation and economic chaos, and the ghosts of vanished forests.

An apologist for South Korea might argue that economically, military rule, by preventing all strikes or labor disputes, can foster investment and accelerate production, that demand for labor will in time lead to improved wages—as in Japan—and that politically, industrial urban life will generate a public opinion which will in time render dictatorship superfluous, even if painful struggles are needed to dismantle it. Mature capitalism may find it, as in Western Europe today, not hard to come to terms with parliamentary democracy—of a suitably restrained sort. Even in Latin America army rule is out of fashion at present, though possibly not for long, since its basic causes have not been removed.

Toward a Postentrepreneurial Epoch

A socialist is left to explain in what way his own methods of industry building have been superior to the South Korean. They, too, have more often than not relied on compulsion; "commandism," or bureaucratic dragooning, has been repudiated in principle but far too widely resorted to in practice. And they have been equally profligate in squandering or poisoning natural resources. Occasionally army men in power have set out to build socialism instead of capitalism, like Siyad Barre in Somalia in the middle 1970s. He received a flow of Soviet arms and advisers, and could bid defiance to clerical obstruction, but he very soon turned away to what seemed the more facile option of starting a nationalist war for territory against Ethiopia. More lamentably, socialism in Eastern Europe, and in the USSR itself, has lost its creative momentum. It has at last been compelled to confess this and, very reluctantly, to let its people breathe fresh air; many other commodities they are still waiting for. One way of accounting for this failure is the Tory contention that socialism goes against the grain, and *must* fail. A kinder one may be that coercion is all right for setting up an economy based on sordid greed, or what N. Hampson has called "the politics of the pig trough,"[26] but not for one that needs the vital spark of idealism. In other words: is socialism repugnant to human nature or dictatorship repugnant to socialism?

We may be forced to look again at some older Marxian ideas and wonder whether socialism can only really come about before it is felt to be necessary (that is, when capitalism has exhausted its historic mission of creating material plenty and has nothing further to offer). There are already symptoms of Japan being ready to accompany or lead the West into a postentrepreneurial epoch and enjoy a rentier existence, placidly buying up Los Angeles and Vancouver and leaving production to the beginners' class, and to robots. A flourishing guided economy like Japan's may prove ideally suitable for translation into socialism, whereas hitherto socialism has too often meant the nationalizing of scarcity.

In any case, capitalism today, not socialism alone, faces many dilemmas which it is poorly equipped to think out. Politics and economics have become inextricably mixed. Today's chancellor of the exchequer is tomorrow's chairman of a finance company, with a doubled or trebled salary. It is hard to say at any moment whether the state is guiding capitalism or capitalism leading the state by the nose. Neither has leisure or taste for long-term planning; both are reduced to hasty, improvised decisions, to get them out of one awkward corner into another—hand-to-mouth tactics with no more distant perspective than the next election or the balance sheet for the next shareholders' meeting. Questioners are referred to the "market" for answers; the economy, like the Newtonian universe, is a self-regulating clock which will go for ever. But the voice of the market is that of the speculator—bull or bear—as the voices of the ancient oracles were those of their priests. And today all governments that have relied on armaments for jobs and profits are faced with a nightmare they never expected to encounter. The Cold War which has been the breath of their nostrils for so many years has suddenly lost credibility, and sweeping arms reductions have become inevitable. The shock must be stunning, worse than a thousand earthquakes. Meanwhile our corner of the universe is rapidly deteriorating; at this rate it will not be much longer inhabitable.

Notes

This chapter originally appeared in *New Left Review,* no. 183 (September/October 1990).

1. L. C. Stevenson, *Praise and Paradox: Merchants and Craftsmen in Popular Elizabethan Literature* (Cambridge, 1984), Chapter 6.

2. G. C. Brodrick, "The Law and Custom of Primogeniture," in *Systems of Land Tenure,* ed. J. W. Probyn (London, 1881), 121.

3. John Brewer, *The Sinews of Power: War, Money, and the English State, 1688–1783* (London, 1989).

4. Ernest Gellner, *Plough, Sword, and Book: The Structures of Human History* (London, 1989).

5. Anon., *General Maxims in Trade* (London, 1713), 168.

6. Tobias Smollett, *Travels through France and Italy* (1766; reprint, London, 1907), 47.

7. Engraving in Fenton House Museum, Hampstead, London.

8. Friedrich Engels, preface to the 1895 edition of Karl Marx, *The Class Struggles in France (1849–50)*.

9. H. Gollwitzer, *Europe in the Age of Imperialism, 1880–1914* (London, 1969), 81.

10. Karl Liebknecht, *Militarism and Anti-Militarism,* trans. G. Lock (Cambridge, 1973), 41.

11. Tom Nairn (quoting David Good), *The Enchanted Glass: Britain and Its Monarchy* (London, 1988), 251–52.

12. Karl Marx, *The Eighteenth Brumaire of Louis Bonaparte,* in *Selected Works,* vol. 2 (Moscow, 1935), 424.

13. K. Marx and F. Engels, *The German Ideology* (1845–46; London, 1938), 73–74.

14. Liebknecht, *Militarism and Anti-Militarism,* 52.

15. Ibid., 65–66.

16. Isaac Deutscher, *The Unfinished Revolution in Russia, 1917–1967* (London, 1967), 10–12.

17. *Chushingura, the Treasury of Loyal Retainers,* trans. D. Keene (New York, 1971).

18. Engels quoted in George Lichtheim, *Marxism* (London, 1964), 125, n. 2.

19. Antonio Gramsci, *Selection from the Prison Notebooks,* ed. Quintin Hoare and G. N. Smith (London, 1971), xci, 118.

20. P. Addison, *The Road to 1945* (London, 1975), 31.

21. *Guardian*, 10 August 1974.

22. From a British television program on Japan today, by A. Sampson, "The Midas Touch," 27 January 1990.

23. E. Seidensticker, *Kafu the Scribbler: The Life and Writings of Nagai Kafu, 1879–1959* (Stanford, 1965), 157.

24. S. E. Finer, *The Man on Horseback* (London, 1962), 159.

25. Richard Gott in the *Guardian*, 30 May 1973.

26. N. Hampson, in H. T. Mason and W. Doyle, eds., *The Impact of the French Revolution on European Consciousness* (Gloucester, 1989), 198.

2

DEVELOPMENT, IMPERIALISM, AND SOME MISCONCEPTIONS

Introduction

"Development" is a large, ramifying, contentious subject. The word itself is appropriately obscure. "Develop," or "disvelop," appeared in English and the Romance languages in the seventeenth century with the sense of unwrapping, unfolding—bringing to light something already in existence, rather than creating anything new. It seems to derive from a medieval Latin word, *falupa,* of unknown origin, for a wisp of straw, presumably straw in which things were wrapped up. Today development is the successor to what earlier generations of Europeans called Progress, a concept inspired by the eighteenth-century Enlightenment and meaning all-around advance in everything that makes up civilization. Material endowments, for more than a very few, were then a distant vision: now, when they are enjoyed by many and visible to many more, they are the chief focus of attention.

In a bird's eye view world history appears to consist of occasional spurts of inventiveness and innovation, like the so-called Neolithic Revolution, interspersed among much more habitual epochs of standing still. In the premodern world there was always development going on somewhere in the form of more land being brought into use, as it was by ploughing up of waste in medieval Europe, cutting down of forests in Russia, digging of irrigation channels in middle and further Asia. This was only lateral extension, not qualitative change, and seldom conduced to any social or political shifts. Neither individuals nor communities are easily stirred out of fixed habits, repetition of things they have always done. "The notorious conservatism of children" offers a close parallel to adult shrinking from change and the unease it always brings with it.[1]

In Asia concern for development was scarcely felt by public authorities except, intermittently, in respect of major water-control works. In Europe, with its smaller principalities and manorial infrastructure, it was felt more broadly by monarchies from the later middle ages onward. A parvenu ruler like the first Vasa, in sixteenth-century Sweden, who had his way to make in the world, treated his kingdom like a careful landowner anxious to improve his estate. Such efforts were spasmodic, and royal ambitions far oftener warlike and destructive or directed to no more than another kind of lateral growth, seizure of territory. Wars of conquest inside Europe represented one form of imperialism, which in protean shapes pervades all history, from the first tribal raid to the latest Wall Street conspiracy. The most elemental definition of imperialism might be the uninvited presence of armed men from outside; their very multifarious motives, and the consequences, still await classification.

Imperialism is interwoven with all discussion of past or present failures of development in the third world, which has only lately emerged from political domination by the 'advanced' nations, while it is not yet free from their financial tentacles. There have been attempts to dismiss its modern version as no more than an optical illusion, a bad dream of peoples suffering from frustrations. It has not often been the straightforward robbery of earlier days, but under one guise or another extraction of tribute has been a very real fact. Two recent studies of colonial southeast Asia reveal a persistent excess of exports over imports, continuing down to independence and displaying clearly enough the predatory nature of the system. During the 1920s alone it totalled about £800 million.[2] In the interwar years Indonesia had an average trade surplus of about $350 million, and its excess exports to the U.S.A. from 1921 to 1941 rather more than balanced Holland's heavy deficit on trade with the U.S.A. It was seldom that more than one-sixth of foreign investment, mostly coming from the metropolitan country, went into manufactures.[3] Industrial growth was proportionately sluggish. It was kept back more positively in the cases where colonial production was deliberately thwarted to prevent competition with manufacturers 'at home'. In Benjamin Franklin's satire on mercantilism, Frederick the Great claims jurisdiction over England, as first settled by Germans like Hengist and Horsa, and prohibits any making of iron and steel, or of hats for sale because 'the art and mystery of making hats hath arrived at great perfection in Prussia'.[4] However flimsy or substantial American grievances may have been, Ireland had solid enough ground for such complaints; it was indeed the classic instance of a colonial economy intentionally injured.

It cannot reasonably be doubted that modern European annexations, and their successor neo-colonialism (with the U.S.A. as chief exponent) have been intimately connected with the appetites of capitalism. It has been persuasively argued by R.J. Hammond that the Portuguese empire in Africa disproves any Hobson-Lenin theorizing: it was not an economic endeavour.[5] This can hardly be taken as typical, because Portugal was itself a backward country; still, it serves as an intimation that in all imperial undertakings there was an admixture of the irrational, or extra-economic. In India under British rule, a possession unique in size, complexity, and long duration, almost every conceivable variant of cause and effect can be found, and to distinguish a basic pattern is a task of special difficulty.

There is much need for objective scrutiny of the whole subject, removal of straw wrappings or unhelpful misconceptions of purposes and their outcome. Some such are recognizble in not a few writings of recent years by third world spokesmen and fellow progressives in the West. Among the theses they have been putting forward, many are not new in themselves, but they have been given a more impressive cast by Marxism, now firmly established beyond the seas and ready to turn Europe's most potent body of ideas against it. This calls for continuing debate among Marxists, and between them and others, and for as dispassionate an approach as possible on all sides. Colonial Marxism has always had a strong infusion of nationalism, which has given intellectuals a link with their countrymen that would otherwise often be lacking. In communist China, hitched on to old Chinese hegemonism or self-inflation, Marxism is apt to look a good deal more than half nationalist. Equally, Europeans of all shades have to remind themselves of the tenacious hold of old ways of thinking and try to free themselves from unconscious prejudices of environment.[6]

Emergence of Capitalism in Northwestern Europe and Not Elsewhere

No investigators have yet succeeded, to more than their own satisfaction, in explaining the genesis of modern capitalism, though they have devoted nearly as much effort to it as explorers did to tracking the sources of the Nile. There was nothing novel about merchant or usurer capital. There had been traders and moneylenders in many parts of the world since antiquity. What was new, and was to be the vehicle of the grand transformation of the world, was industrial capitalism or capital invested in production (its first great domain was English agriculture). This had made a good many false starts earlier on but had always hitherto faded out or been snuffed out. Now at last, during the sixteenth and seventeenth centuries, a convergence of forces pushed part of northwestern Europe, and southeastern England in particular, in a direction that the rest of the world has since followed it in, or wanted to follow.

To put it thus baldly may suggest a "Eurocentric" view, to use a very imprecise and overworked term; it implies a charge, not always unfounded, that Europeans (or "Westerners") regard themselves as a chosen people who having been first in the field with decisive innovations in technology are entitled to a perpetual primacy. By way of corrective it should be recalled that if wide stretches of the earth outside Europe had sunk by that time or were sinking into stagnation, Europe had no immunity from this. Italy was falling behind after a brilliant season; so was Germany, where fresh techniques had been for a while more numerous than anywhere; Poland and most of eastern Europe were in a state of relapse. Even the northwestern corner through which the high road of history happened in that era to run shared with the rest a population physically encrusted with dirt, and mentally with superstition, and formed part of a continent racked by senseless wars, religious persecutions, witch burnings, Turkish invasions, and the arrival of syphilis, accompanied by the pressure of population on food, with a worsening climate helping to spread hunger, often famine, and epidemic plague. All over Europe dominant classes were gaining ground at the cost of a general impoverishment of the masses, Russian peasants forced down into serfdom, English peasants reduced to farm laborers. Another offspring of all this, side by side with capitalism, was Elizabethan tragedy. A lesson to be drawn may be that only under terrible pressures is humanity capable of wrenching itself out of old grooves; at any rate, the experience was not one that any other part of the world has reason to envy.

How a continent in so morbid and miserable a condition could stride forward so swiftly to world mastery may well seem an enigma; the spectacle provokes a query like Cassius's in one of Shakespeare's tragedies:

> Upon what meat doth this our Caesar feed,
> That he is grown so great?

And it has been strenuously maintained that what Europe has fed on, from the outset of its rise, has been the flesh and blood of other climes: in other words, that a great deal of the capital which enriched it was got by ransacking of colonies. Malcolm Caldwell—whose untimely death was a heavy blow to the study of this subject and, it may be added, to the cause of humanity—dwelt in a section of his last book called "The Development of Underdevelopment" on the looting of the other continents, from the fifteenth century, and cited with approval E. Mandel's estimate of a total swag of a thousand million pounds.[7] In Mandel's own words, "it can be stated unhesitantingly" that long-continued brigandage and looting prepared the way for the advance toward industrialization.[8]

Few statements about history can safely be made without any hesitation. Money, or salable goods, can be stolen, but they only turn into capital when applied to productive functions, and this only happens where a groundwork of capitalistic production has already been laid. In England it was being laid in the sixteenth century, when John Bull's career of brigandage was only in its infancy. Spain was then already in receipt of immense plunder from the New World, but the effect was a deindustrializing one, because it enabled the country to buy goods and services from abroad instead of taking the trouble to provide them for itself, while the rest of the bullion was squandered on wars, display, or pious offerings. Nothing could be less correct than A. G. Frank's assertion that seizure of colonial surpluses has always worked toward "generating economic development in the metropolitan centers."[9] By the early seventeenth century, when economic thinking was beginning to dawn, Spaniards were uneasily surmising that their empire was doing them more harm than good, and most historians have thought so ever since. Much the same can be said of Portugal, the other pioneer empire builder. A century later Holland was dropping out of the lead in the march toward industrialism. Whether this was the cause of its turning to more intensive exploitation of its colonies, as Caldwell thought,[10] or colonial bloodsucking was the cause of its loss of economic momentum, clearly ill-gotten gains were no guarantee of progress. It seems much more likely that the vital accumulation of resources took place by way of transfer from poor to rich inside Europe.

Only Western conceit, Caldwell held, made writers like W. Rostow suppose that the West alone could invent industry.[11] Yet it will not be gainsaid that ancient China hit on a whole complex of inventions, none of which occurred to contemporary India or Europe; and what could be done then by China might surely be done somewhere else a millennium later. China failed, or did not care, to follow up its discoveries and wasted gunpowder on firecrackers instead of putting it to its proper uses. A new social force like capitalism was not indispensable for such discoveries to be made, but it was indispensable if they were to be utilized; for this, heavy obstacles had to be broken through. Many of these lay in social psychology. It is another dictum of Frank that factors belonging to the realm of ideology, like the Calvinist work ethic, are never "determinant or decisive but at best derivative or secondary."[12] In terms of any materialist conception of history, this is formally true; yet the more the historian delves, the more he is driven to admit the strength of such intangibles and imponderables. Nonmaterial shackles on economic growth are to be found at the humblest levels. Raymond Firth writes appreciatively of the skill shown by African agriculture in coping with problems of soil or climate, but adds that it has often been hampered by irrational customs, rituals, taboos, as among some Angolan tribes.[13]

In more complex communities resistance to change has been bolstered by vested interests embedded in an old order, influential groups which stand to lose by progress and always know how to identify themselves and their obstructiveness with the cause of religion. Islam proved a very impermeable medium, but so almost as tenaciously did Catholicism, and in Catholic southern Europe industrialism had no native birth. In nineteenth-century Spain it got going in Catalonia, thanks largely to French enterprise, and at a few other points like Malaga where Britons set up factories; but Spaniards were very slow to emulate them. Industry in such an environment was as liable to what may be called "tissue rejection" as the parliamentary rule that Englishmen were anxious to see Spain adopt or the Christianity they wanted India to adopt. Bustling Victorians often deemed frivolous Frenchmen as well as dawdling Spaniards unequal to the exertion, patience, discipline, required for modern industry! Catholic Ireland blamed its torpor on the Protestant ascendancy and on what had happened in the seventeenth century, no doubt with some reason; yet to walk around an Irish town, even as late as the early 1960s, and find it mostly composed of a cathedral, a race-course, and some dozens of saloons might seem explanation enough of the state of the economy.

Religion is of course not the only differential. When Engels visited Canada in 1888, he thought it lamentably sluggish compared with the USA, in which he expected it to be swallowed up.[14] Sam Slick, that genial creation of the early-nineteenth-century Nova Scotian patriot T. C. Haliburton, was always contrasting a stick-in-the-mud Nova Scotia with an energetic though less well-endowed New England at its elbow.[15] But the sharpest contrast came to be that between Ontario, humming with vitality, and neighboring French Canada, buried until the early 1960s in the past, shut up in a sort of spiritual opium den. A Quebec-nationalist writer, M. Rioux, quotes an old French traveler's description of the Québecois spending all they had on dress and ostentation, while English settlers saved up and thought of their children's future;[16] he may have been reminded of La Fontaine's fable of the thrifty ant and feckless grasshopper. Rioux speaks of economic exploitation of French Canada by British in terms implying an authentic colonial relationship.[17] But if backwardness in Ireland was partly the outcome of such exploitation, in Québec it might be said to have caused or invited it. British rule, it should be added, assisted the process by making friends with the clergy after the conquest of French Canada, as useful auxiliaries, and leaving education under their control.

Conservatism could only be challenged where there were social groups ready to take the lead against it. Western European feudalism, Caldwell rightly noted, though without following up the clue, had "peculiar features which made it specially hospitable to the seeds of capitalism."[18] In the building of the early modern state in Europe, and in the religious upheaval of the same era, sections of the lower nobility or gentry played a prominent part, interacting with a prosperous commercial class. A somewhat similar pattern can be detected in the modernization of Japan; in general, Asian feudalism and its élites showed themselves strikingly unfitted for any reception of a new economic order. Down to the end these ruling groups were behaving, almost like automata, in the same identical fashion as their predecessors for centuries before them; mandarin, mullah, maharaja were all, when the Western irruption took place, so many Rip van Winkles, ages behind the times. Every inhabited area had progressed, less or more, during its long history, but almost all seemed to have got into blind alleys or were going round in cycles. Each social-economic structure engendered habits and institutions which stood in the way of any impulse to transcend it. Today the same has happened with capitalism, even where it functions as unsatisfactorily as in Britain.

To attribute paralysis in Afro-Asia and Latin America to their overrunning by the West leaves it, after all, to be explained why they had not forestalled Europe by going ahead long before. Asian civilizations had possessed natural resources as rich, larger populations, superior equipment, more accumulated wealth and, most noticeably of all, fuller state power. China had in addition, over lengthy epochs, far-flung colonial territories, some of them suitable for settlement. There were times when Chinese argosies swept the ocean. Yet they retreated from it, not banished by Western sea power, as might be said of Indian shipping, but from indifference or fear of a few pirates or because the Manchu conquerors in the seventeenth century distrusted the southern coast dwellers and traders. Under whatever dynasty, there was no room for a class corresponding with the bourgeoisie of western Europe to make its appearance.[19] Although appreciable alterations can be observed in the China of the last few centuries of isolation, no such radically new departure was coming in.

India's rulers had a population to tax comparable in size with that of all Europe, most of it at intervals under the single sway of a government based on Hindustan, or the upper Gangetic valley. India exported cloth and other goods; among its chief imports were horses, wastefully used up in warfare, and silver, much of it bestowed on temples; just as much silver from Peru came to a dead end in Spanish churches. Other hoards were piled up by merchants and princes. They were available as Mandel says for investment,[20] but there is very little sign of their actually being invested. Little of an indigenous banking system came into being.[21] If the British were able to carry off such ponderous stocks of wealth from India, these stocks must have been lying idle, waiting for them; it might be said that Britain by bringing them into circulation was rescuing them from sterility, *liberating* them as it professed to be liberating India from many other evils.

Hindu writers have not seldom maintained that medieval India was shaping promisingly until the barbarous inrush of the Turkish Muslims from central Asia. Muslim apologists have often blamed the decay of Islamic civilization on the barbarous onslaught of the Mongols. Both might do well to reflect that societies, like men, are "betrayed by what is false within." Nowadays a number of Indian and other scholars reject the traditional view, shared by Marx, that India was in a state of hopeless incapacity for progress before the barbarous British descent. In the eighteenth century, it is urged, some areas (it may not be easy to locate them on the map) were enjoying sufficient tranquillity to be able to forge ahead. Agriculture was not unskillful and was showing marks of improvement. Caldwell laid stress on the craft skills that India in common with other Asian countries could claim; he may have been unfortunate in picking out cannon founding,[22] for this had stood still for donkeys' years, along with nearly everything else belonging to the kingdom of Mars, in spite of India's perpetual warfare. Prabhat Patnaik in a recent study emphasized the country's complexity of structure, with considerable commodity production and exchange between town and country (though these features had been well to the front in China since at least a thousand years earlier). "Merchant capital was significant, and though the later bourgeoisie was not the literal descendant of the earlier one, there was some continuity."[23] Another observer has noted that some weavers were accustomed to employ others, so that a capitalist road lay open before them.[24]

Agreement among the experts is not yet in sight, and more pessimistic impressions are not confined to Western commentators. Ashin Das Gupta's picture of commercial life in eighteenth-century India is of old ports like Surat and Hugli decaying, trading and shipowning classes shriveling away— fundamentally because Mughal authority was waning—conditions becoming insecure even in the heart of the empire, trading provinces losing touch with each other, while local officials or potentates multiplied exactions from merchants and Marathra armies levied blackmail; activity could grow only in the new European settlements.[25] At Surat in 1732 there was a unique case of merchants rebelling against official demands and hiring troops to protect them.[26] One must suspect that they borrowed this audacity from their European neighbors in the port. Amales Tripathi likewise believes Bengal to have been already in decay before 1757 and the battle of Plassey because of prevailing instability and the absence of a middle class with backbone.[27]

Among the new political entities usurping the place of the Mughals, it is hard to see any qualified to play foster parent to modern industry; and it is common ground among most investigators of development that state action has everywhere been a necessary coadjutor. To stimulate and guide an economy, and keep emergent business and wage-earning classes under restraint without smothering them, was not a task for regimes so closely tied as all these were to the feudal past. Mysore under Tipu Sultan may be the likeliest candidate, and it may be admitted that it was snuffed out by British jealousy and suspicious of its links with the French, as well as by the obsession with territorial gain which Tipu shared with his forerunners all the way back through the weary waste of Indian political history. To whatever was forward-looking in his actions, Mohibbul Hasan does justice in his standard work on him and in his edition of the curious record of the commercial and diplomatic mission sent by Tipu in 1786 to the Persian Gulf and Turkey.[28] Das Gupta, by contrast, does not except Tipu from his strictures on the governments of that time but blames him for crippling business life at Calicut, that thriving old port, by "contradictory and capricious policies." These were designed, it would appear, to create an official monopoly of the pepper trade, like that set up by the strong new Hindu state of Travancore, to the south, where private merchants were either compelled to become government agents or got rid of.[29] Far away in the north the Sikh kingdom of the Panjab survived Mysore for nearly another half-century, with a strong monarchy and army and extensive conquests on both the northwest and northeast. Its landlocked position, so remote from the sea and the new age, clogged it, and a species of feudal baronage was overlaying the earlier democratic leanings of the Sikh community of artisans and cultivators.

Ottoman Turkey exhibits the special case of an Asian country aggressively independent but in close contact from its inception with Europe, for many centuries even incorporating a good part of Europe. If the West enriched itself by force of arms and freebooting, Turkey ought to have been no whit behind. In its palmy days it had the strongest army in the world, for a briefer period a sturdy navy, for a very long time a retinue of dependent territories to exploit; it drew mountains of booty and multitudes of slaves from its wars in both Europe and Asia, and from Africa. Yet nothing came of all this. While Westerners wrote voluminously about Turkey, Turks wrote and read little or nothing about the West and learned from it not much beyond some military methods. After 1600 or so, with decline setting in, they were turning mentally away from Europe, facing toward the East and its comfortable somnolence. Turkish landowners in the Balkans might behave like their neighbors in eastern Europe and employ something like serf labor to produce surplus grain for sale in return for foreign luxuries;[30] but commercialism of this order was more a turning toward a special kind of feudalism than toward modern capitalism; and trade itself, in which Turks once took a share, was left by now, as an inferior pursuit, to Greeks, Armenians, or Jews. Social and mental rigidities became so fixed that the Young Turk revolution of 1908, like the Chinese of 1911, amounted to not much more than an army coup; and in two generations since the Great War and the Ataturk reforms, Turkey has gone on limping. It would be perverse to ascribe this failure to the loss of an empire which for so long did it so little good.

Industrial Revolution and Empire Profits

Capitalism as it evolved in early modern times led on, though not in any straight line, toward the second "big leap," industrial revolution, or the harnessing of mechanical power to production. This intensified very rapidly the distinctive tendency of modern capitalism to produce, instead of simply appropriating, wealth; even if this was partly—first in Britain and then outward in further and further swathes—a cannibalistic process, the machine replacing the handicraft. Why it began about 1770 is a riddle still unsolved. But that its inauguration was financed by Britain's imperial loot, especially from Bengal, is an old conjecture which lately has been having a new lease of life and which by some Indian historians is now apparently taken for granted.

Three main influxes of wealth into Britain in the eighteenth century can be distinguished: income from the West Indian plantations; less illegitimate profit on the export trade to Portugal under the Methuen Treaty of 1803, which diverted to Britain a good part of the gold and diamonds accruing from the short-lived Brazilian boom; and the spoils of Bengal. Portugal underwent a kind of deindustrialization through being swamped with English woolens long before India was swamped with English cottons; but it was the gains from this trade that would find their way most directly into commercial circulation in Britain, and it may be easier to credit them with a share in fertilizing the ground for industrial revolution than the sort of spending that returned planters or nabobs indulged in. India's later importance to Britain may have concentrated attention unduly on Bengal's losses. That stern critic of British misrule in India, W. Digby, wrote in 1901: "England's industrial supremacy owes its origin to the vast hoards of Bengal and the Karnatik being made available for her use." He estimated the total extracted from India between 1757 and 1815 at £1,000 million (a much higher figure than most later ones); and he linked Plassey with the start of the Industrial Revolution, which he put only three years later—"the effect appears to have been instantaneous."[31] Some rupees *may* have percolated by devious channels into Lancashire mills, but not quite so promptly as this. Of any such enormous flow of bullion into Britain, the one inescapable effect must have been headlong inflation. A fourfold rise of prices in sixteenth-century Spain may well have been one of the impediments to industrial advance there; on a smaller scale the windfall of the French indemnity after the war of 1870 seems to have brought only inflation and confusion to Germany.

Mandel is convinced that all Western industrial growth "has been possible only *at the expense* of the so-called under-developed world, which has been doomed to stagnation and repression." He takes as plausible an estimate by Sir Percival Griffiths of British appropriation from India between 1750 and 1800, £100 to £150 million.[32] In a survey of the matter in 1959 John Strachey worked on H. Furber's figure—partly guesswork, as any must be—of £2 million annually in the decade 1783–1793.[33] Over the forty-five years from 1770 to 1815 unearned profit at this rate would add up to £90 million. Strachey reached the conclusion that the drain from India "was by no means the largest factor in Britain's pioneer accomplishment of primary industrialisation," although "it played a very real part."[34] This still sounds convincing.

Colonial gains were coming in from other sources too. But it may be worthwhile to compare sums of this order with what Britain was spending on objects very different from cotton mills. During the same forty-five years the national debt swelled from £128 to £758 million, because of the American Revolution, and then from 1793 to 1815, the wars with Revolutionary and Napoleonic France.[35] This meant an increase of £630 million, or a yearly average of £14 million, raised by internal borrowing, in addition to the massive sums spent out of taxation; which shows what wealth of its own the country—that is the propertied classes—disposed of. War expenditure on this scale, a great deal of it abroad, represented on the whole an enormous diversion of resources away from constructive investment. Secondly, the amount of capital required to start factory industry then (very unlike now) was quite small, trifling by contrast with the outlay on war. Early millowners had to scrape together capital, out of their own and their neighbors' savings, not because the nation was short of funds, but "because they had little access to the big money"; they had, however, equally little need of it.[36] In other words, Britain did not have to shake the pagoda tree in order to get its mechanical looms working. It may have needed India far more, as time went on, to keep them busy. Whether the Industrial Revolution was a response primarily to domestic or to foreign market demand has been much debated, but cotton manufactures, its first fruits, were essentially for export: by 1805 two-thirds may have gone abroad, and this trend continued as the nineteenth century wore on.[37] At the outset a colonial market prominently in view must have been the West Indies, connected with Lancashire by one of the great slave-trading ports, Liverpool, and an area where, at any rate, there were no handicrafts to be ruined by machine competition. But India took an increasing and soon a predominant share.[38]

In many ways the early Industrial Revolution, isolated in its northern valleys, has the air of a random offshoot or mutation. Really it was the outcome of a multiplicity of historical sequences older and newer, but it was nonetheless a breakaway from the rural southern England of stately home and docile farm laborer. This south had already long been permeated by capitalism, but of the earlier phase, and principally agrarian, and it was unlikely by itself to generate the further move to industrialism. Industrial Britain ought to have gone on expanding and have relegated rustic-aristocratic Britain to the background. Down to the first Reform Act and the repeal of the Corn Laws, this seemed to be happening. Thereafter, something like an opposite process supervened, with the industrial north, or its leaders, absorbed or assimilated into a southern plutocracy bolstered by the military and colonial services and by the City of London financial complex, itself increasingly based on empire opportunities, not on manufacture. It may well have been by furnishing the strongest grappling iron between these two discordant Britains of north and south that the empire had its greatest significance.

In the latter decades of the century Britain resembled the frog trying to puff itself up to a bull's size—psychologically, so as to conceal from itself the ebbing of its former preeminence, economically, as Hobsbawm says, to make up for industrial obsolescence by escape into a "satellite world of formal or informal colonies" and dependence on finance and its ramifications.[39] It was now that poverty-stricken India was becoming a linchpin of the British balance of payments.[40] Captive markets had a debilitating effect, and Britain was rapidly overtaken and then left behind by Germany and the USA, which owned no colonies worth mentioning, and which—the USA especially— relied far less on sales abroad. In general, among the European nations those with the most colonies made the worst showing in industrial terms. Spain, Portugal, Holland, Russia are diverse examples of this. Britain was the exception, but only in the preliminary stages of industrialization.

Capitalism is always liable to regression as well as progress. It can count in its checkered ancestry the trader-pirate of Odysseus's day, the slave dealer, the rack-renting landlord, and many similar types, and is ready, given the chance, to slip back into old lawless ways. Colonial profits were handsome, but too large a part continued to be sunk in stately homes and the hiring of platoons of flunkys. Mansions of still wealthier Americans of those days, Vanderbilts and Goulds, in the Hudson River valley, were comparatively modest and have been turned into museums. Even on its own lines, imperial buccaneering was not always a success. As the liberal economist F. W. Hirst wrote soon after the Boer War, "Many of the promoters and speculators who had been most eager for it were ruined"—even though its cost, £250 million, was paid not by them but by the taxpayer. Gilt-edged and many industrial securities fell by 5% to 10%, a shrinkage of capital values portentous enough to shake London's standing as the world's financial center.[41]

Great Britain and India

In a speech in 1942 on self-determination for Indian nationalities, the theoretician of the Communist Party, G. Adhikari, stated what was then an orthodox Marxist view: India's national evolution began with the British conquest and its "shattering of all the old forms of economy," feudal-agrarian relations which debarred India, or any portion of it, from being a nation.[42] It is as certain as anything can be that India could not have grown into a united nation except through all its peoples coming under the same foreign rule. Aspirations to union would otherwise have been very few and as ineffectual as the Pan-African dream. If India would have made more progress on its own, as alleged, it could only have been as a congeries of separate states. Things *might* have been better so, because national consciousness would have kindled more readily on a local basis of common language and tradition; and the afflatus of nationalism may well have been vital to any big economic spurt, such as Japan made. Against this may be set the inevitability of frequent quarrels and the fact that India's capitalists, when history managed to breed them, would have a very large market at their disposal.

For this service, good or bad, Britain rewarded itself handsomely enough, reckoning the dues it collected not much for India to pay in return for law and order or freedom from the internecine wars which would have racked it, as they racked Europe. On the economic plane, whatever may be thought of the political, British rule faces four charges: that it crushed the old native crafts; it did too little to bring India's natural resources into play; it planted very little industry in India; and it put obstacles in the way of industry building by Indians.

Ireland, too, had been given order and a sort of unification by England, a not well-omened precedent; in some ways India's treatment was a curiously atavistic repetition of earlier treatment of Ireland. Import of Lancashire cloth was facilitated by a crippling tax on Indian weavers. It was not a triumph of British skill, Sir John Shore protested, but "a much stronger instance of English tyranny, and how India has been impoverished by the most vexatious system of customs and duties."[43] India had been a partly industrial country, Montgomery Martin declared, and to seek to reduce her to a merely agricultural country would be "to lower her in the scale of civilisation."[44] There is, by contrast, the contention that this decline had been under way well before the impact of machine-made cloth began to be felt in the 1780s.[45] It is obvious, moreover, that handicrafts would have had a losing battle to wage against any industrialism, foreign or native; though the process may have been a complex one with some gains as well as losses. On a more modest level one may see something of this in a people like the Micmac Indians of eastern Canada, who through contact with the white man lost their old art of pottery making but devised better methods of hunting and new styles of clothing and of decoration for it.

As grave as any crippling of old industries, may have been a diversion or deformation of social elements in India with a potential of economic leadership. First to come under British rule and adopt English education, Bengalis had opportunities of government service which might be educative in their way but were a counterattraction to any commercial activity. Something like the *empleomanía,* the thirst for government posts, of contemporary Spain seized on the provinces in turn. Far more deleterious was the landownership introduced by English law, from 1793 when the Permanent Settlement erected large hereditary estates in Bengal. Its evil result of drawing money away from useful pursuits into rack-renting exemplify a general fact, that many of the worst consequences of imperialism have not been dictated by any logical requirements of capitalism but have been unforeseen by-products. Part of the mischief was due to an aristocratic English government only being able, as James Mill wrote, to think of setting up an Indian aristocracy instead of turning its thoughts to peasant welfare.[46] But there was original sin on the Indian side too. Landlordism in English legal guise might be an innovation, but the arts of peasant fleecing were familiar enough. What was taking place was a bonding of an intrusive element with others already present. These landlords were, for instance, often moneylenders as well. Every imperial connection is too apt to bring out the worst of both sides oftener than the best.

When Cornwallis was drafting the Permanent Settlement he was not mistaken in assuming that there was plenty of money in Indian purses which could be applied to buying land.[47] From early days this fund was suffering a second internal drain, through borrowing at high rates by a government always hard up, especially when there were wars to be paid for. Maladies contracted by Britain as a result of wars and "Dutch finance" and a standing debt, with hypertrophy of finance and stockbroking to the neglect of honest industry, were being reproduced on a smaller scale in India. By 1826 government indebtedness was calculated at £28 million;[48] by the time of the Mutiny it had swelled to above £60 million.[49] Most stockholders were Europeans wanting lucrative employment for money not easy to remit to Britain. But a considerable though fluctuating part of the money was Indian. Men of means were quite alive to the charm of safe government loans, which they had never enjoyed before, and here again ancestral moneylending instincts came into play. In 1823 G. A. Prinsep recorded that of loans lately called in, 1.8 out of 7.45 lakhs of rupees belonged to Indians and added: "The Natives are supposed to have a much larger stake in the non-remittable portion of the debt."[50] Tripathi traces a tortuous story of their oscillations between investment in land and in land buying, according to which promised the better yield.

In either case capital was being distracted from the more arduous and hazardous path of industry. This had been part of Europe's experience much earlier, with Spanish *juros* or government annuities in the sixteenth century, and French *rentes* down to the Revolution, sponging up money which might otherwise have looked for productive outlets. Politically, European lenders had been tethered to their governments by becoming their creditors, one reason why the French monarchy lasted so long, and far too long. It was the same in India, and not enough weight may have been given by historians to the effect of loanmongering in ensuring the loyalty of the moneyed class. The government was not blind to it. Lord Hastings justified his heavy borrowing for the Nepal war of 1815 as "identifying the interest of a leading body of natives with ours."[51] Marx quoted a remark of the *Times* in the same vein.[52] Men with their names in the Company's ledgers could not wish to see it overturned in 1857 by the rebels. Nepal was one instance of Indian rupees—as well as soldiers—collaborating in imperial expansion: the conquest of Burma was another, one that led to Indians getting a liberal share in the proceeds of the new colony by means for the most part as parasitic as any of Britain's. In this way, too, the financial élite was led astray, but it followed all too willingly.

At least it had been coming out of its shell and giving some tokens of readiness for better things. "The formerly timid Hindu," we read in a Company report of 1802–03, "now lends money . . . on distant voyages, engages in speculations to various parts of the world . . . erects indigo works in different parts of Bengal" and understands commercial law as well as any European.[53] At that date wealthy Indian dealers could still be looked on "with exceeding hauteur" by British firms in the top flight, but by 1820 British newcomers were glad to come to them for operating capital. "In some cases the native millionaires were admitted as partners in these new firms; but in all instances treated on terms of equality and friendship."[54] Changes following the renewal of the Company's charter in 1833, with India thrown open to European private enterprise, aided "the emergence not only of a middle-class but of a constructive middle-class ideology" in Bengal, represented by Ram Mohun Roy and by Dwarkanath Tagore, a landlord blossoming into "the first Bengalee entrepreneur in the true sense of the term."[55] All in all, "the time seemed ripe for an Industrial Revolution in Bengal under British management, financed by the joint resources of the British and the native capitalists."[56]

Toward midcentury a belated recognition seemed to be dawning on the British mind of the need for constructive measures to promote India's development, hitherto almost totally ignored—or worse. It belonged to the same current as the attack by the bourgeoisie at home on the aristocratic ascendancy. For India, far more than for Britain, the fruits were disappointingly meager. If at home the older ruling class was only partially dislodged, in India there was still less of a shift. Gentlemen whose education was a smattering of Latin and Greek, and whose affiliations were with the southern England of the squirearchy, ran their districts in the spirit of a landowning J. P. keeping his tenants and laborers well in hand. Governors might be autocrats, but they were not in the monarchical tradition of Continental Europe, the school of kings like Louis XIV and their ministers, to whom public works and forms of state-capitalist enterprise came naturally. It was characteristic of this bureaucracy to be content with squeezing revenue out of cultivators and to make up the deficit by selling opium to China, an archaic way of balancing the budget akin to the place in the economy of empire earlier held by the slave trade.

John Capper's book in 1853 was a tirade against British neglect of India, the woefully little done for road building, railways, education, "the petty shop-keeping genius of Leadenhall-street," whose denizens he depicted as fossilized obstructionists.[57] Change *must* come, he exclaimed: "the broad daylight of intelligence is penetrating the hearts and souls of a hundred millions of our fellow-creatures" in "that wonderful land, highly gifted by nature, yet prostrate in superstition and misery."[58] Roads and railways in colonies might serve simply to siphon off more of their wealth, but Capper was not alone among those calling for action in wanting something better for India than a mere plantation economy. A commission of inquiry into public works in the Madras presidency had just issued its first report. Irrigation, this pointed out, enhanced the value of land and thereby the general well-being. "Thus capital accumulates, and with the accumulation of capital comes the love of peace and order, activity of invention, the cultivation and enlargement of the mind, the fine arts, and in a word, civilization."[59] It was a glowing Victorian panorama, innocent of any suspicion of capitalism bringing into the world not peace but a sword. Admittedly "the people of this country are proverbially apathetic and averse to change," but development would rouse them and counteract the "indolent, sauntering way of working" at present the rule.[60] "Native manufacturers are beginning to lift up their heads, and, from the facility with which they imitate European patterns, it seems probable that, if machinery were introduced amongst them, India would again become an exporting nation."[61] It was recommended that money for public works be raised by borrowing in England as well as India to reduce interest rates and avoid starving Indian industry of capital.[62]

What was about to happen, instead of amicable collaboration and burgeoning of new life, was the Mutiny. That cataclysm quenched any pipe dreams by alienating the races far more deeply than before; there had often been contempt on the European side, now there was positive hatred. Railways were at last being built, with military purposes foremost and at the cost of a soaring debt for loans raised in London: previously by far the greatest part of the Indian debt had been held in India. But by this time industrial capitalism in Britain itself was beginning to flag, and India was dauntingly vast, too chock-full of problems for development to be tackled as it might be in a small colony. Britain's empire altogether was out of scale with its limited stock of energy, and it was content to skim off quick profits here and there, from rubber or gold, for instance, without troubling itself over long-term planning.

If Britain was not industrializing India, the question arises why India was not industrializing itself. It was in fact starting to do so, though too slowly. In the Bombay quarter more business spirit was forthcoming than elsewhere, and the cotton mills growing up there, unlike the Calcutta jute mills, were mostly in Indian hands. By 1902 they employed 196,000 workers. Nationalism was sprouting faster than industry, and its spokesmen complained that Indian enterprise was being stifled by foreign rivalry, a British strangehold on banking and external trade. With British capital not setting up cotton mills of its own in India, the government might be more prone to discourage Indian mills, for Lancashire's benefit, instead of giving them the assistance that new industries everywhere required. Transfer of responsibility from Company to crown, and the coming of age of democracy or demagogy, could make India a victim of party politics; and Lancashire, strangely metamorphosed since Chartist days, was turning into an important Tory stronghold. Hence the removal of import duties on cloth, followed in 1896 by an excise on Indian cloth.[63]

There is some cogency in ascribing sluggish growth to these impediments, just as in the argument of the Muslims, before partition, that they could not get a start in business because richer Hindu competitors were always bent on squeezing them out; but it cannot be taken in either case as the whole truth. Lack of tariff autonomy must have played a part; but Japan suffered the same disability during its "takeoff" period, under the "unequal treaties." Distance from any competing country, and transport costs, gave industry in both countries, or in Latin America, a degree of automatic protection. And it was not for want of tariffs that Spanish industry was languishing. Indian millowners took a more realistic view of their position than intellectuals impatient for national progress—a fact with many analogies elsewhere in history. They did not feel the excise duties as a handicap to their coarse cloth in face of Lancashire, but they feared possible competition from handloom weavers, whose product was more like theirs.[64] It has been shown that before 1914 Lancashire cloth, mostly intended for better-off customers, was not in collision with the cheaper Indian mill cloth, selling in the mass market.[65] After that date India gained tariff freedom by stages, ahead of political independence, and by 1938 cloth imports from Britain had fallen by nine-tenths.

An alternative or supplementary explanation was the celebrated "drain" theory, according to which tribute paid to Britain deprived India of capital needed for industrialization. In 1823 it had been reckoned that the annual outflow to Britain, "resulting chiefly from our political relations with Hindostan," stood at £4 million.[66] Measuring the exodus of wealth from 1835 to 1872 by the excess of exports over imports, Dadabhai Naoroji found that it came to a total of £500 million. He deducted from this £140 million of opium revenue, whose real source was China; and he allowed that another £200 million consisted of interest on loans for useful railway building but contended that an India free of tribute could have found capital of its own for railways.[67] Whether it *would* have done so may be arguable. Including the railway payments, his figures for these thirty-eight years average nearly £10 million a year. R. C. Dutt put the annual amount for the last years of the century at £13 million, and held that the loss had been a cause of the recent famines.[68] There could be no doubt, to anyone not turning a blind eye, of what Digby called "the terrible condition of the people, . . . unspeakable and unbearable misery,"[69]—whether because of, or in spite of, British rule. It may be that his intense emotional concern interfered at times with cool reasoning. He fell into some inconsistencies when he protested at English writers expecting Indians "to find capital for industrial enterprises in which they do not believe" and talking of "the want of energy and effort on the part of Indian so-called capitalists"—and when he then went on to assert that wealth could only be built up if the drain were stopped: "India may then be able to pay for her own industrial enterprises."[70]

More important, Digby overlooked that however much India might be having to pay to Britain, there was always plenty of cash in Indian ownership which could have served as capital. India's upper classes must have made far more out of the Indian masses, as princes, landlords, middlemen, usurers, lawyers, than Britain did. It was one of the drawbacks of a parasitic empire that it attracted to itself, and increasingly rested on the support of, all the parasitic elements in colonial society. In the countryside of Bengal this was luridly plain. At the end of the century the fixed government receipts from the landlords there were £2.7 million. Digby calculated the value of agricultural produce as twenty times this amount, or £54 million.[71] If only half the gross product was taken from the unfortunate cultivators by those above them, the latter were pocketing annually about £24 million. This was more than enough to get any number of factories going; instead the sum was frittered away among a series of grades of landlords and lessees, one on top of the other, many of them absentee rentiers. As to what was being carried off overseas, two salient items at least, opium and tea, represented no real deduction from the national stock of wealth; while the country's prime resources, like coal, if not utilized were not being purloined: they lay virtually untouched.

Whether or not a country must have freedom in order to build industry,[72] it must first have the desire to do so, such as European emigrants carried with them to far-off lands, a desire which could only bit by bit break through the thick crust of Asian life—and far more slowly among those with money than those with patriotic ideals. Bengal's emergent middle class had been a very half-baked one, with tenacious conservative attachments. "It was weak and vacillating. It was romantic and escapist. It was torn between the old and the new."[73] Ram Mohun himself, its most vigorous thinker, was a persistent buyer of land. When industry began to be attempted in earnest, it was evident that some groups could make a success of it, like the Parsees who, only half-Indian, were less subject to Indian inhibitions. There were advantages as well as handicaps, including cheap labor; and if the government did not back millowners against foreign competitors it backed them wholeheartedly against their Indian work force: they too benefited by the grand principle of Order, which always chiefly meant keeping the poor in their place. In his hopeful expectation of Indian industry in a near future, Marx underestimated the invisible barriers, the dead weight of the past, and gave too much credit to capitalism as an irresistible transforming force: in reality it, and after it socialism, has been profoundly affected by local backgrounds. Some of the early patriots, like G. V. Joshi and Ranade, were well aware of negative features in Hindu society, absence of mutual confidence and readiness for cooperation, sedentary routine, and paucity of initiative.[74] Most of the capitalists who did come forward belonged, it is true, to orthodox conservative communities like the Marwari, not to the enlightened Westernizing circles;[75] but this has meant their bringing with them into the modern economy sundry encumbrances it would be better without. Soon after independence Nehru lamented that India's capitalists were proving "totally inadequate. . . . They have no vision, no grit, no capacity to do anything big."[76] After another thirty years one of India's foremost industries is still astrology.

The imperial relationship was holding India back, but for more intricate reasons than nationalism has usually recognized. There was an interweaving of inadequacies from each side, with ill results for both, as some observers could see. Charles Trevelyan, one of the first Englishmen to declare that India ought to be governed for the good of Indians, had been sustained by a conviction that "the laws of God are so happily adjusted that, in benefiting the natives, we also benefit ourselves."[77] Translated into the laws of economics, this meant that the more India was helped to improve its income, the more it would be able to buy from Britain. But decades later Naoroji was demonstrating that India only bought, per head of population, the derisory amount of a couple of shillings' worth of British goods yearly, much less than almost any other part of the empire; whereas if it were better off, it would be a far better market. "Will the British merchants and manufacturers open their eyes?" he asked. He repeated the question in 1898 in a lecture at Manchester, in which he urged that the interests of Lancashire and India were really identical. If Indians were enabled to spend even £1 a year on imports, "The word 'unemployed' would vanish from the English dictionary [cheers]."[78]

Dutt's message was the same, and Digby denounced, much as Capper had done, the shortsightedness of the ruling interests, concerned only with immediate gain to the exclusion of "the long and broad view which . . . would have procured greater and yet greater trade prosperity obtained in a legitimate way."[79] No capitalism can afford to take the very long views, but the flaccid British bourgeoisie was less open to them than some of its congeners. British capital investment in India reached a respectable scale only in the 1850s and 1860s: after that it was smaller, year by year, than the interest received; and only a minute proportion of it was in industry.[80] Too little capital was being invested at home also. Hence a lag in technology and an inability to meet "the peculiar and quickly changing demand schedules from countries in the process of industrialization."[81] In the interwar years Germany, Japan, and the USA were outstripping Britain in sales to India.

While materially the two countries suffered from mutually reinforcing defects, Indian idealists were conscious of malign influences on both at a deeper level. Gokhale pointed to a "moral evil" worse than the financial cost of British rule, "a kind of dwarfing or stunting of the Indian race."[82] Dutt, an admirer of Britain in many ways, wrote eloquently of the stunting effect on it of reliance on the exploitation of others. "It is with nations as with individuals; the bread we earn by labour nourishes and invigorates; the food we consume without toil is poison to our system."[83]

Failure to Develop of Other Regions in the Nineteenth Century (Except Japan): Asia, Latin America

Other civilizations might have run out of steam, but it is argued (despite the Ottoman object lesson) that in the era of Western expansion they would have been able, if not held down and robbed by the West, to catch up by emulating it as free agents, as Japan actually did. Thus Caldwell held that backwardness was the result of imperialist coercion, not of "the alleged unsuitability of the societies or people of the Third World to adopt modern technology."[84] It must be noted that acceptance of technical achievements is not the same thing as adoption of the system of production they stem from. West Africans and American Indians as well as Turks were quick to welcome firearms, as soon as these came within reach, but to learn to make them would have demanded new social organs and faculties. It is a contention of Syed Husain Alatas that potentiality for such growth was often blighted by Western conquest; that indigenous trading classes were put a stop to, in Indonesia, for example, by Dutch monopolies and by "institutionalization of the rulers and nobility as the business agents of the Dutch Company."[85] That is, Dutch rule was socially regressive, deepening instead of undermining feudalism; perhaps all the more, though paradoxically, because Holland itself was for long the least feudal, most highly commercialized country of Europe.

Nevertheless, trading classes survived elsewhere, without making any fresh mark. More central to Alatas's case is the proposition that psychological blockages were not native to Asia but were imposed on it by Western domination. As seen through imperialist spectacles, or goggles, the East was idle, shiftless, unreliable, inferior in every way; this loudly trumpeted conviction gradually worked its way into the oriental mind too and hindered it from embracing technology as it would have been ready to do had Asia remained free. Thus "Western colonialism blocked the benefits of Western civilization."[86] It is an intriguing hypothesis and recalls Gokhale's words about the crippling of Indian character. Yet what may really have happened was not that people were pushed down by colonial rule below a level previously attained but that their further progress was held up by colonial rule too long protracted.

It was in fact high time, when the arrogant European came on the scene, for the feudal-bureaucratic strata which had so long stood in the way of movement in Asia, to learn some self-criticism and self-renewal; or, if they were impenetrably self-complacent, for their subjects, into whose minds submission to ruling-class pretensions had seeped in the course of ages, to begin to throw it off. Western criticism—or abuse—was the only starting point there could be, even though, one-sidedly disparaging as it was, it might amount to the psychological bullying stigmatized by Alatas and mutilate as well as humiliate. All this can easily be transposed into the context of the "lower orders" inside Europe, viewed by their superiors not long since very much as "backward" peoples outside Europe were: one more illustration of how closely related are the attitudes of race and class. It was a tenet of middle-class German liberals in 1848, which found its way into the debates of the Frankfurt Parliament, that workmen were too lazy and self-seeking to work without compulsion and hence had no right to citizen status.[87] In France within a few years after the Paris Commune, "the myth of the inebriated, subversive worker had been rooted in the law of the land."[88]

In Japan, under the goad of foreign threats to its independence, the old order was partially dismantled by revolution, but the conditions for such a transformation from within were complex and highly exceptional. Caldwell's suggestion that Java could have done as well as Japan is unconvincing;[89] he takes scarcely any notice of the cultural and mental gulf between them, or their ruling classes, or of Java's far more rudimentary nationhood. His picture of a Japanese people marching forward arm in arm is somewhat idyllic: it leaves out the sweating of the masses by an oligarchy, the rigid police control, the use of female labor shut up in barracks. A UN survey discloses that between 1868 and 1941 rents removed just half of the harvests;[90] it was at the expense of the peasantry that capital was being garnered. In the end social reform was made feasible by the defeat of Japanese by Western imperialism, playing, however egotistically, the part of liberator.

If it is true, as has often been said, that robbery with violence was a sine qua non of European industrialization and that other regions had the ability to industrialize by their own efforts, it must seem to follow that resort to aggression was a prerequisite for them too; with the corollary that it was incumbent on Japan to annex Korea and then embark on the conquest of China and southeast Asia and take the road to the crushing defeat of 1945; and that any other country, such as India, would have had to do the same, whatever dreams its ideologues might indulge in of a new, uncarniverous kind of modernity. And Caldwell, very much a man of peace, seemed to endorse this logic when he said that where industrial raw materials were lacking "the deficiencies could readily be made good by a combination of trade and imperialism," as they were by Japan.[91] An armed scramble of each against all is thus sanctioned, on the astonishing assumption that it was right for Asians, though wrong for Europeans, to propel themselves forward by stealing from others.

No one could have acted on this principle more thoroughgoingly than Mehemet Ali, whose Egyptian career opened in the same year—1799—as the death of Tipu and who might be said to embody ambitions like Tipu's at a higher stage. His Egypt lay close to Europe and had been for three centuries a province of the Ottoman Empire. Its drive toward modernism came in the wake of the French occupation in 1798, with its display of both Western culture and Western barbarism. Bonaparte had broken the back of the old Mameluke lords, leaving the way clear for new blood and new ideas. If only because of Anglo-French jealousies, there was no interference from Europe; on the contrary Mehemet Ali received much praise there and could employ as many Europeans as he liked to drill his army and set up his industries. But there was no national backing for the experiment. There was no native class of businessmen to participate in industry, and state capitalism, while necessary as priming, could not flourish by itself. Troops were enrolled by conscription and trained by flogging. Mehemet himself was an outsider (like Tipu's father in Mysore), a soldier of fortune from Albania. As soon as he had an army, he plunged into adventures abroad; his objective was not an Egyptian nation but a smaller replica of the Turkish empire. His whole program remained artificial and had broken down long before the British took over the Nile valley from his successors in 1882.

A few states, like Siam, escaped annexation; others avoided it long enough to make clear how much or little it was in them to turn over a new leaf. Modernization from above was attempted by a bevy of rulers who, like the reformers in Japan, saw the risk of their thrones being washed away by the Western tide: Mahmud II in Turkey, Mongkut in Siam, Mindon in Burma, Kuan Hsü in China. They all failed. China's élites refused to heed the signs of the times more than fitfully and feebly; they were too inflexibly set in their old ways. When the masses rose against them, they showed that they had nothing to learn in ferocity from any white conquistadores. Destruction of life in the putting down of agrarian and colonial revolts in nineteenth-century China must have very greatly exceeded the total loss inflicted by the Western overrunning of Afro-Asia. And whereas the machine gun pointed, however crookedly, toward the future, the executioner's sword was wielded by the dead hand of the past. Some relief, but no forward movement, was provided by Inner Mongolia and Manchuria, where from the later nineteenth century Chinese migrants were settling in millions, on a scale comparable with the British emigration to North America, and largely dislodging the native inhabitants. After a hundred years of European intercourse modern-style industry was still in its infancy, and this cannot be attributed to any Western veto. In European possessions like Hongkong and Singapore Chinese businessmen flourished; they helped to finance the revolutionary organization which led to the setting up of the republic in 1911. M. N. Roy, in the early 1920s one of the first Indian communists, and one of the first Marxists to essay a study of Chinese history, saw how inextricably mingled were feudal and moneyed forms of exploitation and how hopeless was the outlook of too many literate Chinese. "Not able to understand the causes for the deplorable stagnation of their national life, they make a virtue of it."[92]

Latin America presents a special case because it was an offshoot of Europe, was never more than loosely controlled by Spain and Portugal, and for a century and a half has been formally independent—and yet is still lethargic. To many it has seemed not too hard to account for this in terms of geography, racial disharmony, religion, the Iberian social and cultural legacy. A. G. Frank's interpretation looks by comparison overingenious and schematic. Like Alatas, he views colonialism as withering all countries exposed to it, but for an opposite reason. It did not withhold capitalism from its possessions:

on the contrary, Latin America was drawn only too firmly into the capitalist orbit from the beginning, but with a subordinate or "satellized" status which molded it in such a way as to make fuller development forever impossible, except through revolution and socialism.

Frank makes the large admission that in stressing "satellite" relations heavily, he has neglected points like the class composition of capitalism.[93] A great deal of what he has to say about it rests on an elementary confusion between merchant and industrial capital. Sixteenth-century Spain was *not*, in any modern sense, a capitalist country, its colonies could be so far less. It had traders, money manipulators, some landlords selling from their estates in urban markets like Seville. On the strength of features like these we could regard the Arab empire, as described by M. Rodinson,[94] or the Roman empire even earlier, as capitalist. If Spanish America failed to develop, so did Spain. Its premature decadence is so patent that Frank has to attribute it to Spain being "satellized" in turn by a commercially stronger England.[95] His whole world is a set of Chinese boxes, with nearly everyone satellizing or being satellized. But Spain was in decline while it still had the best army in Europe, as well as the biggest empire in the world; and to equate English commercial penetration of Spain with the Spanish conquest of Mexico is a descent into mere metaphor, leaving "imperialism" destitute of any real meaning. Similarly the relation between North and South within the USA is treated as "fundamentally the same" as the colonial relationship,[96] a notion which overlooks crucial differences.

All leading groups everywhere responsible for development or the dearth of it have been creations of "the world capitalist system"[97]—a generalization singularly inappropriate to Japan, self-isolated for two and a half centuries. Much of Frank's analysis of Latin America is an attempt to prove that there is no place for bourgeois revolution there because everything is already bourgeois, or capitalist, including agriculture. The hacienda or large estate, which to most observers has appeared so feudal, was, he insists, an offspring of merchant capitalism. Rural Brazil is "an integral part of the entire capitalist metropolis-satellite structure."[98] This may be true in an obvious sense, but a slave plantation in Alabama also belonged to a world economy predominantly capitalist; a Polish demesne in the seventeenth century, worked by serf labor, might be selling its produce to Amsterdam; an Indian peasant today may be in debt to a moneylender who has borrowed funds from a bank. If all these phenomena are qualify as "capitalist," there is nothing to hinder us from transforming the world in a twinkling, like stage scenery. Frank's own presentation of agrarian Brazil is hard to reconcile with his thesis; it shows what others have emphasized, an obstinate survival of feudal traits under a surface of bourgeois legality. Many landowners, like the cocoa growers of Bahia, are, as he says, speculators rather than producers. They may make an extra profit out of collecting products from their tenants and marketing them; feudal lords in central Europe were doing the same thing four centuries ago, he might have added. He denies that Chilean *hacendados* have ever been "feudal landowners sitting on their isolated rural holdings":[99] it scarcely seems that he would admit any feudalist short of a Merovingian magnate on his autarchic domain.

In all this there seems no elucidation of why Latin American capitalism should function so differently from European; there is only the perpetually invoked formula of the tainted satellite, suggesting some kind of ritual impurity or doctrine of karma. Yet Frank does usefully raise some awkward conundrums. He is within his rights in saying that the terms "feudal" and "capitalist" have both been far too loosely used; he himself is by no means the only sinner. Marxists have been as guilty as others, and if Frank is disposed to see a vague "capitalism" everywhere, they have been as ready to descry a hazy "feudalism" at every end and turn. Historians have not devised terms for the multitude of intermediate agrarian forms, especially those off the main road of European history. It goes with this that they are poorly equipped to define what "bourgeois revolution" can or should mean in the countryside or what variant shapes it may take. These perplexities lend appeal to the hypothesis put forward lately by some Indian Marxists of a distinct "colonial" mode of production, specific to the epoch of modern imperialism.[100]

In Frank's scheme of things the failure of Latin America to add economic independence to the political self-government achieved in the early nineteenth century was inescapable, because all aspirations to it were hedged in by the capitalist framework.[101] This, too, sounds doctrinaire, because no other framework existed, and also because of the rapid success of the USA, which has to be explained away on the ground that the USA while tied to Britain was not exposed to so heavy a metropolitan pressure.[102] On the contrary, the impact of Britain's strenuous mercantilism might have been expected to be far weightier than that of Spain's languid imitation. To say that satellites were paralyzed by being impregnated with "the same capitalist structure and its fundamental contradictions"[103] leaves us in the dark about how capitalist Europe itself was forging ahead—under the impulsion, surely, of these very contradictions.

It was much rather because of the clash of class interests (combined with the philosophy of *mañana*) that most of Latin America was failing to achieve self-sufficiency. It might take the form of a collision between the interests of merchant capital, based on the ports and on import-export trade, and those of the hinterland;[104] though what the interior provinces, of Argentina for instance, had at the outset in the way of manufacture was only old-fashioned handicrafts, and it cannot be taken for granted that these would have blossomed spontaneously into modern industries. In Chile free trade and wheat exports triumphed over protection and industrialism because this suited the dominant landowning class, not because any outsider had power to compel it. Frank is entitled to say that opposition to industrializing efforts by two presidents, Montt in the 1850s and Balmaceda in the late 1880s, was encouraged by Britain;[105] but foreign influence did not decide the issue. Active meddling by Europeans was only occasional; they were always at cross-purposes; there could be no question of an occupation of any country. Rather, it might be said that security from any such menace deprived South America of the spur which set Japan in motion.

As we come nearer to the present, from British hegemony to American, the danger of open or covert intervention has become much more real. Even so, denial that any country once "satellized," or now undeveloped, can ever move forward on capitalist lines,[106] has too much resemblance to the Marxist dogma in the 1930s, following the world slump, that capitalism was now finally moribund, that the spirit of growth had transmigrated to the USSR. In recent decades Mexico has got quite far, despite the perilous proximity of its northern neighbor. Great social inequalities persist, but Mexico has "long since left the ranks of the world's poor countries." Four-fifths of industrial output has come from private enterprise, but state capitalism (or what in India is called the "public sector") has had an important role in aiding and sustaining it: in an old saying, "one hand washes the other."[107]

Under the Brazilian military regime an expansion more artificially organized from above has had to depend still more on state-capitalist underpinning: by 1977 this covered two-fifths of the two hundred largest enterprises, and private capital was feeling some dismay at this outcome of a seizure of power advertised as the rescue of Brazil from socialism.[108] In Asia what may be termed "military capitalism," pioneered in many ways by Japan, has been in the limelight. It has meant forced marches toward industrialism by regimes feeling obliged to compete with a nearby country which might stir up their own people against them: Pakistan's government with India, Taiwan's with China, South Korea's with North. In some of these countries, smaller and more vulnerable and therefore more amenable than Brazil to foreign tutelage, "multinational" corporations can take the place of state enterprise. They provide high-level technology, while dictatorship and martial law, under American sponsorship, guarantee an obedient labor force.[109] With these assets industrial growth—which American capitalism has all along been readier than British to promote—can be phenomenally rapid, though its benefits will be very slow to percolate down to the people. Some glimpses of the brutality of the process were afforded by the widespread protest movement of May 1980 against army rule in South Korea.

Conclusion

A dozen years ago a banking expert sent by President Johnson during the Vietnam War to report on southeast Asia wrote: "If there is to be more peace and less war on this planet, . . . we are going to have to promote something called development as a means of accommodating more of the millions in the world who are struggling to get a foothold."[110] Promotion of "military capitalism" has been America's chief response, and one result is that competition of cheap labor like South Korea's is worrying older industrial lands, including Japan. One of capitalism's deepening contradictions lies here. For the victims of the experiment it may be said to represent only the harshest of many paths that have been tried up and down the world, all in some degree painful. Planned development nowadays can be, in more favorable political conditions, less of an ordeal than the last century's chaotic growth; it can scarcely be made smooth and easy. There is besides the immovable obstacle that the earth has not resources to support industrialization on the prodigal Western scale for all and that if this *were* possible the planet would be reduced to a desert.

But there are many other reasons for hoping that the Third World, so critical of "Eurocentrism," will not want to ape the Western economy of waste too slavishly. Its idealists have been on the lookout for new pathways from the first. Even while nascent Indian nationalism was most avid for factory industry, patriots like R. C. Dutt were hopeful that "something of the home industries will survive the assault of capitalism"; a self-employed artisan or farmer, they were convinced, was superior to the wage laborer "in dignity and intelligence, in foresight and independence."[111] Gandhi was echoing this thinking with his spinning wheel, though his utopia, within the boundaries of a rigid class society, was unrealizable. African writers have regretted, among the things swept away or swept aside by imperialism, "the communal, anti-capitalist (and not merely pre-capitalist), cooperative, democratic, fraternal values" of an older day.[112] Among Québec separatists there are some who have no wish to see their province catching up in acquisitiveness with British Canada or the USA and choose to think of its future in a wider aspect of civilization than material output alone.[113] In this light it can appear good fortune to have been left behind for a while and by virtue of this to have the chance now not only of making headway but of making it in the right direction. All who have been thinking in ways like this have doubtless been small minorities, but force of circumstances may turn out to be on their side.

Notes

This chapter originally appeared as Occasional Paper No. 13 (1981) of the University College of Wales-Swansea Center for Development Studies.

1.   P. Gay, "On the Bourgeoisie: A Psychological Interpretation," in *Consciousness and Class Experience in Nineteenth-Century Europe,* ed. J. M. Merriman (New

York, 1979), 192. This volume might be called a study of development and underdevelopment.

2. F. H. Golay, "Southeast Asia: The 'Colonial Drain' Revisited," in *Southeast Asian History and Historiography*, ed. C. D. Cowan and O. W. Walters (Ithaca, N.Y., 1976), 368, 379. Cf. Malcolm Caldwell, "South East Asia from Depression to Re-occupation," *Sri Lanka Journal of the Humanities*, December 1976.

3. Boudhayan Cattopadhyay, "Foreign Private Capital in South and East Asia on the Eve of the Second World War," in *Essays in Honour of Professor S. C. Sarkar*, ed. Barun De et al. (Delhi, 1976), 783, 814.

4. "An Edict of the King of Prussia" (1773). An earlier precedent was the cutting down of spice trees by the Dutch, to secure a monopoly of shipments to Europe.

5. R. J. Hammond, *Portugal and Africa, 1815–1910: A Study in Uneconomic Imperialism* (Stanford, 1966), x; cf. 65, 66, 139.

6. U. Melotti accuses European socialists of being accustomed "to pass off imperialist and racist ideas . . . by dressing them up as orthodox Marxism": *Marx and the Third World* (London, 1977), 9.

7. M. Caldwell, *The Wealth of Some Nations* (London, 1977), 55.

8. E. Mandel, *Marxist Economic Theory* (London, 1962), 441.

9. A. G. Frank, *Capitalism and Underdevelopment in Latin America* (New York, 1967), 3.

10. Caldwell, *The Wealth of Some Nations*, 76.

11. Ibid., 66.

12. Frank, *Capitalism and Underdevelopment*, 96.

13. R. Firth, *Human Types* (London, 1975), 60, 71ff.

14. See, e.g., Engels's letter to F. A. Sorge from Montreal, 10 September 1888.

15. T. C. Haliburton, *The Clockmaker* (1836).

16. M. Rioux, *La Question du Québec* (Montreal, 1978), 36–37.

17. Ibid., 228.

18. Caldwell, *The Wealth of Some Nations*, 54.

19. On this subject it is worthwhile to read L. Dermigny, *La Chine et l'Occident: Le Commerce à Canton au XVIIIe siècle, 1719–1833* (Paris, 1964), Part 2, Chapter 1, and Conclusion. Cf. Melotti, *Marx and the Third World*, Chapter 16, "The Long Stagnation of Societies Based on the Asiatic Mode of Production," e.g., p. 103 on the "suffocating State power" which prevented moneyed classes from attaining the freedom of action "that in the West opened the way to capitalism." Chapter 17 is on China.

20. Mandel, *Marxist Economic Theory*, 442.

21. See L. C. Jain, *Indigenous Banking in India* (London, 1926). Irfan Habib describes the use of something like bills of exchange but concludes that such financial practices were not leading toward industrial capitalism: "Banking in

Mughal India," in *Contributions to Indian Economic History,* ed. T. Raychaudhuri (Calcutta, 1960), 10ff., 20.

22. Caldwell, *The Wealth of Some Nations,* 70.

23. Prabhat Patnaik, "Imperialism and the Growth of Indian Capitalism," in *Studies in the Theory of Imperialism,* ed. R. Owen and B. Sutcliffe (London, 1972), 212.

24. Cf. H. B. Lamb, "The 'State' and Economic Development in India," in *Economic Growth: Brazil, India, Japan,* ed. S. Kuznets et al. (Chapel Hill, N.C., 1955), 464. "By the eighteenth century India had attained a very high degree of development in preindustrial terms." Lamb goes on to blame the British connection for the failure to evolve further.

25. Ashin Das Gupta, "Trade and Politics in 18th-century India," in *Islam and the Trade of Asia,* ed. D. S. Richards (Oxford, 1970), 181, 183–84.

26. Ibid., 192–93.

27. Amales Tripathi, *Trade and Finance in the Bengal Presidency, 1793–1833* (Bombay, 1956), 258.

28. Mohibbul Hasan, *History of Tipu Sultan* (Calcutta, 1971) and *Waqai-i Manazil-i Rum: Diary of a Journey to Constantinople* (Bombay, 1968).

29. Das Gupta, "Trade and Politics," 197–98.

30. F. Braudel, *The Mediterranean and the Mediterranean World in the Age of Philip II* (London, 1972–73), 725.

31. W. Digby, *"Prosperous" British India: A Revelation from Official Records* (London, 1901), 30–33.

32. Mandel, *Marxist Economic Theory,* 441–43.

33. J. Strachey, *The End of Empire* (London, 1959), 63.

34. Ibid., 68.

35. F. W. Hirst, *The Stock Exchange* (London, n.d.), 39–40.

36. E. J. Hobsbawm, *Industry and Empire* (Harmondsworth, 1969), 75.

37. Ibid., 48; cf. 53: "the expansion of trade connected with the colonial system was stupendous."

38. See M. Barratt Brown, *After Imperialism* (London, 1963), 45ff., on the greater importance of India as a market for cloth than as a source of loot.

39. Hobsbawm, *Industry and Empire,* 191.

40. See S. B. Saul, *Studies in British Overseas Trade, 1870–1914* (Liverpool, 1960).

41. Hirst, *The Stock Exchange,* 69, 71–72.

42. G. Adhikari, "Pakistan and Indian National Unit" (London, n.d.), 19.

43. Sir John Shore quoted in Romesh Dutt, *The Economic History of India in the Victorian Age* (1903; reprint, London, 1960), 108–9.

44. Montgomery Martin quoted in ibid., 114.

45. Das Gupta, "Trade and Politics," 202. He adds: "It must be clearly realized that the industrial revolution did not break up a growing healthy structure of trade. It delivered the coup de grâce to a languishing commerce."

46. James Mill, *The History of British India* (1818; abridged ed., Chicago, 1975), 489.

47. Tripathi, *Trade and Finance*, 18.

48. P. Auber, *An Analysis of the Constitution of the East-India Company* (London, 1826), 292. Cf. 294: "The Company's bonds are a very marketable security, and present an eligible investment."

49. Figures in Dutt, *The Economic History of India*, 217.

50. G. A. Prinsep, *Remarks on the External Commerce and Exchanges of Bengal* (London, 1823), 12–13.

51. Tripathi, *Trade and Finance*, 178.

52. *Marx-Engels on India* (Moscow, 1959), 125–26.

53. Tripathi, *Trade and Finance*, 138.

54. J. Capper, *The Three Presidencies of India* (London, 1853), 381–82. He had been editor of the *Ceylon Examiner*.

55. Tripathi, *Trade and Finance*, 250–251.

56. Ibid., 266.

57. Capper, *The Three Presidencies*, 355.

58. Ibid., v–vi.

59. *Parliamentary Papers*, 1852–53, vol. 74 (East Indies, Public Works), par. 287.

60. Ibid., pars. 298, 300.

61. Ibid., App. L.

62. Ibid., par. 488.

63. See Dutt, *The Economic History of India*, 539: "The Conservative party were bound by many pledges and semi-pledges to the Lancashire voters."

64. Bipan Chandra, *The Rise and Growth of Economic Nationalism in India . . . , 1880–1905* (Delhi, 1966), 139–40.

65. A. P. Kannangara, "Indian Millowners and Indian Nationalism before 1914," *Past and Present*, no. 40 (1968).

66. Prinsep, *Remarks*, 17–18. On pp. 64–65 he alludes to "the Indian tribute to Great Britain."

67. Dadabhai Naoroji, *Poverty and Un-British Rule in India* (London, 1901), 33–34. Cf. Chandra, *The Rise and Growth*, 706: "the drain theory was revolutionary in its political implications." (Chapter 13 of Chandra's book is titled "The Drain.")

68. Dutt, *The Economic History of India*, 344, 528.

69. Digby, *"Prosperous" British India*, 17.

70. Ibid., 192. Yet in 1868 W. W. Hunter was expatiating on the "vast store of surplus capital, ever keenly on the look-out for investment . . . which forms so striking a feature in the mercantile economy of Bengal": *Annals of Rural Bengal* (London, 1897), 51.

71. Digby, *"Prosperous" British India*, 549.

72. Barratt Brown argues that it must: *After Imperialism*, 160, 164.

73. Tripathi, *Trade and Finance*, 223.

74. Bipan Chandra, *The Rise and Growth*, 74, 81. K. Davis, "Social and Demographic Aspects of Economic Development in India," in Kuznets et al., *Economic Growth*, 314–15, concludes that "social impediments" to progress added up to "a rather impressive amount of obstruction."

75. Bipan Chandra, *The Rise and Growth*, 84–85.

76. S. Gopal, *Jawaharlal Nehru, a Biography*, vol. 2 (London, 1979), 98.

77. J. Rosselli, *Lord William Bentinck: The Making of a Liberal Imperialist, 1774–1839* (London, 1974), 185.

78. Naoroji, *Poverty and Un-British Rule*, 629.

79. Digby, *"Prosperous" British India*, 262–63.

80. Bipan Chandra, *The Rise and Growth*, 91–93.

81. H. Venkatasubbiah, *The Foreign Trade of India, 1900–1940* (Delhi, 1946), 81.

82. Gokhale quoted in Dutt, *The Economic History of India*, 574.

83. Dutt, *The Economic History of India*, 613.

84. Caldwell, *The Wealth of Some Nations*, 80.

85. Syed Husain Alatas, *The Myth of the Lazy Native* (London, 1977), 196–97.

86. Ibid., 20–21.

87. G. A. Kertesz, in *Intellectuals and Revolution*, ed. E. Kamenka and F. B. Smith (London, 1979), 72.

88. S. Barrows, "After the Commune," in Merriman, *Consciousness and Class Experience*, 213.

89. Caldwell, *The Wealth of Some Nations*, 71–72.

90. Mandel, *Marxist Economic Theory*, 473.

91. Caldwell, *The Wealth of Some Nations*, 68.

92. M. N. Roy, *A Marxist Interpretation of Chinese History* (abridged ed., Boston, n.d.), 14, 83–84. At the same time Roy censured those who exaggerated China's difference from Europe and judged it unable "to absorb the conquests of modern civilisation."

93. Frank, *Capitalism and Underdevelopment*, xiv.

94. M. Rodinson, *Islam and Capitalism* (Harmondsworth, 1977), Chapter 3.

95. Frank, *Capitalism and Underdevelopment*, xi.

96. Ibid., 245.

97. Ibid., 94.

98. Ibid., 198.

99. Ibid., 89.

100. See Hamza Alavi, "India and the Colonial Mode of Production," in *The Socialist Register, 1975,* ed. R. Miliband and J. Saville (London, 1975). On pp. 193–94 he lists other writers on the theme, including Jairus Banajee.

101. Frank, *Capitalism and Underdevelopment,* 55–56.

102. Ibid., 12.

103. Ibid., 10.

104. See, e.g., H. S. Ferns, *Britain and Argentina in the Nineteenth Century* (Oxford, 1960), Chapter 2.

105. Frank, *Capitalism and Underdevelopment,* 72–73, 79ff.; cf. 287.

106. A denial too often and too readily repeated, as Sutcliffe remarks: "Imperialism and Industrialization in the Third World," in Owen and Sutcliffe, *Studies,* 174.

107. M. S. Baratz, "Mexico," in *Economies of the World Today,* ed. C. Wilcox et al. (New York, 1976), 93–94, 103–4.

108. Bruce Handler, in the *Guardian,* 9 February 1977.

109. In South Korea, as R. Whymant writes, "Strikes are illegal, workers' pay has lagged behind inflation, there is no minimum wage law, labour laws on work conditions are flouted with impunity" (*Guardian,* 6 November 1976).

110. Eugene Black, *The Alternatives in Southeast Asia* (London, 1969), 153.

111. Dutt, *The Economic History of India,* 518–19.

112. T. Hodgkin, "Some African and Third World Theories of Imperialism," in Owen and Sutcliffe, *Studies,* 110.

113. Rioux, *La Question du Québec,* Chapter 11.

3

COLONIAL AFRICA AND ITS ARMIES

One of the prizes of empire has always been a supply of colonial soldiery, for use on the spot or elsewhere. It is likely to be cheap, and its employment draws off warlike elements that might make trouble. All the old empires raised troops from subjugated provinces; some, like the Assyrian and the Roman, came to rely far more on colonial levies than on their own manpower. Tribesmen from Numidia or Mauritania were among Rome's innumerable recruits, and involvement in the wars of other countries has been through the ages one feature of a vast African diaspora. In Muslim India, whose rulers could seldom rely on their own subjects, African as well as many other foreign swordsmen were familiar figures: they were known as "Habshis"—blacks, or Abyssinians. An English traveler in the seventeenth century came on them in Ceylon, at the capital of the king of Kandy. "He hath also a Guard of Cofferies or Negro's, in whom he imposeth more confidence, than in his own People."[1] As late as the end of the nineteenth century the Nizams of Hyderabad kept a disorderly rabble known as the "African Bodyguard."[2]

In Europe a Negro battalion took part in the French siege of Gaeta in 1806, and for a bonus of fifty centimes the men were encouraged to run and pick up enemy shells and try to remove the fuses before they could explode.[3] Before the twentieth century Africans were frequently made use of in the Americas, though there were obvious risks in arming members of the slave race. Individual masters would hesitate, as French planters did,[4] but governments at a pinch were bolder. Brazilian Negroes fought well against Dutch and French invaders in the seventeenth century. In Jamaica in 1728, when the authorities could not depend on their poor whites, mostly Irish, in case of Spanish attack, they formed a corps of Negroes who were to be posted behind them and ordered to shoot any who turned tail.[5] To Tom Cringle, watching a militia parade in Kingston, the blacks looked a good deal more martial than either the white men or the mulattos.[6] Argentina during its struggle for independence made use of free Negroes and Mulattos and then filled the gaps with slaves.[7] Later on the dictator Manuel Rosas, aided by his amiable daughter Manuelita, won the impulsive loyalty of the blacks, who furnished him with spies inside every family and with retainers not to be bribed by any rival.[8] North Americans, too, drew on Negroes in the course of their War of Independence, which was to bring so little freedom to the black man; and when Melville served in the navy he found a slave among his messmates.[9] Long after emancipation, black men in the American army represented a sort of "colonial" soldiery.

Thus, long before the "scramble for Africa," the fighting qualities of some of its people had been known abroad, while its discords made it easy for outsiders to secure a following. Warfare in many forms was endemic, from tribal skirmishes to quite large-scale encounters. An eighteenth-century Portuguese explorer was impressed by the power of one Kazembe, or ruler, in the Congo whose troops were "remarkably well disciplined, and very orderly in their behaviour."[10] Although the continent had lagged far behind in weaponry, it showed a precocious quickness to learn. West Africa's long history of organized warfare was enlivened from the Middle Ages onward by the advent of horse and gun, and states and dynasties rose and fell on the tides of conquest. An early Dutch agent there warned his employers of African skill in the use of "muskets and carabines," and deplored the facility with which these weapons could be obtained.[11]

Portugal, the pioneer, was always short of manpower, and defended its scattered strongholds in Africa as in Asia chiefly with local levies or mercenaries. A victory over the Congolese was won in 1665 by an army of "3,000 African bowmen, 200 European troops, 150 settlers, and 100 African riflemen."[12] Defoe's Captain Singleton, crossing the continent, could only trust his captured porters with bows and lances, and wanted them to think the white men's firearms supernatural;[13] but the Portuguese leaders had no fear of putting them into the hands of black recruits, too divided among themselves to think of combining against their masters.

By the nineteenth century Angola had a second-line force known as the *guerre preta* or black army, "raised on a vassal basis by chiefs of the coastal belt whom the Portuguese had terrified, corrupted, or otherwise persuaded into co-operation."[14] For any expedition against a tribe of the interior it proved easy to obtain soldiers from another tribe hostile to it. There were normally more black troops than white,[15] despite Angola's growing number of white settlers, while a visitor to Guinea in 1936 paid tribute to Portugal's success in running it with 264 African volunteers under six white officers and eleven NCOs.[16] For some years after rebellion broke out in Angola in 1960, there was hesitation about relying on black troops, but by 1968 they were back in the line. According to an official statement in that year, a quarter of them were still volunteers, but opponents asserted that the proportion was really far smaller.[17]

As a rule, in colonial Africa only limited forces were required for policing heterogeneous populations with little or no national character. Resort to formal conscription was exceptional; indirect modes of compulsion were commoner. In either case there were affinities with slavery, and these revealed themselves from time to time, not only in the Portuguese empire where enslavement of black man by white lingered longest. Cut off in Egypt with a dwindling army—a premonition as it were of France's later dwindling manpower—Bonaparte ordered all Mamelukes from eight to fourteen years of age to be drafted and trained for service.[18] For more immediate purposes he was asking the sultan of Darfur in the Sudan to send shiploads of black slaves down the Nile[19] to be turned into defenders of liberty, equality, and fraternity. There was always likely to be a sub-Saharan ingredient in armed forces in northern Africa. When Mehemet Ali of Egypt was building a European-style army he invaded the Sudan partly in search of supplies of slaves to swell its ranks;[20] unluckily for him, all but 3,000 of the 20,000 brought to Assouan by 1824 cheated him by dying. Dinka tribesmen continued to be inducted as slaves into Sudanese units of the Egyptian army.[21] Servitude in indigenous forms went on. In the Great War a Sierra Leone chief thought himself entitled to impound the bounties due to seven of his "domestics" who joined or were pushed into the army, had any of them survived; and most of the carriers raised both there and in French West Africa were bondsmen.[22]

From the commencement of the long-drawn-out French conquest of Algeria, a generation later, native levies were being enlisted. Some Turkish *spahis* (*sipahi, sepoy*) marooned there joined, and *chasseurs spahis* began to be set on foot from material partly French, partly local. By 1914 there were seven regiments, and the corps lasted until Algeria regained independence. A Kabyle tribe, the Zwawa, which had been in the habit of supplying mercenaries to the Turks, in 1830 offered them to the French; though a few years later they deserted to the enemy under the influence of religious fanaticism, and from 1841 the "Zouave" corps was exclusively French.[23] Other local recruits became the *tirailleurs algériens*. A British officer observing the operations against the Kabyles in the late 1850s noticed how easy it was to enroll defeated tribesmen as irregulars eager to join their conquerors in plundering other villages with which they were feuding.[24] He noticed also that while the French stimulated zeal by allowing a few natives to win commissions, they took care—unlike the British in India before the Mutiny—not to trust their native soldiers with artillery.[25] After all of northwest Africa came under French rule, opinion held Moroccan recruits to be "by far the best," with Algerians second and Tunisians last.[26]

Senegal was occupied by the French in the time of the Second Empire,

and in 1857 its first administrator, Faidherbe, set on foot the first battalion
of *tirailleurs sénégalais*. From 1885 there was a regular mode of recruiting,
through chiefs who "often resorted to tyrannical methods to impress their
young subjects into French service"[27]—methods destined in the long run to
undermine their own ascendancy. It was with the troops thus acquired that
the rest of French West Africa was subdued. Reliance on local fighting men
obliged the French to fall in with local custom. Hope of plunder was the
volunteer's chief inducement, "and the regular distribution of captives was
the most efficient way to secure his continued loyalty. That female prisoners
were euphemistically called *épouses libres* did not make them any less a form
of payment.[28] In 1890 *tirailleurs soudanais* were added, in 1891 Hausas. In
1900 all black African units were incorporated in the army under the generic
title of *tirailleurs sénégalais,* though the Senegalese were now only the biggest
single contingent.[29]

Britain depended both at home and in India on voluntary enlistment, and
it was natural for the same practice to be followed in Africa. In West Africa
the military mind was never entirely satisfied with the material at hand. Burton
referred disparagingly to a Gold Coast Corps disbanded after mutinying in
1862.[30] "The West African people," according to two very recent writers,
"may be broadly divided into Negro, or debased races, and the finer types";
though they add that both species shared, when in uniform, "the useful
attributes of cheerfulness and loyalty."[31] Experiments began early. During
and after the Napoleonic wars Africans were enrolled in several units, most
prominently in the West India Regiments, which after 1840, with a Royal
African Colonial Corps reconstituted as one of them, took over garrison
duties in both West Africa and the Caribbean.[32] In 1863 some freed Hausa
slaves were formed into "Glover's Hausas," or the Lagos Constabulary, and
in 1873 some of these served under Wolseley in the sixth Ashanti war. They
were, it was said, so scared of guns that "they would hang them up in trees
and actually worship them," but a Scots officer succeeded in licking this
unpromising material into shape.[33] In 1897 a group of units were amalgam-
ated into the West African Frontier Force.

As British control spread over Nigeria, the Muslim north offered a recruiting ground which must have reminded Britons of northwest India. In 1914
the Nigeria Regiment, as one constituent of the West African Frontier Force,
was formed out of a miscellany of earlier formations, like the one put together
by the Niger Company.[34] It had not been intended to serve outside its own
region, and when in 1916 it was decided to raise a Nigerian Brigade for the
campaign in German East Africa, men from each company were invited to
come forward. Many northerners did, "but in the south matters were not
nearly so good." An NCO assured an officer that they would go wherever
they were ordered, but they would not *volunteer* to go so far from home: "a
man was a fool to leave his wife and family, home and comfort, for war and

discomfort."[35] A more sensible attitude, or one further removed from the instincts of the true fighting breeds, could scarcely be imagined. There were still Europeans who deemed Nigerians and West Africans at large only fit for porter work.

Europe's standing armies were often built up in the sixteenth century round a nucleus of foreign mercenaries, and this pattern can be found repeating itself in Africa. A police force was set up in the German Cameroons in 1891 which included Hausas and Dahomans, to whom were added men from Togo and the Sudan. In 1895 a regular *Schutztruppe* or "protective force" was instituted.[36] It was kept up to the mark by flogging, but its function was to protect German interests, not the population, against which it was guilty of much high-handed conduct. "Natives have an almost innate tendency to exploit their fellows," one scholar commented[37] somewhat fatuously. Germans could virtuously point to their "protectorate Troops Law" of 1896, which restricted native levies to the scale needed for police duties, and eschewed any militarizing policy like that of the French.[38]

In the Congo Free State the first nonwhite soldiers were collected from Zanzibar, Nigeria, and elsewhere;[39] then men were drawn from certain provinces whose inhabitants the Belgians regarded as "martial races." Grogan, the Cape-to-Cairo traveler, accused them of tapping the wrong tribes, degraded and vice-sodden cannibals. "Most natives can be touched in their pride or sense of the responsibility of a soldier's position," he wrote. "But these brutes are mere brutes."[40] It might be replied that they were wanted, in the bad early days of the Congo, for brutal business. Grogan alleged also that instead of being supplied with provisions, they were too often left to supply themselves, by "commandeering."[41] Subsequently each province was called on for a quota, but down to 1914 some furnished more men than others, and even after that date, more sergeants.[42]

In eastern Africa, too, European power found its first props in soldiers from outside. But many areas were well stocked with "martial races" of their own. Livingstone's letters reflect a very marked dichotomy between two types of people, one remarkably pacific, the other aggressive and predatory. This was a situation favorable to intruders, with the slave dealers from the coast, Arab or Portuguese, in the lead. They were attended by fighting men culled from "such tribes as exhibited the qualities of ruthlessness and courage of a far higher order than that possessed by their victims."[43] These "more virile" natives were of Wakuma, Masai, Yao, and Zulu stock. An unfriendly witness, a South African officer writing on "The Natives and Their Military Value," paid the Wakuma and Masai the compliment of crediting them with physiognomies "much closer to those of Europeans' than most Africans could boast; and he pointed out that British, Belgian, and German *askaris*—this Arab word became the standard term for soldier in the whole region—were drawn from the same districts, some far off in the Sudan.[44] That some peoples, or classes, are more martial than others is a fact, but one due to social circumstances and conditioning, and liable to rapid change. Europeans were too apt to see if it is an unchanging genetic fact, on a par with their own inborn superiority.

Askaris of the true breed "simply loved being soldiers."[45] Army life was the one least out of harmony, in this new age, with their old habits: they took no interest in the schools and clerkships that European rule brought and that other African communities eagerly clutched at. There were marked differences of temperament among the martial races themselves, with a dividing line between those amenable to strict army training and those impatient of it. Organized drill and discipline have been the hallmark of modern European warfare and were giving Europe the mastery of the world. Willingness to submit to them is a social phenomenon of complex origins but must be connected with habituation to authoritarian rule. Zululand was developing both a despotic monarchy and a code of military obedience not equaled perhaps anywhere in old Asia. Masai, seminomadic pastoralists, shone as irregulars or as scouts or guides. By contrast, some of the men who put on uniforms took so readily to the parade ground that they could be seen going on with their exercises in their free time. "For drilling and parade," a British observer concluded, "the native mind shows great keenness and aptitude. . . . Smart and well-disciplined they are most punctilious in all military services."[46]

It was out of this stuff that the King's African Rifles (KAR) were embodied in 1902: by 1914 they mustered twenty-one companies, veterans of a long series of minor campaigns.[47] This regiment was a fusion of three that had come into being in Britain's East African territories. These, too, started with a nucleus of outsiders. The Central Africa Regiment, in Nyasaland, began with Indian soldiers, mostly Sikhs; the Uganda Rifles with a very mixed bag of Sudanese, among them Egyptians and tribesmen; the first East Africa Rifles were another hotchpotch, taken over from the private army of the Imperial British East Africa Company.[48] It was the same story with the Northern Rhodesia Regiment; it consisted at the outset, in 1894, of two hundred Sikhs, volunteers from the Indian army, forty Zanzibaris, forty Arabs, sixty-nine Makua recruited with Portugese permission in Mozambique, along with "negro irregulars" from a medley of local tribes.[49] There would be obvious difficulties in the way of turning such a scratch lot into an effective force, but at least its motley ingredients would never combine either with one another or with the surrounding population against their paymasters.

In German East Africa, where the last revolt was not quelled until 1907, the first members of the *Schutztruppe* set up in 1891 were likewise strangers, most of them Zulus, Somalis, Sudanese, Swahilis, or coast "Arabs."[50] As German power pushed inland, it drew on tribes like the Wasakuma and Angoni. "Particularly fruitful was the area around Tabora, in the centre of the territory, the land of the Wanyamwezi, which produced a large proportion of the German force."[51] Others came from British territory, among them men previously in battalions of the King's African Rifles disbanded in 1911 as superfluous,[52] an illustration of the artificiality of colonial frontiers in Africa. Enlistment was for five years and could be renewed; native NCOs were usually long-term men. The German authorities, it was credibly enough reported, "assiduously encouraged their Askaris . . . to consider themselves in every way superior to the mass of non-military natives and as a class apart from their fellows." They proved very "receptive of the military cult," behaved like men of a higher caste, and looked altogether different from the rest, "in whose demeanour the sense of inferiority and the timidity engendered by years of oppression was very noticeable."[53] This was not much unlike the relative status of army and civilians in Hohenzollern Germany. Every two askaris shared a "boy," or batman. They were "very vain and proud," their commander from 1914, von Lettow-Vorbeck, found, and there was no getting rid of such customs.[54] Like all the other forces, they had besides an indispensable train of carriers, "ruga-ruga," who might be given some military lessons. When the censorious Grogan reached a post in Tanganyika, he was for once delighted with what he found. "The German black troops keep splendid order, and the station has the most flourishing air. I am a great believer in the Germans' African methods."[55]

After their initial duty of helping to "pacify" their own region, colonial levies might be utilized further afield. Angolan troops were used in the 1880s against rebels in Mozambique.[56] When the Italians attacked Ethiopia, a large part of the army defeated at Adowa in 1896 was composed of men from their African possessions.[57] Ethiopia itself had been expanding of late by methods akin to those of the European empires, absorbing into its army warriors from the areas overrun by the dominant Amharas. In the British case it was the strain of the Boer War a year or two later, with white men alone in action, that led to East African detachments being employed far away from their homes. In 1899 some men of the Central Africa Regiment were sent to Mauritius; they were allowed to take one wife each but fell foul of the Creole inhabitants. Next year others from the same corps found themselves in the Gold Coast and in Somaliland fighting the "Mad Mullah."[58] Somalis of northern Kenya made useful soldiers and policemen, though they tried to insist on being accorded a better status than ordinary Africans;[59] and it was lamented that some of "the riff-raff to be found about the bazaars of sea-port towns" had been allowed to get into the army and infect the solid, reliable "up-country" Somalis.[60] The French had started earlier, using Algerians in their Crimean and Italian wars, and at the end of 1913, of 76,000 men engaged in the occupation of Morocco, 12,000 were Senegalese.[61] Here was the same process that India had gone through, a kind of snowballing through which a small investment of European manpower could yield large returns.

The Great War embroiled Africa as well as Europe, and, unlike the Boer War, it ranged European and African together on both sides—a disagreeable surprise to "those who said that hostilities would be confined to Europe, and that war between two white races in a black man's country was unthinkable."[62] Nigerian and Gold Coast units helped to round up the Germans in the Cameroons before joining in the vastly more arduous campaign in East Africa. They were wanted there because of heavy mortality from sickness among the white troops. Nigeria's first contingent, in 1916, was made up of 2,402 African soldiers with 125 British officers and seventy British NCOs; their own mortality was to be heavy enough.[63] Indians taking part, including Baluchis, Kashmiris, Panjabis, Pathans, were joined by Portuguese and Belgians with their African auxiliaries. Besides all these there were South Africans, who gave deep offense to the Nigerians by addressing them as "boys," as they were accustomed to do with all black men at home;[64] and for part of the time the commander-in-chief was Smuts. Altogether, if Leipzig was a Battle of the Nations, this was a war of the races.

As in the Boer War, a huge sledgehammer was being brought to bear on a very small band of opponents, but now most of these were black men. While the Indian corps was getting ready, its commander, Brigadier General A. E. Aitken, stated tersely: "The Indian Army will make short work of a lot of niggers."[65] Lettow-Vorbeck's memoirs describe the capture of four Indian companies and their British officers, and "the warlike pride with which our Askari regarded the enemy; I never thought our black fellows could look so distinguished."[66] It was thanks in great measure to the quality of these men that his tiny army "engaged, from first to last, the attention of 372,850 British, and surrendered twelve days *after* the Armistice."[67] He began the contest with 2,540 askaris and enrolled 11,000 more in the course of it; he could scrape together about 3,000 Germans.[68] There were times when the "splendid bearing" of the Africans breathed fresh confidence into despondent Europeans,[69] and in the remnant which finally laid down its arms, reduced to 1,323 men, askaris outnumbered Germans by nearly eight to one. An English settler who served against them testified that "as a rule the German, black or white, fought us clean and fair."[70]

Immense devastation fell on some areas; thousands of villagers were carried off by the rival forces as porters. Kenya alone paid for the war with an estimated 46,000 African lives.[71] Meanwhile the KAR expanded to a strength of nearly 32,000, including some captured German askaris,[72] and at the end of the war their victory parade at Nairobi was a stirring occasion.[73] Glory had been dearly bought, but there was at least the novel sensation of a spectacle in which ordinary Africans could take pride.

In the Great War, writes Lord Wavell, "for the first time in history coloured troops were used in warfare on the continent of Europe."[74] They came mostly from India or Africa. Their coming was not unforeseen. Britain's regular army was small, and France, in the best position to tap the African supply, was heavily outnumbered by Germany. Use of colonial troops to make good the deficiency had found its loudest advocate in Colonel Mangin, most of whose career before 1914 was spent in the colonies. In 1910 he wrote a book, *La Force noire,* which made a strong impression on many other army men and politicians. In the same year he headed a mission charged to explore the potential of West African manpower as the raw material of war, and the Assembly approved a plan to raise 20,000 more *tirailleurs* within the next four years.[75] From 1912 any shortage was made up by compulsion: district headmen had to supply quotas of *appelés,* for four years with the colors. The burden was depicted as a light one, only one man per thousand it was said officially. Similar measures were introduced in Madagascar and Indochina. It was becoming a cliché to refer complacently to Africa as "un immense réservoir d'hommes, prêts à défendre la patrie." When the expected war came, it brought 1,918,000 men from the colonies to France, 680,000 of them combatants, and for Frenchmen the reality of their empire became for the first time thrillingly alive.[76] There had always been critics who urged the folly of sending the country's soldiers away to remote corners of the globe; now empire was proving itself an asset, instead of a liability, to national defense.

In French black Africa about 215,000 soldiers were mobilized during the Great War, of whom 157,000 were sent abroad and about 30,000, a very high ratio, killed.[77] To bring in recruits, considerable pressure was exerted, both in this and in the Second World War, through chiefs or headmen, who were government cats-paws, and through Muslim religious leaders who, having a status of their own, could drive bargains with the French in return for inducing their disciples to take service instead of helping them, as they often did at first, to dodge it.[78] In 1915 some of these soldiers were at Gallipoli, and the Muslims among them, as among the Indian units, were pitted against their Turkish coreligionists. Sir Ian Hamilton, the Allied commander, was not much pleased to see them. "These niggy-wigs were as awkward as golly-wogs in the boats," he confided to his diary after watching practice landings,[79] and he was soon disgruntled because "the proportion of white men in the French Division is low; there are too many Senegalese."[80] He objected again when the French withdrew some of their own troops and noted that "the Turks dropped manifestos from aeroplanes along the lines of the Senegalese calling upon these troops to make terms and come over now that their white comrades had left them to have their throats cut."[81] Turkish propaganda filtering through the Sahara combined with discontent at home against the French demands for more men to cause a serious revolt in 1916.[82]

But it was on the western front that most of the French African troops were deployed. During the retreat from Mons, Douglas Haig observed that a neighboring French corps included Moroccans, "chilled and depressed" in their light tropical wear.[83] A vanguard of Senegalese reached the trenches of Artois that same autumn, and "literally died of cold";[84] their superiors had not troubled to think about climate or clothing. Winter camps were then formed for them on the Riviera, and they did much good service; their habit of massacring prisoners struck alarm into the enemy.[85] It was in 1917, after the costly failure of many offensives, that the highest hopes were pinned on them, as men who could be counted on to break through any line, to display something like the *furia francese* of former days or the whirlwind of a Highland charge. They were known as "Mangin's blacks"; he was now at the head of the sixth Army, cast for a prominent role in the great new attack mounted by Nivelle, and was impatient to make good his doctrine of Africa as the sword arm of France. "Mangin was a killer, and he looked the part,"[86] but most of his victims were to be his own men. "In the spring," wrote Brigadier General Spears, who was with a British corps on the flank, "long trains hauled their cargoes of black chattering happy sub-humans to the area where presently the heaviest fighting would take place"[87]—language graphically expressive of the white man's feelings about his black cannon fodder.

But instead of a "wild savage onrush," when their day of glory arrived on 16 April 1917, they were so numb with icy rains that they could scarcely crawl forward. "They got quite a long way before the German machine-gunners mowed them down." In the confusion, French as well as German guns were firing on them. Of 10,000 engaged, 6,300 were casualties, the rest broke into panic flight. It was a "heart-breaking spectacle," says Spears, but he adds consolingly: "As they ambled back they soon recovered their composure. Fear had probably never penetrated their thick skulls."[88] On the murderous battles of July and August the following year Ludendorff was to comment: "The French had sent into action a remarkably large number of Senegalese and Moroccans and had endeavoured to spare their own people."[89] As Spears remarked, the French turn of mind was "unsentimental"; and their own men had sometimes mutinied. We are told that they have "gratefully remembered" Senegal and its sacrifices;[90] but gratitude seems to have confined itself after 1918 to monuments in Dakar in honor of the "morts pour la patrie."[91]

When Smuts was laying down the command in East Africa he paid tribute to "the native troops, who make splendid infantry . . . they have done magnificent work."[92] At the end of the war he sounded a warning against allowing the Germans back into Africa, where they might raise formidable armies and use them to conquer other territories and build an economic and military power which "might yet become an important milestone on the road to world Empire."[93] At the peace conference when the mandate system was being devised, governments administering backward populations, especially in central Africa, were forbidden to militarize them. This was meant to protect whites at least as much as blacks, but the French strongly objected to any such restraints.[94] Fears continued to haunt the South African mind of "hordes of native soldiers," trained by white rulers, who might be "a grave menace to European civilization on the continent"; the Italian conquest of Ethiopia would make possible "the rapid preparation of a native army formidable in numbers and military spirit."[95] Norman Angell believed that this had indeed been Mussolini's prime motive: "we shall find Italy with a million black conscripts, not to fight in Africa but in Europe."[96]

France's occupying forces in the Rhineland after 1918 included some blacks, partly, it must be supposed, as a means of rubbing their defeat into the Germans. Others were being employed in "pacifying" Syria and Morocco. Recruiting diminished after 1920 and in the interwar years averaged only about 10,000 annually—one sixth of what the army had pressed for—of whom two men in three were conscripts. Economically and socially, "the results of conscription were generally condemned as disastrous";[97] they were vividly depicted by the anthropologist Goer.[98] It was General Franco who brought African soldiers to fight again in Europe, this time in a civil war. His Moors appear to have been supplied by their feudal chiefs, at so much a head. According to a pro-Franco Spanish writer, about 80,000 were raised; he adds that "The Moorish soldier was generally excellent, showing blind obedience toward his Spanish officers."[99] George Padmore warned the left in Europe to be on its guard against similar use of African soldiery elsewhere and pointed out that "one-third of the French standing army garrisoned in France is composed of colonial professional troops."[100]

In the Second World War black Africa supplied the French with 160,000 men. In Nigeria 121,652 men were raised. Chiefs and notables were expected to persuade young men to come forward, and "possibly moral pressure was sometimes used"[101]—which may possibly be an understatement. Both Nigerians and KAR took part in 1940 in the liberation of Ethiopia, where prisoners included 11,732 Africans along with 10,350 Italians.[102] Later they served in Burma; and they demonstrated what had often been questioned, that complicated modern equipment was not beyond their ability to master.[103] During 1945–54, 56,000 black troops were sent to fight for France in Indochina, and then 30,000 in Algeria. Portugal went on with the same tactics until 1974; in 1976 Rhodesia was trying uneasily, under the spur of necessity, to raise more black mercenaries.

Egypt, never formally annexed, had to be allowed officers of its own. A training school for officers in the Sudan was set up in 1905.[104] But this was exceptional. The KAR came out of the Great War under the leadership of 1,423 British officers assisted by 2,046 British NCOs.[105] That only white men could be qualified to command was a general axiom of colonial armies; not mainly because of educational or technical requirements, which India, for example, could easily meet, but because white status had to be kept up and large-scale mutiny made improbable. This was still more essential in

Africa because of the absence of large numbers of European troops to provide a counterweight. Since native troops had no leaders of their own, it was easy to maintain that without white officers they would always be helpless. This was only a logical extension of a conviction that European peasants or workmen could only make good soldiers when led by men of the higher classes. Any broad gulf whether of class or of race is likely to foster a mystique of "leadership."

Both Senegalese and north Africans could stand heavy shellfire, Spears considered, but when their officers were knocked out, "they were apt to become a general nuisance if not a danger."[106] "No single factor is of greater importance with colonial troops than the choice of suitable European leadership," writes the historian of the KAR, and he finds one reason for the Italian collapse in Africa in 1940 in "the poor quality of many of the officers and NCOs serving with the native regiments."[107] He describes the inexperienced British askaris of that time as shaky at first. "Africans tend to be better in attack than in defence" and to be "credulous" and "quickly affected by rumour," easily unnerved by tactical retreats.[108] Clearly this is likely to be the case with any soldiers who have no leaders of their own kind. In East Africa, as in most areas, chiefs seldom joined the army, preferring to ingratiate themselves with authority by getting others to join instead. Bechuana and Basuto soldiers in the Second World War had an advantage here: some of their chiefs were with them, with the rank of RSM, and could "lead and advise, exhort, bring news, explain difficulties"—and being largely Christians, they had native pastors with them as well.[109]

Between white officer and black private, one stumbling block was language. In the British case, ability to communicate with the men was less readily acquired in Africa, where most officers were regulars who came out from their own regiments for a short term only, than in India. East Africa's lingua franca, "kitchen Swahili," was very simple, a member of the KAR in its later days remarked, but some officers and NCOs never learned it; this he thought "totally unforgivable," the more so as many askaris had to learn it as a new language, besides a modicum of English.[110] To one Englishman washed into the KAR by the Second World War, relations between the regular officers, despite their very poor linguistic attainments, and their men seemed reasonably good: those between British regular NCOs and Africans much less so, because they were apt to be puffed up by their novel importance.[111]

How army service affected Africans and Africa is a question too little explored. Colonial forces were small at most times, and recruiting grounds as a rule restricted; they were likely to be—as in the Panjab or for that matter in the British Isles—the poorest, most backward areas, outside the mainstream of African life. This was so in French West Africa; in Nigeria "the best recruiting areas were those furthest from the regional capitals, in economically depressed parts"[112] chiefly in the north and the "middle belt." In Uganda they lay in the north, "among ethnic groups possessing a reputation for martial skills and few other economic opportunities."[113] This very backwardness, however, could mean that army life had all the more effect in shaking up the individual or group, and through them the archaic societies they belonged to. It could be, as for Amerindians and other preindustrial peoples, an intro-duction, for want of a better, to a modern world of gadgetry, of time regulated by clocks and watches; it was a bridge between past and present. In British eastern and central Africa "it is difficult to over-estimate the significance of the European military machine" in mixing together members of different communities, scattering people far and wide in the same way as work in the mines did.[114]

Soldiering and mine working had much in common, in the recruit's removal from his home, isolation, subjection to discipline; of the two, the army may be thought, in peacetime at least, the more humane employer. In western Africa it did something to undermine indigenous slavery, by offering one of the new occupations that bondsmen could run away to.[115] To men from very poor districts a very modest allowance of food and clothing was luxury. A force like the KAR provided an elementary education, as well as medical care, and some training in hygiene and domestic science for soldiers' wives; all this could give the recruit a better opinion of himself, along with an improved physique.[116] In its later days it had a training school where men leaving the ranks could turn themselves into craftsmen or welfare officers.[117] There was always a trickle of men ending their service after a shorter or longer term, carrying their new acquirements with them; it was noticeable in the Congo that they were often so completely detached from their old moorings that they preferred to settle in the towns instead of going back home.[118] After both world wars the trickle became a flood. In the Second World War espe-cially, with its far more complex requirements, recruits had to be sought from wider sections of society, as well as in greater numbers; from south as well as north, in Nigeria as in India. Men who went abroad often came home with altered ideas about themselves and their world. After 1945 an observer wrote of Africans, whose horizons till lately had been bounded by their villages, returning from battlefields in Europe or Burma with new vistas before them and a thirst for education, the "white man's juju," as the bringer of "wealth, power, and success," the three things needed for happiness in life.[119]

Politically, the consequences of the colonial army system may have been on the whole less good, but they were very mixed. Sometimes service might intensify old tribal loyalties and rivalries. These could hamper smooth running, as an officer noted,[120] but they had their uses too. It was for a long time the practice of the KAR to have half of a company made up of Yao and half of hereditary foes of theirs like the Angoni, although by 1926 it could be said that "all the Nyasaland troops have proved themselves so reliable that such a precaution is not really necessary."[121] Mutinies between 1895 and 1900 made the Belgians decide that the Congo army must be "ethnically integrated down to the squad level"; when another outbreak in 1944 disclosed that there had been carelessness about this, "it was reiterated that at least four ethnic groups had to be represented in each platoon."[122] It must have been largely due to such measures that mutinies were on the whole uncommon, by comparison with India, up to 1857.

Conversely, army service, with this shuffling up of elements, might have a detribalizing influence and make for a new, wider union. In East Africa it was sometimes found that men serving British and Germans did not hesitate "to fight against their blood brothers."[123] Or members of diverse tribes might come together in a common loyalty, cemented by a regiment's traditions, ceremonies, and songs.[124] In an epoch when old social ties were loosening, and many individuals were cast adrift, this might supply a new brotherhood or "family." And in some degree such coming together might contribute to the molding of Africa's new nations. In the Belgian Congo the "Force publique," with its wide catchment from all the provinces, could be deemed "the most truly national Congolese institution."[125] Nevertheless, it broke up the moment independence came, partly for want of an officer cadre of its own. During the world wars, especially the second, colonial governments in need of recruits had to make some appeal, as in India, to "national" feeling, and when Nigerian troops were fighting far away from home, it was easier to think, or talk, of "Nigeria" as an entity. Yet on the whole, few Nigerians came to think of the army as "theirs," as a part of a nation.[126]

Dividing and ruling might be practiced between army and people as well as between soldier and soldier. Sometimes its results came about without intention, as at Freetown at the end of the nineteenth century when there was rioting between the West African Regiment and the populace.[127] Soldiers culled from backward areas "were quite ready to suppress rebellions against colonial rule that might arise elsewhere."[128] In Morocco the French could be accused of utilizing Berbers from the hills against Arabs of the towns.[129] In Mozambique toward the end, the Portuguese were playing on tribal enmities, hiring Makua against Makonde;[130] the worst atrocities of the repression may have been caused by these tactics. In Guinea, Fula tribesmen were set against the rebels, and attempts were made to set Cape Verdeans against main-landers.[131]

Colonial forces did contribute to emergent nationalism, indirectly or directly. Their achievements in foreign wars could stimulate African self-respect; in the early 1920s West African spokesmen were declaring that if black men had been good enough to take part in the Great War, they were good enough to take part in running their own governments.[132] In Senegal "blacks who had been feted by whites in France for their victories over another white race, began to doubt the innate superiority of the whites."[133] France, like

Portugal, went on with the game too long and again ignored religious feeling. There was resentment at the use of black troops in Algeria: a serious matter for a government "well aware that the Algerian and Moroccan troops which were used in Indochina" were now "the hard core of the rebel army in North Africa."[134] In British Africa, where this goad was lacking, things went differently. As in India, the "martial races" played little part in freedom struggles. Kikuyu were not taken into the KAR, John Gunther found, because, like Bengalis, they were reckoned "too intellectualized and unreliable."[135] Only six years later another visitor to Kenya was writing: "The Kikuyu, so long contemptuously dismissed as a rabble of cowardly 'Kukes,' have gone through fire"—one tenth of their whole community, he thought, had been killed or arrested.[136]

A decree of 1889 authorized Senegalese to be commissioned,[137] but few were in fact commissioned until after 1949, when officer training was embarked on as part of a program of black army expansion.[138] When the French left Africa they planned to retain military control. The British might have been expected toward the end to see their interest in training plenty of African officers, to leave behind as pillars of British influence and stability. Whether from lack of political foresight or from army prejudice, they trained very few. Absence nearly everywhere at independence of a competent and socially influential officer class—such as emerged in India during the Second World War—was by no means an unqualified misfortune. But in sum the armed forces bequeathed to the new Africa by the colonial régimes were small, badly equipped, and poorly led. So far they have been, as those of Latin America have always been, more of a nuisance than an asset.

Notes

This chapter originally appeared in Brian Bond and Ian Roy, eds., *War and Society: A Yearbook of Military History*, vol. 2 (London, Croom Helm, 1977).

1. Robert Knox, *An Historical Relation of Ceylon* (1681; reprint, Dehiwala, Ceylon, 1966), 65. I owe this reference to Dr. T. Barron.

2. J. E. Harris, *The African Presence in Asia* (Evanston, Ill., 1971), 102–5. Lord Macarthey found at Macao in 1794 an unimpressive company of Negro or mulatto infantry; see J. L. Cranmer-Bying, ed., *An Embassy to China* (London, 1962), 219.

3. P. de Ségur, *Un Aide-de-camp de Napoléon* (1873; Nelson ed., Paris, n.d.), 303.

4. E. Fieffé, *Histoire des troupes étrangères au service de la France* (Paris, 1854), vol. 1, 278–81.

5. H. O. Patterson, "Outside History: Jamaica Today," *New Left Review*, no. 31 (1965): 39.

6. M. Scott, *Tom Cringle's Log* (1836), Chapter 11.

7. T. H. Donghi, "Revolutionary Militarization in Buenos Aires, 1806–1815," *Past and Present,* no. 40 (1968): 87, 97.

8. See D. F. Sarmiento, *Facundo* (1845), and A. W. Bunkley, *The Life of Sarmiento* (Princeton, 1952), 84–85.

9. Herman Melville, *White Jacket* (1850), Chapter 90.

10. B. Davidson, *In the Eye of the Storm: Angola's People* (London, 1972), 77.

11. B. Davidson, *Africa in History* (London, 1968), 194.

12. D. M. Abshire and M. A. Samuels, eds., *Portuguese Africa: A Handbook* (London, 1969), 43.

13. Daniel Defoe, *The Life Adventures and Piracies of the Famous Captain Singleton* (Everyman ed., London, 1922), 62, 65.

14. Davidson, *In The Eye of the Storm,* 111.

15. Abshire and Samuels, *Portuguese Africa,* 209–10; cf. 407.

16. Ibid., 103.

17. Davidson, *In the Eye of the Storm,* 112.

18. J. C. Herold, *Bonaparte in Egypt* (London, 1962), 211–12. A "Mameluke corps" of Copts and others, who accompanied the French when they went home, was later formed (241, 391).

19. Ibid., 316.

20. H. Dodwell, *The Founder of Modern Egypt: A Study of Muhammad 'Ali* (Cambridge, 1931), 63–65.

21. R. Davies, *The Camel's Back: Service in the Rural Sudan* (London, 1957), 129–30.

22. J. Grace, *Domestic Slavery in West Africa . . . , 1896–1927* (London, 1975), 166, 221.

23. W. H. Chaloner and W. O. Henderson, eds., *Engels as Military Critic* (Manchester, 1959), 81–82.

24. H. M. Walmesley, *Sketches of Algeria during the Kabyle War* (London, 1858), 344ff.

25. Ibid., 29ff., 51.

26. C. G. Haines, ed., *Africa Today* (Baltimore, 1955), 57.

27. S. P. Davis, *Reservoirs of Men: A History of the Black Troops of French Africa* (Chambéry, 1934), 64.

28. A. S. Kanya-Forstner, *The Conquest of the Western Sudan: A Study in French Military Imperialism* (Cambridge, 1969), 272.

29. See War Office, *Handbook of the French Army,* 1914 ed., 71–73; *Larousse* encyclopedia, "Sénéal."

30. Sir R. Burton, *A Mission to Gelele, King of Dahome,* ed. C. W. Newbury (London, 1966), 187n.

31. Col. A. Haywood and Brig. F. A. S. Clarke, *The History of the Royal West African Frontier Force* (Aldershot, 1964), 11.

32. C. Fyfe, *A History of Sierra Leone* (Oxford, 1962), 215. Numerous references to military history will be found in the index, under "Army."

33. W. Baird, *General Wauchope* (Edinburgh, 1901), 41.

34. N. J. Miners, *The Nigerian Army, 1956–1966* (London, 1971), 12, 26.

35. Capt. W. D. Downes, *With the Nigerians in German East Africa* (London, 1919), 44.

36. H. R. Rudin, *Germans in the Cameroons, 1884–1914* (London, 1937), 193–94.

37. Ibid., 197.

38. Dr. H. Schnee (an ex-governor of German East Africa), *German Colonisation Past and Future* (London, 1926), 79.

39. V. A. Olorunsala, ed., *The Politics of Cultural Sub-nationalism in Africa* (New York, 1972), 206.

40. E. S. Grogan and A. H. Sharp, *From the Cape to Cairo* (Nelson ed., n.d.), 294.

41. Ibid., 295.

42. Olorunsala, *The Politics*, 201, 281.

43. Brig. Gen. J. J. Collyer, *The South Africans with General Smuts in German East Africa, 1916* (Pretoria, 1939), 18.

44. Ibid., 16–17.

45. I. Grahame, *Jumbo Effendi: Seven Years with the King's African Rifles* (London, 1966), 56.

46. Capt. R. V. Dolbey, *Sketches of the East Africa Campaign* (London, 1918), 23. Cf. W. Lloyd-Jones, *KAR, Being an Unofficial Account of the Origin and Activities of the King's African Rifles* (London, 1926), 106: "The African askari loves drill . . . he is a real joy to a good 'drill.'" Haywood and Clarke, *The History*, 323, tell of West Africans giving themselves extra drill.

47. Lt. Col. H. Moyse-Bartlett, *The King's African Rifles: A Study in the Military History of East and Central Africa, 1890–1945* (Aldershot, 1956), 259.

48. Ibid., 3, 11, 51.

49. W. V. Brelsford, *The Story of the Northern Rhodesia Regiment* (Lusaka, 1954), 4.

50. Brig. Gen. J. H. V. Crowe, *General Smuts' Campaign in East Africa* (London, 1918), 27; Maj. J. R. Sibley, *Tanganyikan Guerrilla: East African Campaign, 1914–1918* (London, 1973), 17–18.

51. Sibley, *Tanganyikan Guerrilla*, 18.

52. Crowe, *General Smuts' Campaign*, 29.

53. Collyer, *The South Africans*, 18–20.

54. Gen. von Lettow-Vorbeck, *My Reminiscences of East Africa* (London, n.d.), 24.

55. Grogan and Sharp, *From the Cape to Cairo*, 121.

56. R. J. Hammond, *Portugal in Africa, 1815–1910* (Stanford, 1966), 183.

57. See A. H. Atteridge, *Famous Modern Battles* (London, n.d.), Chapter 10, "Adowa." Other accounts differ as to the ratio of African troops in Baratieri's army.

58. Moyse-Bartlett, *The King's African Rifles*, 29–30, 33.

59. I owe my knowledge of Kenyan Somali soldiers to a seminar paper by Miss Mahassin El-Safi on Somalis in Kenya at Edinburgh University in February 1971.

60. Lloyd-Jones, *KAR*, 216–17.

61. War Office, *Handbook of the French Army*, 114–15.

62. C. J. Wilson, *The Story of the East African Mounted Rifles* (Nairobi, 1938), 9.

63. Downes, *With the Nigerians*, 46.

64. Ibid., 54–55.

65. B. Gardner, *German East: The Story of the First World War in East Africa* (London, 1963), 17.

66. Lettow-Vorbeck, *My Reminiscences*, 61.

67. J. Terraine, *Douglas Haig: The Educated Soldier* (London, 1963), 136.

68. Lettow-Vorbeck, *My Reminiscences*, 19.

69. Ibid., 142.

70. Wilson, *The Story*, 28.

71. Sir C. Lucas, ed., *The Empire at War*, vol. 4, Africa (Oxford, 1925), 236–37, 272–73; Davidson, *Africa in History*, 255.

72. Sibley, *Tanganyikan Guerrilla*, 116.

73. Moyse-Bartlett, *The King's African Rifles*, 415.

74. *New Cambridge Modern History*, vol. 12 (1960), 263.

75. Davis, *Reservoirs of Men*, 109–110; S. H. Roberts, *History of French Colonial Policy (1870–1925)* (London, 1929), 332.

76. Roberts, *History*, 605.

77. Exact figures are not known, and estimates vary somewhat; this is by Davis, *Reservoirs of Men*, 156.

78. C. Cruise O'Brien, "Chefs, saints et bureaucrates: La Politique coloniale au Sénégal," in *Sociologie de l'impérialisme*, ed. Anouar Abdel-Malek (Paris, 1971), 214–14.

79. General Sir Ian Hamilton, *Gallipoli Diary* (London, 1920), vol. 1, 104.

80. Ibid., vol. 1, 192; cf. 195.

81. Ibid., vol. 2, 226, 236–37.

82. V. Thompson and R. Adloff, *French West Africa* (London, 1958), 120.

83. Haig quoted in Terraine, *Douglas Haig*, 96–97.

84. Brig. Gen. E. L. Spears, *Prelude to Victory* (London, 1939), 203.

85. A. Horne, *The Price of Glory: Verdun 1916* (Harmondsworth, 1964), 308.

86. Ibid., 228.

87. Spears, *The Price*, 264–65.

88. Ibid., 490, 504–6.

89. Ludendorff, *My War Memories, 1914–1918* (English ed., London, 1920), 676.

90. M. Crowder, *Senegal: A Study of French Assimilation Policy* (rev. ed., London, 1967), 95.

91. There were long delays after the Second World War before any compensation was awarded to black veterans: Thompson and Adloff, *French West Africa*, 228–29.

92. Smuts quoted in Downes, *With the Nigerians*, 267.

93. Smuts quoted in the introduction to Crowe, *General Smuts' Campaign*, xvi. Cf. a long memorandum by Curzon, in December 1917, on the perils of a German militarization of Africa: W. R. Louis, *Great Britain and Germany's Lost Colonies, 1914–1919* (Oxford, 1967), 94–95.

94. League Covenant, Art. 23, Clause 5; H. W. V. Temperley, ed., *A History of the Peace Conference of Paris,* vol. 2 (London, 1920), 239–40.

95. Collyer, *The South Africans,* 16–17, 19.

96. Norman Angell quoted in Padmore, *Africa and World Peace* (London, 1937), 236.

97. Thompson and Adloff, *French West Africa,* 227, 232; cf. Roberts, *History,* 332.

98. G. Gorer, *Africa Dances: A Book about West African Negroes* (London, 1935).

99. R. de la Cierva y de Hoces, "The Nationalist Army in the Spanish Civil War," in *The Republic and the Civil War in Spain,* ed. R. Carr (London, 1971), 199.

100. Padmore, *Africa,* 235.

101. Miners, *The Nigerian Army,* 14.

102. Brelsford, *The Story,* 83.

103. Moyse-Barlett, *The King's African Rifles,* 573.

104. Sir H. Macmichael, *The Anglo-Egyptian Sudan* (London, 1934), 147.

105. Moyse-Barlett, *The King's African Rifles,* 413.

106. Spears, *The Price,* 265.

107. Moyse-Bartlett, *The King's African Rifles,* 573, 685.

108. Ibid., 572.

109. See D. H. Barber, *Africans in Khaki* (London, 1948), 86–87; B. Gray, *Basuto Soldiers in Hitler's War* (Naseru, 1953), 52–53. Mr. C. Himsworth kindly lent a copy of this work to me.

110. Grahame, *Jumbo Effendi,* 35.

111. Information from Professor G. A. Shepperson, 3 December 1975.

112. Miners, *The Nigerian Army,* 27.

113. Olorunsala, *The Politics,* 80.

114. G. A. Shepperson, "Military History of British Central Africa" (a review of Moyse-Bartlett, *The King's African Rifles*, in *Rhodes-Livingstone Journal* 26 (1959): 24, 26.

115. Grace, *Domestic Slavery*, 168.

116. I am indebted for this to an article kindly shown to me in advance of publication by the author, Dr. A. Clayton, of the Royal Military Academy, Sandhurst: "Communication for New Loyalties: African Soldiers' Songs."

117. N. Farson, *Last Chance in Africa* (London, 1953), 177.

118. Olorunsala, *The Politics*, 200–201.

119. D. M. McFarlan, *Celabar: The Church of Scotland Mission, 1846–1946* (Edinburgh, 1946), 165–66.

120. Grahame, *Jumbo Effendi*, 56–57.

121. Lloyd-Jones, *KAR*, 47.

122. Olorunsala, *The Politics*, 201.

123. Dolbey, *Sketches*, 23.

124. This is the main theme of the article referred to in note 116 above.

125. Olorunsala, *The Politics*, 241.

126. Miners, *The Nigerian Army*, 32; cf. 30, on complaints of disorderly behavior by some recruits, especially during the Second World War.

127. Fyfe, *A History*, 596.

128. Miners, *The Nigerian Army*, 2.

129. S. Smith, *U.S. Neocolonialism in Africa* (Moscow, 1974), 153–54.

130. Abshire and Samuels, *Portuguese Africa*, 423.

131. B. Davidson, *The Liberation of Guiné* (Harmondsworth, 1969), 62.

132. Davidson, *Africa in History*, 277.

133. Davis, *Reservoirs of Men*, 166–67.

134. Thompson and Adloff, *French West Africa*, 231.

135. J. Gunther, *Inside Africa* (London, 1955), 364.

136. E. S. Munger, letter from Nairobi, 14 March 1955, in E. S. Munger, ed., *African Field Reports, 1952–1961* (Cape Town, 1961), 247.

137. Davis, *Reservoirs of Men*, 66.

138. Thompson and Adloff, 231–32.

4

EUROPE AND THE WORLD: THE IMPERIAL RECORD

Earth is sick,
And Heaven is weary, of the hollow words
Which States and Kingdoms utter when they talk
Of truth and justice.
—Wordsworth, *The Excursion*, Book 5

A hundred years ago a Lhasa official said to a Briton from India: "Thibetans like to remain in their own land; how is it that the English are always craving for the territories of others?"[1] It was a question with a very wide bearing, considering that so much of history has been a matter of peoples trespassing on one another's soil. In modern times Europeans have done so most conspicuously. It may be reckoned to them as a sign of grace that they have learned to be capable in some degree of self-criticism over their conduct; it is unlikely that Roman intruders, Chinese, Arabs, or Turks ever acquired this capacity, except over some odd particular outrage. But far louder today than any self-reproaches of Europe are recriminations from the countries that it annexed or meddled with. Looking back on its collective past, contemplating its present condition, this "Third World" more and more loudly demands reparation by way of a better share of our planet's good things. Edmund Burke could only recommend the suffering and oppressed to await the final proportions of eternal justice; today, the poorer nations are as little inclined to follow such advice as the poorer classes.

Their claims rest on charges of injury, plundering, and impoverishment by the West, not of a material kind alone. On the other side there are benefits, tangible or less ponderable, to be set against what was appropriated. In some ways at least, it is scarcely possible not to recognize a heavy balance against Europe. But to draw up an account sheet, with every ramifying consequence included, would baffle any but the eye of Omniscience. O. Henry has a story about a well-meaning young man, inheritor of an ill-gotten fortune, who is anxious to make restitution; a carping socialist convinces him that to make good all the secondary and tertiary evils it was responsible for would more than swallow up all his money.

What is most easily discernible among the gains and losses belongs to the material sphere; to translate it into moral terms is harder, and a task historians

are little qualified to undertake. Ever since they turned into a regular professional body, a hundred years ago, they have prided themselves on a strict
objectivity, eschewing any concern with ethics (though not always with patriotism). What meaning history without regard to morality can possess, they
have not explained. Giambattista Vico thought of men unconsciously fulfilling
the purposes of Providence; others in search of a meaning may sometimes
feel drawn to a comforting notion of an automatically functioning distribution
of good and ill, like the self-adjusting market of the economists. Portuguese
and later Europeans descended on Asia and Africa to enrich themselves by
fair means or foul, but they brought with them a wide range of useful new
plants and animals.

One complication is that Europe through most of its annals has been closely
entangled with its neighbors. Rome spread over parts of Asia and Africa as
well as much of Europe; Ottoman sultans reigned over parts of Europe and
Africa as well as of Asia. A clear-cut antithesis of Europe and its neighbors
has only emerged in recent times. Not all its governments were colony seekers;
some were only over a brief span. All countries within the European orbit
benefited however, as Adam Smith pointed out, from colonial contributions
to a common stock of wealth,[2] bitterly as they might wrangle over ownership
of one territory or another. The latest, if not last, colonial wars were fought
by single countries, but with enough backing from others to make all the
capitalist West their accomplice. Much devastation by the Portuguese in
Africa was carried out with equipment supplied by NATO.[3] But since 1917
an always deeply divided Europe has been split in a new way, with the
peculiarity of a large expanse of Asia continuing to be linked with Russia
and sharing its socialist orientation. Neither camp has failed to put its own
interests first, but those of the USSR, and Eastern Europe since 1945, have
been substantially more in harmony with those of the Third World, and their
dealings with it far less open to censure.

Badly as Europeans might often treat colonial peoples, they were ready to
be quite as brutal with one another when conflict broke out between nations
or, as in Spain in 1936, between classes. This had its counterpart in the
way non-Europeans were accustomed to harry one another, until they were
partially restrained from doing so by the European ascendancy. German
propaganda had an axe to grind, when Germany was being deprived of its
colonies after the Great War on the grounds of unfitness to rule, with its
tale of Hottentots—"doomed to degeneration and extinction by their own
vices"—getting into South-West Africa and preying on the villainous Her-
reros, who in turn, until the coming of the German flag, preyed on the hapless
Berg-Damaras.[4] All the same, Africa and most of the Third World really were
a *Dar-al-Harb,* a realm of war, no peaceful Garden of Eden for the "merchant-
thieves of Frangistan" to break into.

One feature that stands out is the surprisingly high proportion of Africa and Asia, including both India and China, under alien or half-alien rule. West African societies frequently consisted of an intrusive people superimposed on an earlier one, ethnic discord taking the place of Europe's class discord; further south the Matabele dominance over the Mashonas of what is now Zimbabwe was of a similar character. Frantz Fanon's dictum that "it is the settler who has brought the native into existence"[5] overlooks all this. Revolts of many kinds were endemic; so were wars. Most of the black slaves carried off to the Americas were war captives sold by African kings or chiefs to white dealers for gunpowder or rum. It may, of course, be that this business would not have reached such staggering dimensions without Europe's gunpowder to inflame African strife. Similarly, it was with firearms improved by inter-course with the West that Mehemet Ali, the Albanian tyrant of Egypt, got control of most of the Sudan, where "the slave trade rapidly developed into the major industry," with annual negro-hunting expeditions on a grand scale.[6] It cannot be too surprising if Europeans sometimes felt that nothing they did to them could be worse than what these "natives" did to one another.

Entities such as we call "Burma," or "Holland," are largely fictions or optical illusions. Each name covers a welter of jarring groups, and among these some on both sides might do well or badly out of the operations of imperialism. A good many who came to grief fully deserved their fate. The vicious Oriental potentate or the barbarous tribal chief was not always a figment of Western imagination; there were many ruling classes that their peoples were far better off without. Numerous Europeans were enriched by their empires; many others who took part in the building of them travailed or perished, as little rewarded as Egypt's pyramid builders of old. European forces suffered appreciable losses in fighting one another for colonies before 1815, and though their losses in battle with Afro-Asian antagonists were nearly always small compared with the other side's, they underwent all the torments of hunger and thirst and were swept off in multitudes by disease.

How does the account stand between England and Wales, and how might a free Wales have turned out? We cannot guess how many promising new beginnings may have been crushed underfoot by juggernauts like the Roman legions; and we must ask whether, even if most of the old world from China to Peru was to all appearance in a sorry condition, there may have been enough vitality here and there to throw off the winding-sheet of the past. Many of its spokesmen in recent years have thought so, and some have endorsed "development theory" arguments that their countries are "underde-veloped" only because Europe made them so. It is soothing to a poor country's self-esteem to be assured that its poverty has been due to foreign exploitation, not to any defects of its own; and its well-off classes will welcome the assurance as removing any share of the blame from them. Yet, to believe that any countries outside Western Europe were capable of moving forward on their own is not easy; the dead weight of ages lay heavily on them. Japan was able to advance by imitation of the West; it must seem unlikely that any others, or more than a very few, could have emulated it, though some made fitful efforts.

Most of Asia outside the Far East and Turkey and nearly all Africa were brought under European occupation. Among the survivors, some lost part of their territory, as Siam did to France, Persia to Russia, Mexico (most flagrantly of all) to the United States. The term "semicolonial," in vogue in the later nineteenth century, suggests aptly enough the status of nearly all. It was the creed of the Old China Hands, the Western traders at Hong Kong or Shanghai, that China existed to furnish them with quick fortunes and that their governments' duty was to make sure that it did so. There is not much in the condition of these countries, while they had freedom of action, to favor belief in their capacity for progress. A French observer in Afghanistan soon after the first British occupation in 1838–41 testifies that the feudal lords and clerics denounced the British "because under them they could not practise their iniquities"; commoners rose against them because blinded by prejudice, but they soon regretted them.[7] Spain had reacted similarly to the Napoleonic occupation, Afghanistan is reacting similarly now to the Russian. In an account of the disorderly state of Turkey about the same time, we read of a governor of Mosul who "rushed out one night, mad with drink, to murder at pleasure"; Stratford Canning, the British ambassador, who "took a very elastic view of his responsibility," was exerting himself to save Jews, Greeks, Armenians from massacre.[8] This may seem a highly colored picture, but it remains true that the Ottoman empire's endeavors at reform were spasmodic at best, interrupted by many backslidings, and wholly inadequate in their outcome.

Conquest and occupation were grievous experiences; whatever beneficial results might ensue, the cure was at best a harsh one, like old-style surgery without anesthetics. Only in the light of their tragic vision of history could Marx and Engels contemplate conquest as sometimes a chapter of human progress. Conservatives have been fond of warning us that human nature is not good enough for socialism, but they have judged it quite good enough for imperialism, which must put a far heavier strain on it. No evidence could contradict more flatly than imperialism's record the judgment of Dr. Johnson that a man is never more innocently employed than when he is making money. The first modern empires, or in the case of Spain's empire, what was left of it after the early nineteenth century, remained to the end unregenerate, much as Spain and Portugal made only laggard progress at home. Their worst consequences were unintended, the work of germs exported from Europe along with its human marauders. Diseases assisted the acquisition of Spanish America, though they reduced its value, by inflicting on a vulnerable population a demographic disaster beside which the Thirty Years War, or even the Black Death, was a trifle.[9]

Spanish and Portuguese greed wore a religious cloak; bourgeois Holland and England represented a new society that took naked class division for granted, without holy water or feudal camouflage, and could regard a frank confrontation of higher and lower races as no less natural. It was in the worst days of tooth-and-claw philosophy that the newest empires were hatched. King Leopold's Congo marked the lowest depth that European behavior outside Europe could reach; it cast before it the shadow that was to turn into Hitler's empire inside Europe. Ugly happenings have accompanied all conquest; it may be said for modern Europe that whereas Assyrians or Romans boasted of their worst doings, Europeans have preferred to throw a veil over them. They were guilty of nothing worse than many things perpetrated at the same time within the non-European world by its own men of might, during the Abyssinian expansion in the nineteenth century, for instance, or the reoccupation of Sinkiang by a Chinese army after the Muslim rebellion. At times, European example may have done something to inflame the ferocity of others. Western conduct during the joint campaign of 1900 in China against the Boxers cannot have had a wholesome influence on the Japanese taking part; but there was seldom much need of the white man's tuition.

A complex society like Europe's could not forever be content with crude spoliation: other and better motives were felt, or had to be simulated, and might come to acquire real meaning from force of repetition. In one form or another they had floated for very long on the surface of empire. They are readily discernible among Romans or Chinese and in religious guise among Muslims. In Europe other refining and softening influences were at work. Among them Enlightenment thinking, with its interest in other races and its humanitarian leanings, has been recognized as a forerunner of the antislavery movement.[10] In addition, social friction in Europe, with the French Revolution as its loudest eruption, and the religious revival it did much to bring about stirred misgivings about rights of exploitation and helped to inspire the principle that colonial rule ought to be beneficial to both sides.

As the nineteenth century went on, the civilizing mission became an article of conventional faith. It could be clothed, as it was in France, either in spiritual drapery, to satisfy Catholic voters, or cultural and scientific, for secularists. Baron Macaulay cherished the thought that if Britain should someday lose India, its gift of civilization would be imperishable. In the midst of their quarrels among themselves, Europeans could praise one another for improving conditions in their colonies. Russian expansion east of the Caspian, an Englishman wrote in 1883, had been "of immense benefit to the country, . . . an unmixed blessing to humanity": slave-raiding and brigandage had been suppressed, commerce protected.[11] Inveterately antitczarist as he was, Karl Marx concurred; he could sound so robust a civilizer as to be termed by a recent commentator "merely another mid-Victorian."[12]

It became clear very early to some of the best European minds that if Europe was to civilize other races, it must look to its own blemishes. Enslavement of native peoples was the evil that stirred up most controversy. Debate began in the first days of the Spanish coming to America, a triumph hailed by the contemporary historian López de Gómera as the greatest event since Christ, bringing the blessing of baptism and release from a long catalogue of vices like idolatry, sodomy, and polygamy.[13] It threatened the recipients with the more dubious blessing of reduction to serfdom on the settlers' *encomiendas,* or feudal estates, or in the silver mines. Las Casas, the missionary bishop whose book *The Destruction of the Indies* came out in 1539, was only the most eloquent of the Indians' defenders. Men like him wanted natives to be accepted and treated as human beings, and it was their doctrine that prevailed in Spain, officially at any rate, over the rival thesis of Sepúlveda that they were scarcely human, natural slaves whom it was proper to treat as chattel.

In its own, however distorted fashion, Europe often really was a civilizing presence, and its aspirations could be authentic, if never unmixed with less lofty impulses. But they could readily fall into self-deception or serve as a mask for hypocrisy. Profession and practice were never the same and might be grotesquely far apart. Milton's manifesto composed in 1655 on behalf of the Protectorate, to justify the war with Spain which led to the seizure of Jamaica, rehearsed standard national and imperial themes, among them sympathy with the downtrodden inhabitants of the Americas and religion as England's primary incentive, one that ought to unite Englishmen of all parties.[14] Next year an English translation of Las Casas was prefaced by a condemnation of Spanish crimes and an assurance that any English acquisitions, by contrast, would bring liberation.[15] In the West Indies of the era that followed it might have been said, as in England in the time of Stephen and Matilda, that God and His angels slept.

"There can be no doubt," one of the buccaneers invading what was to be Rhodesia declared, "that the Mashonas will improve immensely under the civilising influence of our rule."[16] Japan was quick to pick up Western catchphrases and made "celestial salvation of the oppressed" its warrant for occupying Korea. When Italy was attacking Libya in 1911, there was a cascade of rhetoric about the Crusades and Lepanto, in a style, as an Italian historian of the war writes, which today seems bewildering.[17] Professor Zimmern thought of the Great War as putting the copestone on "the principle of the trusteeship of the ruler on behalf of the ruled" and quoted the Kenya White Paper of 1923 on England's "mission" to train the inhabitants " 'towards a higher intellectual moral and economic level,' " part of its "benevolent despotism" everywhere in the colonial empire.[18]

There were always sceptics who declined to take at its face value the imperial password of being cruel only to be kind. Livingstone saw many things more clearly than they could be seen from Europe and derided the optimism of "minds enlightened by the full jet of the oxyhydrogen light of modern civilization."[19] At the end of the nineteenth century, Winston Churchill, in his younger and better days, inveighed against the hollowness of imperial rhetoric, the distance "from the wonderful cloudland of aspiration to the ugly scaffolding of attempt and achievement," a gap "filled with the figures of the greedy trader, . . . the ambitious soldier, and the lying speculator."[20]

Goodwill during a great part of the nineteenth century was concentrated on the abolition of the slave trade and colonial slavery. It was most vigorous in Britain. Agitation about the plight of blacks might sometimes be, as objectors like Dickens suspected, a substitute for reform at home; but it is quite as likely that by educating public opinion, it helped to pave the way for social amelioration at home as well. It may be viewed as part of the all-around advance of the middle classes; this advance slowed down later as the millocracy joined forces with the landed aristocracy and its confederates in the City, whose ambitions were turning increasingly toward colonial gains. Campaigning for the rights of other races was carried on by bodies like the Aborigines' Protection Society or the opponents of the opium trade. But the support they received did not come up to what the antislavery movement had been able to arouse.

Public protest against imperial misrule never disappeared. It belonged to a European tradition stretching back through Burke and the trial of Warren Hastings to Cicero and the Verrine orations; it was something inconceivable in any non-European empire. At the beginning of the nineteenth century Sir Thomas Picton was recalled from his governorship of Tobago and convicted of allowing a woman suspect, under old Spanish law, to be tortured. He was acquitted on appeal, and lived to die at Waterloo. In the far graver scandal over Governor Eyre of Jamaica in 1865, "the intellectual flower of the country" joined in the protest, with J. S. Mill in the lead;[21] though it is noticeable in this case that while the thinkers were on the right side, the men of feeling and fancy—Carlyle, Ruskin, Tennyson—were on the side of the criminal and carried majority opinion with them.

Mitigation of the harshest features of German rule in Africa was the outcome of remonstrances by both Catholics and Socialists. But an enlightened public opinion broad enough to be effective was rare. A Commons speaker in 1814 lamented that in the British mind faraway Hindus were mysterious beings, "as if they were not composed of flesh and blood, nor had passions and desires, as the rest of the human species."[22] Old Mr. Willet in *Barnaby Rudge* was not much different from the run of his fellow countrymen in thinking of all remote lands as "inhabited by savage nations, who were perpetually burying pipes of peace, flourishing tomahawks, and puncturing strange patterns in their bodies."[23] At a superior social height we hear from Osbert Sitwell of a London house in 1914, soon after the Delhi Durbar, "sumptuously frescoed by Sert, with designs of elephants and howdahs and rajahs and pavilions and melons and bulrushes in sepia and gold."[24] In these hues

India offered a theatrical backdrop for the gambolings of a plutocracy; to the many it brought an occasional thrill. In a great measure empire and its heroic trumpet calls were "pure escapism";[25] an imaginary empire would have served the stay-at-homes almost as well, and when the Hollywood film dawned, an alternative outlet for fantasy became available.

With a public mind so frivolous, adequate scrutiny of colonial affairs was not to be expected. A critic of Dutch rule emphasized the incapacity of voters in Europe to weigh questions about territories on the other side of the globe;[26] and their possession by Europe's leading democracies could have a stultifying effect on parliamentarism. Gladstone in opposition found fault with a Tory MP for asserting that "the people of India were most happy and contented" and proving it by the absence of complaints in a heavily censored press.[27] From the Treasury bench he would see India through the other end of his telescope. As colonial nationalist movements grew up, it usually seemed to them that parties of the Left and Right in Europe had the selfsame deaf ear for their appeals, however noisily they might disagree on domestic issues. In the climacteric years of the revolt of Afro-Asia the average Westerner's response was at best indifference. Little notice was taken of the horrific massacres by the French at Sétif in Algeria in 1945 or in Madagascar in 1947;[28] after eight years of the Algerian war a conspiracy of silence still prevailed in France, the disgusted Sartre wrote.[29]

Peer Gynt in old age, looking back on a lifetime of racketeering and slave dealing, epitomizes modern Europe's ransacking of the other continents. Individual Europeans could be sensitive to fine issues through an awareness of Europe's preeminence and responsibility; on far more, the political or psychological effects must have been mostly bad. Bitterli points out that the Portuguese entering Africa were encountering societies where slavery was habitually practiced,[30] and the same is true of the British and other slave traders who followed in their footsteps. In the early nineteenth century four-fifths of the revenue of Angola came from a tax on the export of slaves.[31] Europe was in danger of being barbarized by its contact with barbarism. In our own day the grisly epidemic of police torture infecting so much of the world has had some of its starting points in attempts to subdue colonial unrest by terror.

During the nineteenth century imperialism was, as W. J. Mommsen says, convenient for "deflecting the attention of the rising middle classes from the constitutional issues they should have been coping with,"[32] while colonial possessions enhanced the prestige and self-confidence of ruling classes and helped them to keep their ground. Materially, investors often did very well out of the Third World; morally, far less well. About the end of the century, G. E. W. Russell drew a gloomy picture of upper-class luxury, depravity, and decadence. "The power of the purse is everywhere felt, if not seen," he wrote with the occupation of Egypt and the Boer War in mind. "It regulates our journalism. It pollutes our domestic politics. It governs our foreign relations."[33] Corruption in high places must be reckoned among the causes of the reckless policies which brought about the Great War; for Europe the war brought retribution, but a good share of the cost and suffering fell on its dependencies.

Some part of the mediocre success of the civilizing mission can be ascribed to mutual incomprehension, that is, to the difficulty or impossibility of any meeting of minds within the unnatural walls of an empire. Like the triumvirs in *Julius Caesar,* colonial rulers were always prone to suspecting "millions of mischief" behind loyal smiles. Failure to penetrate the native mind nagged at the all-powerful white man. "Every person with any knowledge of the African soul," according to an official German statement, "knows how well the negro is able to conceal his real feelings" from his master.[34]

With the gulf separating ruler and ruled, it is not to be wondered at that civilizing missions were envisaged chiefly in negative form, as the freeing of benighted peoples from bad rulers and then from bad habits. Spain might be said to have liberated Mexico from its Aztec tyrants, much as Turks at the same moment were liberating Hungary from its seigneurs; both had a firm conviction of bringing deliverance from the bonds of superstition. Suppression of abuses could fit in better than positive measures of improvement, even famine relief, with Europe's nineteenth-century faith in laissez-faire, most assertive in Victorian England. There such evils as public hangings, boy chimney sweeps, or cockfighting were being put a stop to. All peoples have indulged in regrettable customs, from "ploughing by the tail" in Ireland to cannibalism, a blemish of various climes including, it has been suggested, Aztec Mexico[35] and parts of the Pacific, where it was a stumbling block to Robert Louis Stevenson's sympathy with the islanders.

India's Muslim overlords had frowned on suttee, but did not effectively ban it; British rule ended it, though less promptly than could be wished. Like other social reforms, this required the support of progressive Hindu thinking, but such thinking derived primarily from foreign ideas and without foreign lawmakers and policemen would for an indefinitely long time have been impotent. Further steps came sluggishly, and the blame is not easy to apportion. There was always a legitimate doubt as to how far outsiders could interfere with practices sanctioned by religion, like child marriage. For government to tamper with them might be risky; not to do so might make it seem to be washing its hands of responsibility. In the twilight of the Raj the book *Mother India,* by an American admirer of British rule, Katherine Mayo, was vituperated by Indian patriots as a compendium of imperial and racial prejudice. A British heretic in India observed that if the place was really like that, after so many years of British management, it was time for his countrymen to go away.[36] A tacit answer was that the Caliban disposition of its inhabitants made it impossible for any Prospero to do much with them beyond preventing them from biting and scratching one another.

Apart from hesitant social reform, the gift that Western rule prided itself on bestowing was order, that watchword of governors in the colonies as of Metternich and the Holy Alliance in Europe. It had more of an affirmative and novel quality in Asia because it implied a guarantee of private rights, seldom safe under any of the old regimes; above all, security of life and, almost as important to the European mind, property. Administration in Calcutta, one of Britain's new urban creations, might have many vices, but "the god Property was respected here as it was everywhere that people spoke English," and wealthy Indians were happy to take up residence in the city.[37] When William Hickey quarreled with a native broker he owed money to, and fiercely ordered him out of the house, the Bengali went straight to a lawyer and took out a writ of *capias ad satisfaciendum*.[38] Needless to say, British or other Western law benefited chiefly those who could learn how to manipulate it; to the rustic its niceties were a mystery, and he hankered for old modes of dealing out justice, rough and ready but at least comprehensible. In less sophisticated Africa, even so civilized a representative of Europe as Dag Hammarskjöld might seem to share with ordinary Europeans a conception of order as first and foremost the safeguarding of *their* property and interests.[39]

Functions undertaken, as a rule inadequately, by colonial authorities included those concerned with what is known today as "nation building." In some measure they were helping to build nations by the simple act of bringing together heterogeneous communities, subnationalities like India's or principalities like Malaya's. There were, however, cases of deliberately opposite tactics, as when the French split up Vietnam into separate compartments or cut off Lebanon from Syria. But the birth of a nation could be hastened in either case by colonial rule provoking resentment and national movements being launched. For these, or for any progress, ideas were as indispensable as economic change, as were institutions, administrative or legal or political, in harmony (or not too much out of harmony) with them. Administrators were not likely to think of trying to release popular energies and to help men and women to expand more fully into human beings. Still, such schoolrooms as they provided might at least open new horizons to a minority. Printing was a newcomer everywhere except in the Far East, and newspapers, even though never allowed to operate without interference (they suffered from it in most parts of Europe too), could help to kindle a political spirit; towns, the cradles of nascent nationalism, could begin to acquire a civic quality they had never possessed outside Europe.

Without Western infusions, colonial discontents could have found no better expression than the sterile *jihadism* which had failed to avert European usurpation. Nationalist movements infallibly met with an unfriendly official reception, but its sharpness varied widely. British reactions were on the whole the mildest, and the eventual British withdrawal was far less bloodstained than most others. All the same, it was preceded toward the end by a shrinkage of liberal principles and a stiffening of police activity in the face of the challenge of nationalism and of trade unionism. Leonard Barnes was writing in 1939 of a drastic curtailing of African civil liberties by new penal codes and of authorities licensed to intern or deport at their own whim.[40] In 1947, a Fabian writer with experience of Africa portrayed the frigid manner of bureaucrats of "the sullen, somnolent, dyspeptic type" and remarked that conventional officialdom could function not too inadequately while things were quiet but that "as soon as a 'native' turns dynamic and intellectual, he becomes an enemy."[41]

It was clear to Fanon that there were urban dwellers in northern Africa—workmen, shopkeepers, petty bourgeois—who could enjoy a modest prosperity under their foreign rulers, so that the nationalist parties they adhered to were not excessively militant; a true revolutionary force, he believed, was to be looked for only among the peasantry. In some fields colonial power was assisting, not merely allowing, its wards to flourish—or some of its wards: it may be salutary to recall the warning of a seasoned witness that there is "no necessary connection for good or ill between public works and native welfare."[42] In India its salient achievements were irrigation canals, roads, and railways; it left behind a relatively good infrastructure of communications and transport. But beyond this, and some investment mainly in the extractive enterprises of mine or plantation, there was far too little in British or other colonial territories of the material progress that Marx had looked to as the second phase of the civilizing mission.

After thirty-six years in Somalia, it had to be admitted, no more had been accomplished than establishment of order; economic growth was nil and taxes were stiff.[43] Writing in 1909, Sir G. Molesworth was indignant at Indian disaffection. "The Government of India is the purest administration in the world, and forms a brilliant contrast to the Parliamentary administration of Great Britain, which day by day grows more corrupt." Yet he was constrained to regret that Indians, in spite of their wonderful government, were woefully poor and industrially retarded; Britain ought to have encouraged their cotton mills instead of hampering them.[44] Pressure from Lancashire had too much to do with policy; there was besides what an Indian historian calls "a nagging fear of the industrialisation of the Eastern peoples."[45]

Lack of rapport between government and people was another handicap. Public works like canals could be constructed by fiat; where public confidence and cooperation were required, bureaucracy fumbled. Its measures to combat cholera in western India early in this century aroused resentment because there were no channels through which they could be explained to the man in the street. At Lyallpur in the Punjab it set up an impressive agricultural research station, but to persuade illiterate, suspicious peasants to take its good advice was another matter. A local man employed in public relations told me of the method he had devised: he sat under the village tree dispensing hints about aphrodisiacs, a topic of never-failing interest to the rustic, and then led the discussion to improved seeds or tillage.

Hammond called his book on Portuguese Africa "a study in uneconomic imperialism," and C. Southworth concluded that colonies had been "an unprofitable venture" for France.[46] Not, however, for a good many Frenchmen; advocates of colonialism had private nests to feather, and many of the losses and gains of empire meant a transfer of wealth from pocket to pocket within the colony-owning country and by other circuits within the colonies. How much the common man in Europe shared in the profits is a disputatious question. Gollwitzer's opinion is that on the whole imperialism helped to improve conditions in Europe, in part directly, in part through international rivalry making better health and efficiency acceptable national goals.[47] This might, of course, have come about otherwise; and colonial greeds had much to do with the feuding that led to both world wars.

How much, again, the Third World contributed to capital accumulation and industrialization in Europe has long been argued. Many have suspected that the white man's burden of riches had its start in colonial plunder; for example, not a few Indian scholars have urged that loot from India was the prime motor of modern England's prosperity. Against this it may be recalled that loan capital was plentiful in eighteenth-century Europe; anyone could borrow, from Holland especially, at low rates. By the time of the Industrial Revolution very large reserves had been built up in England itself. Admittedly, colonial tribute helped to swell them. Fernand Braudel lends his weighty support to those who stress its importance, for industrializing Britain in particular. "It was this extra share which enabled Europeans to reach superhuman heights in tackling the tasks encountered on the path to progress." He calls attention, however, to the price this exacted from the British masses.[48] Here, once more, "Britain" might be enriched but a great many Britons impoverished. Multitudes were condemned to starvation, more still subjected to traumatic change. From this point of view, West Indian rum, sugar, tobacco, Chinese and then Indian tea, can be seen as tranquilizers, at least as efficacious as Methodism, which helped to reconcile Europe's poor to their lot. Desire for these luxuries could make men want better wages to buy them with; this might make for discontent, but also for harder work.

In the colonies the costs of empire fell most heavily on peasants, almost everywhere the majority. In India taxation, chiefly of the villager, was already severe before the British advent, and land tax continued throughout the nineteenth century to provide a disproportionately large part of the revenue required for running the administration and for maintaining a powerful professional army, Indian and British, which not only policed India but shared in imperial campaigning far and wide. In Egypt under the British, soldiers went on being conscripted as before; it was the French who relied most on this system, especially in Africa. Any such practice carried with it inevitable abuses, worst of all when it came to conscripts being brought to Europe and the Middle East to fight in the battles of the Great War.

Too often Europeans were parasites on colonial peoples; in addition, their rule gave fresh opportunities to swarms of local predators, to whom indeed its profits quite largely went. Old forms of slavery continued to be widespread in Asia,[49] and some of their beneficiaries could be useful auxiliaries of foreign power. Hereditary debt bondage lingered on in the Indian countryside all through the British period. Newer types of parasite might be generated by the new order; frequently they came from outside. Indian moneylenders found their way into Burma, and much Burmese land found its way into their hands; in French Indochina rice milling and most other commercial activities were cornered by Chinese,[50] who would be an awkward legacy of colonial rule after it came to an end. Transformed into a mercantile (and very loyal) community by the magnet of Bombay, Parsees had a lucrative share in the smuggling of opium into China, on which British India's balance of payments for so long depended.

In such a case the native predator shaded into the collaborator, of whom every empire stood in need. All administration had to be carried on, more or less, through local intermediaries, who often could be only loosely controlled; they might be an obstruction between even a well-intentioned government and its subjects. At their best they were of a type most in evidence in India, trained as understudies of British officials and gradually winning equal status, public servants with standards of conduct unimaginable in the India of any earlier times. Far less wholesome was the employment of sections of earlier ruling classes as assistants or as buffers between government and people. After the Mutiny the remaining Indian princes were kept on under British patronage; analogous procedures were adopted in Egypt and Malaya, by the French in Indochina and Morocco, and by the Russians in Bokhara. Where suitable collaborators were not forthcoming they might be created, like the landlords set up in India, first of all by the Permanent Settlement in Bengal, whose consequences were an incubus to the province until after independence.

More straightforwardly, the required middlemen might be produced in some colonies by the coupling of white men and native women, whose offspring occupied a middle ground in terms of race as well as of rank. Commandeering of women was one of the many species of tribute levied by the white man, most blatantly in the slave plantation areas of the Americas, and in southern Africa. It had been another accompaniment of conquest all through history; modern Europe was the first to abandon it, if never completely.

Churchill in Africa was alive to the perils threatening native peoples "abandoned to the fierce self-interest of a small white population," full of "the harsh and selfish ideas which mark the jealous contact of races and the exploitation of the weaker."[51] It was in settler regions that ethnic groups which could be dubbed "primitive" came most easily to be classed as "superannuated races" and to be expected to go under in the struggle for survival. That "savage tribes disappear before the progress of civilized races" was deemed by a Rev. Thomas Atkins, who visited Tasmania in 1836, "a universal law in the Divine government."[52] To expedite their departure might be reckoned a kind of euthanasia. Mrs. Bates, who spent half a lifetime studying and caring for Australian aborigines, was convinced that there could be no future for them.[53] "History" was often invoked, most loudly by American expansionists, as equivalent to destiny or heavenly decree, in order to justify things that might cause qualms of conscience. "We can't stop history in full course," the British statesman in Joyce Cary's novel declares. "And history is going all against the primitive—it always did."[54]

Communities not wiped out were disrupted in many ways, some of which might in the long run prove beneficial; the worst disruption took place where Europeans were allowed to settle and deprive cultivators of their land, reducing them to helotry as many of the smaller peasantry of Europe were being reduced. This happened in parts of Africa suited to white settlement but also here and there in Asia where plantations were being laid out—in Ceylon and the Indian hills or in Indochina. A British writer on Africa praised the Convention of London of 1884, after Majuba, because it sought to shelter Africans from "the unscrupulous aggression of the Boers."[55] In reality such protection could amount to very little, and when the Union of South Africa was set up in 1910, any attempt to shield the other races against the whites was virtually abandoned. Since then British capitalism has taken an energetic hand in their exploitation.

Refusal to be drilled into fixed work habits, useful chiefly to settlers, was a leading criterion of "primitiveness." In one guise or another, labor was an essential part of the dues exacted from colonies. Taxation might take the form of corvée work. When slavery was given up, its place was taken by the "coolie emigration" from India and China,[56] often not much better than slave dealing under a new name. West Indian plantations and Malayan tin mines were ready customers. More irregular modes of recruitment, like the "blackbirding" that went on in the Pacific, added to the total. That natives should be summoned to work seemed so obvious that it could be endorsed by some Socialists. Fourrierist plans for settlements in north Africa not infrequently hinged on conquests followed by obligatory labor services.[57]

Asians and Africans were called on not only to toil, but to do so with vigor and enthusiasm. A gospel of work, with Thomas Carlyle for one of its authors, became an essential part of the civilizing mission. Like the quality of mercy, work had the double merit of blessing both him who gave and him who received; for the giver it was educational and usually the only education that came his way. Multatuli, in his novel, invented a Rev. Mr. Twaddler of Amsterdam who was fond of preaching on the conversion of the Javanese, now happily rescued by Dutch power from heathen darkness and only needing to be "led to God by labour."[58] A German ex-governor and apologist for his country's methods quoted with relish the words of Joseph Chamberlain: "I believe it is good for the native to be industrious, and we must bend every effort to teach him to work."[59] There must be suitable penalties, in the German view, for "the frequent laziness and insubordination of native workers or servants"; masters must be authorized to exercise "a light paternal correction."[60] Smuts accused Alfred Milner of failing to grasp, unlike Cecil Rhodes, that unless an African is "compelled to work by firm persuasion he is very likely to prefer a life of ease, lying happily in the sun."[61] Depravity indeed, which the white man could feel a clear duty to banish, but which his forceful tutoring was only too likely to deepen.

The term "race" came into Europe in the sixteenth century; appropriately, in view of its hazy meaning, its origin is unknown. It has been asserted that racialism as we know it is no older than modern nationalism and imperialism. There is some truth, though not the whole truth, in Freyre's claim for Brazil of "racial democracy"; Portuguese emigrants were too few to avoid blending with other breeds, and this could lead to such fusions as Brazil's musical idiom and dances. It has been said, too, that belief in racial inferiority is an intellectual rather than a moral error, and its being shared in some degree by a man like Marx goes to confirm this. But it was also very much an extension of belief in the inferiority of the lower classes within Europe; this helped to make it a ubiquitous component of European thinking. A curious reflection can be found in that popular fable *The Wind in the Willows,* with its clear-cut demarcation between the civilized animals who sing Christmas carols or doze by the fire over a sheet of rhymes and the vicious denizens of the Wild Wood. Its climax is a barbarian invasion, repulsed after a heroic fight. It came out in 1908, the year when Kenneth Grahame retired from the secretaryship of that sacred fane of civilization, the Bank of England.

Exponents of racism like Sir Richard Burton were fond of saying that Africans themselves admired light complexions.[62] In India, too, such a feeling can be traced to a long-continuing drift of incomers and conquerors from north to south; so also in Europe after the Romans. Somalis could be credited with "proud bearing and a superb carriage bespeaking their consciousness of a racial superiority over their neighbours."[63] The white man par excellence, the Englishman, stood at the summit of a hierarchy. When a British proconsul ascribed to his countrymen "that power of government which . . . is the prerogative of their Imperial race,"[64] the pride of rule of an aristocracy was being democratized into a virtue of a whole people, mostly perfectly innocent of it. The Labour Party when it appeared on the stage was not free from some comparable underlying assumptions; its thinking about areas like the West Indies showed marks of a "racial typology" when their fitness for self-government had to be weighed up.[65]

According to a Frenchman who knew India, the English were less good than the French at getting on with Asiatics, because of "that stiffness, punctilious etiquette, and domineering tone, which they adopt everywhere."[66] According to an Englishman, French manners were stamped by "absolute ignorance and insolent disregard" of the character and feelings of subject peoples.[67] Dutchmen were apt, as they themselves were aware at times, to alienate notables by their contemptuous attitude.[68] British rudeness may have had the excuse of serving as a substitute for the violence more habitually indulged in by most other colonialists, a relief for the bottled-up irritations of a life of exile. Britons in India seldom went much beyond beating their servants, in the style of the apoplectic Major Bagstock, retired to London with his dusky attendant, in *Dombey and Son*. Unwillingness to be on social terms with "natives" could have the good result of compelling those who smarted under it to turn to their own countrymen instead, thus giving national movements a broader base.

Conservatives in France or Britain today like to suppose that their former subjects remember them with esteem; however, the gratitude felt by educated Asians or Africans has not been to Western bureaucrats, businessmen, policemen, but to Shakespeare—India's national poet, as he has been called—or J. S. Mill or Descartes. But what these men gave might have to be paid for by a diminished vitality of old cultures. Success inflamed the West with a "naïvely egocentric" conviction that "civilization and culture were synonymous with the Western varieties."[69] Complaints of European misrepresentation of the character and way of life of other peoples have multiplied of late, adding a new chapter to older charges of imperial abuse of strength. Edward Said condemns, too sweepingly, the "Orientalism" of travelers, explorers, and scholars writing about the Middle East; Alatas pursues a similar theme in further Asia.[70] It is hard to specify the harm done. Unflattering accounts of Afro-Asian life may have paved the way for occupation of more territories by preparing Western opinion to think it always justified. Lamartine evoked an Orient conscious of its failure and longing to be taken under Europe's wing.[71] Asian self-respect may have been undermined only among those few who could read what was said about them, but these may have been rendered more anxious to Westernize themselves, at the cost of cutting themselves off further from their own kin.

Yet "Orientalists" initiated fruitful studies in many fields, introduced nations to their own past, and taught them to think of their future. A similar ambivalence pervaded religious thinking. In the antislavery agitation the churches in Britain distinguished themselves, with Nonconformists the most zealous; so did missionaries from many lands in educational and medical work in the colonies. It was a common suspicion among white men that "Christianity might produce dangerous notions of democracy, of human equality";[72] between missionaries and settlers or officials there was only limited intercourse. On the other side of the medal, they could be regarded in Afro-Asia as agents of imperialism, and so in fact they often were, as in the Spanish and Portuguese empires, which always relied heavily on ecclesiastical machinery, or in the French penetration of Indochina. Some Protestants in China could welcome war, even an Opium War, as a battering ram to break down obstacles to the Gospel; in 1900 some punitive expeditions against Chinese villages were led by American missionaries.[73] It was as hard for mission workers as for other white men and women to feel much patience with a traditional life that appeared to them nasty, brutish, and short, as it still too often does to visitors. Such impressions throng the record, for instance, of the Scottish Presbyterian mission in the Punjab, where the inner "darkness of superstition and sin" seemed to match "the abhorrence of soap and water," "the accumulated filth," of the outward man.[74]

It was part of Fanon's case that colonialism quickly subverts inherited culture, and seeks to "dehumanize" by stifling it without offering a satisfactory replacement and by merely subjecting a useful minority to an education modeled on its own. To detach an élite from the mass was a strategy not unknown inside Europe; Slovenes in Hapsburg Hungary who wanted education had to turn themselves into Magyars. The colonial intellectual's groping for a national identity, so poignantly felt by Fanon, must have been still more tormenting for Africans, with their nonliterate background; although Asia's literature, philosophy, and useful knowledge, apart from being little shared in by the masses, were in some respects worn out and sterile before contact with the West galvanized the Chinese and others into revitalizing them. North Africa was in a similar but more forlorn state. In sub-Saharan Africa art and myth were more a heritage of entire communities, but this meant that they were bound up with the noxious as well as the more admirable features of communal life.

Still, Europe should be better able today to sympathize with regrets over cultural disruption, because industrialism and modernism have had the same blighting effects on its own life that European ascendancy is accused of having had elsewhere. A few Europeans have been learning to appreciate the arts and practical skills of other climes, Indian classical music, for example; far more have been having their wits addled by a counterinvasion, as in Roman times, of Eastern astrology and mumbo jumbo, while a vacuum in popular art has been filled up by the synthetic jazz culture of America.

"Cultural imperialism" could be displayed most blatantly in elementary education. To keep their subjects docile, it has been said, rulers present them with an image of the world meant "to increase their alienation and passivity" by showing it as "a fixed entity," incapable of change.[75] South African schoolbooks are compiled in this spirit; in Namibia children are taught that the Germans were "invited by warring tribes" to come in and establish peace among them.[76] More broadly, empire ideology combined with arrogance has been well calculated to convince its underlings of their inadequacy. No record, perhaps, of the painful psychological trauma this can inflict is more graphic than the Tunisian writer Albert Memmi's *Portrait du colonisé*. Alatas is indignant at the hangover of colonial mentality in his Malaya.[77] At the 1984 meeting at Tashkent of the Afro-Asian Writers' Association a spokesman recalled that this body had been set up in 1958 because of a growing consciousness of "the incredibly difficult, sometimes agonizing process of 'spiritual decolonisation.'"[78] Intellectuals must have been the most directly affected, but the diffusion of plagues like alcoholism suggests widespread damage.

Sooner or later conditions in many colonies brought to the front new or half-new classes which could lead the way, fumblingly enough, toward independence. Where imperialism nurtured, as it was only too well able to, an indiscriminate hated of everything associated with it, the struggle might be blind and unconstructive, or fall back into religious bigotry. Muslim countries have been more than usually prone to such regression. Mahdism— that "new poor emerging out of the African darkness," as it seemed to Europe[79]—made a deep impression on them in the late nineteenth century. The present "Islamic revival" contains many questionable ingredients; they are most obtrusive in the clerical regime in Iran since the fall of the Shah, who with his huge foreign armory and backing had been proof against any more rational opposition. By the West, always two-faced in such matters, fanaticism in Iran is loudly condemned, because a nuisance to Western interests, but in Afghanistan it was loudly applauded, because there it embarrassed only Moscow.

Some countries formerly under Western sway have reached genuine independence, such as India by one path, Vietnam by another. Many more have passed since 1945 into the limbo of neocolonialism, whose affinities are with the "indirect rule" cultivated in some colonies and with the handling of "semicolonies" or "spheres of influence." It could be resorted to with little harm to imperial concerns, because colonialism had left both a material infrastructure and a human basis in Westernizing groups willing to cooperate and in a position to benefit. Europe prepared the ground, the United States reaps more and more of the harvest. Its hegemony has, on the one hand, quickened the shift away from direct colonial rule, on the other, done its best to frustrate any further advance toward real freedom.

Hopeful observers have counted on Western capital to help to develop the backlands for the sake of worthwhile markets. On the whole it seems content rather to dump surpluses and extract raw materials. Things are steadily worsened by the population explosion: the negative bent of most of the good done by Europe shows in the curbing of epidemic disease without the economic development needed to absorb and check the resulting numbers. Emigration confers opportunity on a few, at the cost of some loss of human resources. New York is crowded with Indian and Filipino doctors and surgeons who ought to be working at home.

Shortcomings of both rulers and ruled in colonial times must be blamed for the poor calibre of political leadership in most newly freed countries. Imperialism chose some dubious associates, a habit carried much further by the United States. Colonial rule was superimposed on earlier, deep-rooted patterns, so that it cannot bear sole blame. Governments like the British in India may have reinforced some mischievous legacies of the past by making so much use of "martial races." Some armies they left behind have a deplorable political record, and some of the dictatorships thrown up by them have reverted to the habits of aggression so rife in Afro-Asia before the Europeans: the Sudanese in the non-Arab south, the West Pakistani in east Bengal, and the Indonesians in Timor. In each of these cases there has been an accompaniment of wholesale bloodshed. We are very far from fulfillment of Fanon's vision of the Third World coming into the vanguard, utilizing Europe's ideas but remembering its high crimes and misdemeanors, and "starting a new history of Man."[80] For some years China purported to be doing this, but those years have gone by.

How cogent is the claim of ex-colonies for compensation, or how likely to carry conviction to Western publics? In recent times Germany has acknowledged a debt to the Jews; ironically, payment has been made to the state of Israel, whose debt to the Palestinians it has displaced is equally undeniable. So is the compensation promised but not paid by the United States to Vietnam. When we look further back into history, things become more puzzling. State debts can be transmitted from age to age, and the sins or follies of the fathers thus visited, with biblical warrant, on the children. But it would be difficult to say how far back responsibility for acts of conquest and spoliation can be assigned or measured; and if restitution is due from European conquerors, it must be due from others as well. There were Persian and Afghan invasions of eighteenth-century India as well as European. India, it may be remarked, has exerted itself to make amends for age-old cruelty to its aboriginal peoples by reserving places for them in colleges and government service.

Another way of looking at the question may be to say that if humanity was ever to break out of the ruts it had got stuck in, some region had to lead the way. Europe led, and if it ransacked other continents, it subjected itself to centuries of wars, upheavals, and religious furies—calamities which may well have been a necessary ordeal, the initiation rites of industrial society. Any benefits of this ordeal the rest of mankind now has a chance of sharing at far lesser cost and far more quickly. If Bengal helped to foot the bill for Britain's industrial revolution, in the long run India would be among the gainers. An album in the India Office Library of Pictures of Kashmiri crafts-men at work in the 1850s shows a goldsmith with spectacles on his nose. The blessing represented by the spread of this single, simple invention round the globe is incalculable.

A corollary is that the West, having no real need now to squeeze the Third World, ought to free itself from the continuing temptation to do so by eliminating from its social structure the factors making for exploitation of other peoples. In every social order throughout history there have been such elements, stimulating aggression in one or another of its countless forms. In the case of modern Europe and its American offshoot it is capitalism that has been most to blame. Human nature is not totally depraved, as Christianity has taught, but it is extraordinarily mutable or malleable in this raw youth of its evolution; how it shapes depends, as that great Welshman Robert Owen was one of the first to perceive, on the environment it is exposed to. Colonialism has an analogy in the ill-treatment since history began of women by men. The men of today cannot make up for this, but they can join with women in reforming the institutions which guaranteed their subjugation.

Urban man everywhere has adopted European clothes; more important, something like a common moral code has made its way everywhere, in the limited sense at any rate that such evils as the slave market, which Europe renounced and by example or compulsion brought others to renounce, today have few if any defenders; and that others such as torture have few confessed though many secret practitioners. On the open space thus cleared there is room for an edifice of social ethics of a more positive cast, uniting humanity in common effort. It is long since the malady of "two Englands," rich and poor, side by side, began to be deplored; "two worlds" on one small planet would be the same evil disastrously magnified.

Notes

This chapter originally appeared in Moorhead Wright, ed., *Rights and Obligations in North-South Relations* (London, Macmillan, 1986).

1. "Summary of Events," *Asiatic Quarterly,* July 1866.

2. Adam Smith, *The Wealth of Nations,* Book 4, Chapter 7, "Of Colonies," Part 3 (opening).

3. Bruno da Ponte, *The Last to Leave: Portuguese Colonialism in Africa* (London, 1974), 60–61.

4. German Colonial Office, *The Treatment of Native and Other Populations* (Berlin, 1919), 31.

5. Frantz Fanon, *The Wretched of the Earth* (1961; trans. C. Farrington, Harmonds-worth, 1967), 68.

6. M. D. Theobald, *The Mahdiya: A History of the Anglo-Egyptian Sudan, 1881–1899* (London, 1951), 7–8, 10–11.

7. J. P. Ferrier, *Caravan Journeys and Wanderings* (English ed., London, 1857; reprint, Karachi, 1976), 186.

8. S. Lane-Poole, *The Life of Lord Stratford de Redcliffe K. G.* (London, 1890), 199, 201.

9. C. M. Cipolla, ed., *The Fontana Economic History of Europe: The Sixteenth and Seventeenth Centuries* (London, 1974), 10n; F. Braudel, *Civilization and Capitalism, 15th–18th Century,* vol. 3, *The Perspective of the World* (trans. S. Reynolds, London, 1984), 393–94.

10. See, e.g., U. Bitterli, *Die "Wilden" und die "Zivilisierten"* (Munich, 1976), 426–27.

11. C. Marvin, *The Russians at Merv and Herat* (London, 1883), 269, 276–77.

12. R. Robinson, in *Oxford and the Idea of Commonwealth,* ed. F. Madden and D. K. Fieldhouse (London, 1982), 31.

13. L. Hanke, "More Heat and Some Light on the Spanish Struggle for Justice in the Conquest of America," *Hispanic American Historical Review* 44 (1964): 296–97.

14. *The Prose Works of John Milton,* ed. J. P. St. John (London, 1848), vol. 2, 349ff.

15. Bartolomé de las Casas, *The Destruction of the Indies,* trans. J. Phillips (new ed., New York, 1972). Much can be learned about the ancestry of the civilizing mission in England from J. McVeagh, *Tradefull Merchants: The Portrayal of the Capitalist in Literature* (London, 1981).

16. W. A. Wills and L. T. Collingridge, eds., *The Downfall of Lobengula* (London, 1984), 306.

17. G. Malgeri, *La Guerra Libica (1911–1912)* (Rome, 1970), 48.

18. Sir A. Zimmern, *The Third British Empire* (London, 1926), 13, 40, 53.

19. *Livingstone's Missionary Correspondence, 1841–1856,* ed. I. Schapera (London, 1961), 282 (13 September 1855).

20. Winston Churchill, *The River War* (London, 1899), 26–27.

21. M. St. J. Packe, *The Life of John Stuart Mill* (London, 1954), 469.

22. *The Speeches of Robert Richards, Esq., in the Debate in Parliament on the Renewal of the Charter of the Hon. East India Company . . . , 1813* (London, 1814), 50.

23. Charles Dickens, *Barnaby Rudge* (1841), Chapter 28.

24. Osbert Sitwell, *Great Morning* (London, 1949), 257; cf. 215.

25. W. S. Hamer, *The British Army: Civil-Military Relations, 1855–1905* (Oxford, 1970), 217.

26. Multatuli [E. D. Dekker], *Max Havelaar* (English ed., New York, 1927), 235–36.

27. William Gladstone quoted in *Hansard,* vol. 251, 1880, col. 922ff.

28. Fanon, *The Wretched of the Earth*, 62.

29. Ibid., preface by J. P. Sartre, 25.

30. Bitterli, *Die "Wilden" und die "Zivilisierten"*, 96.

31. R. J. Hammond, *Portugal and Africa, 1815–1910* (Stanford, 1966), 46n.

32. W. J. Mommsen, in *Nationality and the Pursuit of National Independence*, ed. T. W. Moody (Belfast, 1978), 128.

33. G. E. W. Russell, *Collections and Recollections*, Series 2 (London, 1909), 63; cf. 275ff.

34. German Colonial Office, *How Natives Are Treated in German and French Colonies* (Berlin, 1919), 29.

35. M. Harris, *Cannibals and Kings* (London, 1977), Chapter 9.

36. Lt. Col. Arthur Osburn, *Must England Lose India?* (London, 1930), 11.

37. A. Calder, *Revolutionary Empire: The Rise of the English-Speaking Empires* (London, 1981), 590.

38. *Memoirs of William Hickey*, ed. A. Spencer (London, 1913), vol. 3, 151–52.

39. C. C. O'Brien, "The Congo, the United Nations, and Chatham House," *New Left Review*, no. 31 (1965): 8.

40. Leonard Barnes, *Empire or Democracy?* (London, 1939), 165–66.

41. L. Silberman, *Crisis in Africa* (London, 1947), 5–6.

42. J. S. Furnivall, *Colonial Policy and Practice* (Cambridge, 1948), 322.

43. D. Jardine, *The Mad Mullah of Somaliland* (London, 1923), 30.

44. Sir G. Molesworth, *Economic and Fiscal Facts and Fallacies* (London, 1909), Chapter 41.

45. P. S. Gupta, *Imperialism and the British Labour Movement, 1914–1964* (London, 1975), 154.

46. Hammond, *Portugal and Africa*; C. Southworth, *The French Colonial Venture* (London, 1931), 131.

47. H. Gollwitzer, *Europe in the Age of Imperialism* (London, 1969).

48. Braudel, *Civilization and Capitalism*, 386–87, 581, 641.

49. See B. Lasker, *Human Bondage in Southeast Asia* (Honolulu, 1950).

50. Southworth, *The French Colonial Venture*, 100.

51. Winston Churchill, *My African Journey* (London, 1972), 25, 118.

52. See A. Montagu, *The Nature of Human Aggression* (London, 1978), 84–85, 169.

53. Daisy Bates, *The Passing of the Aborigines* (London, 1972).

54. Joyce Cary, *Prisoner of Grace* (London, 1954), 280.

55. E. Sanderson, *Africa in the Nineteenth Century* (London, 1898), 282.

56. See P. C. Campbell, *Chinese Coolie Emigration to Countries within the British Empire* (London, 1923); H. Tinker, *A New System of Slavery: The Export of Indian Labour Overseas, 1830–1920* (London, 1974).

57. See M. N. Mashkin, *Frantsuskie Sotsialisti i Demokrati i Kolonialnii Vopros, 1830–1871* (Moscow, 1981).

58. Multatuli, *Max Havelaar*, 129; cf. 239.

59. See A. H. H. Schnee, *German Colonisation Past and Future* (London, 1926), 135. Cf. Hammond, *Portugal and Africa*, 156, 160.

60. German Colonial Office, *The Treatment of Native and Other Populations*, 125.

61. J. C. Smuts, *Jan Christian Smuts* (London, 1952), 93.

62. C. Bolt, *Victorian Attitudes to Race* (London, 1971), 134.

63. Jardine, *The Mud Mullah*, 19.

64. Lord Cromer, quoted in Sir A. Colvin, *The Making of Modern Egypt* (London, 1906), 350.

65. Gupta, *Imperialism and the British Labour Movement*, 260; a recurrent theme of the book.

66. Ferrier, *Caravan Journeys and Wanderings*, 341; cf. 372.

67. Sanderson, *Africa in the Nineteenth Century*, 101.

68. C. R. Boxer, *The Dutch Seaborne Empire, 1600–1800* (Harmondsworth, 1973), 259–61.

69. M. Leiris, "Race and Culture," in *The Race Question in Modern Science* (Paris, 1956), 97.

70. E. W. Said, *Orientalism* (London, 1978); S. H. Alatas, *The Myth of the Lazy Native* (London, 1977).

71. Said, *Orientalism*, 179.

72. Bolt, *Victorian Attitudes to Race*, 118.

73. Jane Hunter, *The Gospel of Gentility: American Women Missionaries in Turn-of-the-Century China* (New Haven, 1984), 6, 171.

74. Rev. J. F. W. Youngson, *Forty Years of the Panjab Mission of the Church of Scotland* (Edinburgh, 1896), 252, 276–77.

75. Paulo Freire, *Pedagogy of the Oppressed* (Harmondsworth, 1972), 109.

76. Ann Harries, in *Anti-Apartheid News* (London), April 1984.

77. S. H. Alatas, *Intellectuals in Developing Societies* (London, 1977).

78. *Soviet Weekly* (London), 1 October 1983.

79. W. Baird, *General Wauchope* (Edinburgh, 1900), 89.

80. Fanon, *The Wretched of the Earth*, 254.

5

IMPERIALISM AND REVOLUTION

"Established custom," Dr. Johnson wrote after his tour of Scotland, reflecting on the Union of 1707, "is not easily broken, till some great event
shakes the whole system of things, and life seems to recommence upon new
principles." At another point in his narrative he looked further back, to the
years of the Commonwealth, and thought of brute force as a mainspring of
historical progress. "What the Romans did to other nations, was in a great
degree done by Cromwell to the Scots; he civilized them by conquest, and
introduced by useful violence the arts of peace."[1] We may qualify this by
recalling Milton's dictum that what conquerors like the Romans brought to
peoples like the Britons might be either elevating or debasing and enslaving.[2]

There is room for much disagreement over the relative significance in
history of a society's internal pulses and the influences reaching it from outside.
It is a problem bearing on all world history and in a special degree on the
story of conquests and empires, the effects on one people of subjugation by
another. This ubiquitous phenomenon took on a new character in modern
times, in the centuries of Western ascendancy marked by the coming of
capitalism and the accompanying growth of technology, thanks to which
conquerors have always had—as they did not always have in earlier times—
a superiority at least on the material side of life. What gains or losses have
resulted for the many countries subjected to Western occupation or interference is a question all the more important because direct colonial rule has only
very recently been coming to an end, and indirect control or 'neocolonialism'
is still widespread.

Western thinking has usually favored the view that colonialism, despite
much that is shameful in its record, rescued backward or stagnating societies
by giving them better government and transformed them by drawing them
out of isolation into the currents of the world market and a world civilization.
Marxists (European Marxists at any rate), who have given more thought than

most to the subject, have often concurred in this judgment, so far as the postulate of a general lack of forward movement in the precolonial world outside Europe is concerned; they have been sceptical about most of the positive benefits claimed for colonial rule and have had more to say about its predatory motives. An awkwardness is observable here in the Marxist theory of history, derived as it was from European evolution. Seeking rational explanations, it has been attracted by whatever may appear a logical interaction and unfolding of forces within a complex; yet when looking away from Europe it has felt obliged to conclude that history has been kept going, at a certain stage, or got back into motion, only by the intrusion of external forces. The symmetry of the theory is thus upset. So far as the inhabitants of Africa were concerned, the European intervention beginning in the fifteenth century was purely accidental and therefore irrational.

It was of course no accident in terms of *Europe's* development. Broadly, it may be said that western Europe revolutionized itself, over many centuries; eastern Europe had new ways of life thrust on it from above, by Westernizing rulers like Peter the Great, and most of Afro-Asia, still more, from outside. Even within the West, each of the great revolutions—Dutch, English, American, French—owed very much to foreign ideas and leaders with knowledge of foreign countries; more than one also to foreign armed aid. Revolutions may be, or seem, short and sharp, but social change, as Fernand Braudel says, cannot come about quickly in sudden bursts.[3] Hence genuine transformation cannot be imposed simply from above. It is almost as unlikely to come about simply from below. Mao stood for a literal faith in the self-transforming potential of the Chinese peasantry; but many struggles of earlier times had failed to demonstrate this.

A rough distinction may be drawn between *growth,* due primarily to internal evolution and ferment, and *change,* which may come about most often through external intrusion; and the deepest alterations may be supposed to have come about through a convergence of the two factors, a phenomenon extremely rare in the history of both modern and older forms of imperialism. From the penetration of one society, ripe for change, by another with some superior attainments, a third may be expected to emerge, distinct from both though inheriting much from each.

If force can be the midwife of history, as Marx termed it, a new life must be supposed already existing, struggling for birth. In Europe successive rebirths had been taking place ever since the fall of Rome; elsewhere they are much harder to descry, and Western eyes at any rate have often failed to make out any symptoms of an approach to them. Feudal-type rebellion was as common in Indian history as peasant revolt in Chinese. Yet, by the eighteenth century, Europe and Afro-Asia were existing in separate compartments; in the West time had been running faster, while the others had not even been able—or had not wanted—to make a clock. There had been no lack of novelty in Asia, partly the outcome of contacts of one region with another; shifts in styles of government, new fashions in philosophy, religious movements waxing and waning, though these were seldom more than revivalist outbreaks, turning back to the past. Of more lasting value were fresh achievements in literature and the arts. But by far the greater part of all this was confined to the upper walks of society, or the "superstructure," and left the mode of production and its toilers untouched. Muslim rule brought various technical as well as cultural innovations into India, affecting agriculture as well as handicrafts; but it brought no basic change, economic or social. Frequently such alien dominion may have had on balance a tendency to perpetuate rather than to sweep away.

Whether such directionless eddying can continue indefinitely, if not broken in on from outside, or whether there must be some limiting point at which political or cultural variations on the ground bass of an unchanging economy must come to an end may be arguable. Whether it is moral and psychological exhaustion rather than economic that threatens to bring a civilization to an end, or perhaps the two things combined, may also be a question. China's long inanition after a brilliant start suggests forcibly that a society has only limited potentialities of progress, sooner or later to be suffocated by an accumulation of vested interests and conservative instincts. Everywhere in Afro-Asia these grew to be strong and immobilizing. Chinese merchants and moneylenders grew rich by collaboration with the bureaucracy, and their ambition then was to gain entry to the mandarin class and bask in its prestige, very much as moneymakers in early modern Europe wanted to turn themselves or their sons into landowning gentlemen. An Asian writer highly critical of the West has acknowledged the absence in the East of a functioning "intellectual community"[4] with the ability to view critically its own society. This was an especially vital lack for, unlike developments in Europe, it was accompanied by the failure to emerge of an authentic "bourgeoisie"—a class geared to capital accumulation and industrial production. In the East, priestcraft held dominion over men's thinking. Everywhere in the once stirring Islamic world stagnation had set in, a charmed sleep from which it had no power to rouse itself.

Even allowing for European self-complacency and prejudice, it may not be too surprising that Europeans coming in contact with Asia's élites soon felt unable to take them very seriously. Chinese mandarins were at first an exception, but as time went on and familiarity increased, they came to share the contempt bestowed on all "Celestials" of the "Heavenly Kingdom." "The Chinese," a British representative in China, J. F. Davis, wrote in 1840, "have much of that childish character which distinguishes other Asiatics," the result, he thought, of their minds being cramped by despotic rule.[5] Asian infantility was indeed a prevalent Western impression. In the Canton trade, "sing-songs"—musical boxes and the like—were more in demand than any other Western products; Europeans in India found high society in the Mughal empire which had been established by new invaders from Muslim Central Asia during the sixteenth century fascinated by gewgaws such as whistles or mirrors. Persians, though talented, are "just like children," a British diplomat of this century declared.[6] Westerners reared on Descartes or Bentham had some reason for impatience with the antiquated nonsense that passed for learning or wisdom at Al Azhar, the celebrated Cairo seminary, or the Hanlin Academy in Peking whose members were the cream of Chinese scholarship.

European expansion has left behind it the problem of how much it did to transform retarded continents or open the way at least to their renovation. Little of the sort can be credited to the Portuguese or Spanish pioneers, and not much more to the early Dutch or English who followed on their heels. Modern colonialism entered a new phase after the great events of the later eighteenth century: the Industrial Revolution and American and French Revolutions. As far away as China, Lord Macartney on his embassy in 1793–94, an unsuccessful attempt to persuade the government to open its doors to foreign trade and diplomacy, met with an "indistinct idea" of some grand upheaval in Europe. Perhaps it was the example of 1789 that made him forecast chaos if the Chinese should revolt against their masters, the Manchus, whose ancestors had taken possession of China in the seventeenth century.[7]

In Europe itself few nations had the capacity to turn over a new leaf, and progress had to be set in motion by assaults on archaic regimes, like Napoleon's triumph over Prussia in 1806. French armies going out to emancipate Europe and staying to exploit it had some resemblance to the Europeans who were going out into Afro-Asia. The Younger Pitt was indignant at the revolutionary government's order to French generals to "liberate" occupied territories from their rulers;[8] conservatives by the Ganges or the Yellow River must have felt that this was just what British generals were being sent out to do. By many Europeans, Karl Marx among them,[9] their doings could be viewed as bearing the promise of a new age, as a rough but necessary cure for an inveterate sleeping sickness. Colonial rule might aspire to a radical, utilitarian overhauling of old societies, a blend of the work of the rising bourgeoisie and of its predecessors, enlightened despots of the breed of Frederick the Great or Joseph II of Austria.

Eighteenth-century India was going through the breakup of the Mughal empire and on the political surface was much more in a state of mutation than most of Asia. Having lost its largely synthetic unity, the country was going through something like a "warlord" era, a period of power struggles that in most areas had little meaning. India, unlike China, was a theatre of very diverse ethnic and linguistic composition, where forces of dislocation could work themselves off in local ambitions (the prowess of the Maratha armies, for example, had at most a subnational character) or in ideological currents such as the Sikh creed represented in a limited locality. Both the

Maratha and the Sikh movements were hardening into old feudal molds before the time came for them to face the European challenge. Altogether, India showed very little preparedness to react to this positively.

The Far East was a distinct continent, with a character of its own (which in some respects had its closest parallel in Europe) and, despite much diversity, a common culture originating from China. It was here that Western intervention was to have its most revolutionizing effect, even though colonial occupation did not ensue except in Indochina. In the Far East, unlike Asia further westward, foreign impact met with and released mounting internal pressures toward change. Since the seventeenth century both China and Japan had practiced isolationism; but with old structures of authority and ideas ossifying, their rulers could not ban internal unrest as easily as foreign intercourse. Paradoxically, India, always freely open to aliens from far and wide, proved better able to keep its old habits unaltered. There, two powerful religions, Hinduism and Islam, mutually hostile, were equally vigilant guardians of established social relations. Beyond their eastern limits an eclectic mixture of Confucianism, Buddhism, and indigenous cults like the Taoist in China and the Shinto in Japan ensured a lower intensity of religion and a less potent damper on criticism or innovation. Ultimately it would make for a lesser barrier than in India or the Islamic world against adoption of Western modes, whether under capitalist management as in Japan or socialist as in China.

A further difference was that these kingdoms of the Far East had a kind of national sentiment scarcely known to India or Islam, though usually hitherto less outward-looking, less aggressive than Europe's. Vietnam had tenacious memories of wars of resistance against China. Korean poetry through the ages was tinged by a similar spirit.[10] In Japan the centralizing control of the Shogunate, the military-feudal regime of the dominant Tokugawa family in the seventeenth and eighteenth centuries, assisted growth of collective feeling,[11] and neo-Confucian orthodoxy was being modified by thinking of a more Japanese cast, with a Shinto admixture. Something like what Europe called "public spirit" can be discerned in all these countries. It must have owed a debt to Confucian stress on principled concern with the affairs of this world, instead of private hope of escape to a better one.

Complexities of economic change underlay a growing restlessness. In China there had been "centuries of prosperity and growth," including growth of population, which swelled the towns and promoted interregional trade,[12] though it also perilously worsened land hunger and agrarian tensions. In Japan under the Tokugawas a rice economy was giving way to a money system, partly as a consequence of the feudal lords being compelled to spend half of each year in the capital.[13] Writings on economics were one feature of the sophisticated urban life reflected in Japanese novels of the eighteenth century. Economically, however, as well as politically, the catalyst of contact with the West was needed to precipitate radical change. In China before the second half of the nineteenth century there was scarcely any sign of a "putting out" method of production, that forerunner of industrial capitalism in the West; Japan was closer to the goal, but the restraints of a feudal society were a heavy impediment.[14] Everywhere the *idea* of capitalism, the entrepreneurial spirit, was wanting. It had dawned first, for very complex historical reasons, in northwestern Europe: elsewhere, so far as may be seen, it was only from outside that it could reach the moneyed classes capable of adopting it, somewhat as the idea of socialism has not been generated within the working class but has been brought to it by middle-class theorists.

In both China and Japan from the later eighteenth century peasant revolt was endemic. In China it weakened but could not transform the fabric of the old order, until eventually it swelled into a communist-led revolution. In Japan the share of rural disturbances in rendering the Tokugawa system no longer viable is debatable. Discontent higher up in society gave the failing Shogunate most anxiety. It was fanned by cupidity for foreign trade and its profits, and for Western wares, firearms among them, and by curiosity about Western knowledge, beginning with medical science. Chinese and others have commented that Japan could take to these things readily because it had always been borrowing, and its standard culture was more Chinese than native. Transition was greatly smoothed by the availability of a Mikado, a legitimate sovereign who could be brought out of his dynasty's long seclusion at Kyoto and stage-managed by reformers. There is both resemblance and contrast between this and the action of the sepoys at Delhi in 1857 in proclaiming as their liege lord the octogenarian pensioner in the Red Fort who was the last of the Mughal emperors. In each case a people faced with Western cannon was turning back to an old monarchy for a symbol, if no more, of its independence; in the Japanese case, unlike the Indian, there were social forces capable of establishing under its auspices a new order of their own fashioning.

Confrontation with the West made it plain to an energetic wing of the samurai, or lower nobility, that the policy of seclusion was no longer practicable in a realm so much smaller and more vulnerable than China. This class could enter partnership with businessmen alert to the opportunities of the time, on the basis of a capitalist industrialization able to sustain up-to-date armed forces and hence indispensable for national survival. The process could not be smooth or unruffled; the rebellion of the powerful Satsuma clan in 1877 was a quite violent affair. But it remained an internal broil among sections of an upper class divided from its inferiors by a broad gulf. No mobilizing or awakening of the masses took place. In China and Vietnam modernization was to be far slower and more painful, and in the end the masses would be brought fully into the arena. A British trade report summed up the Far East from an angle typical of undemocratic Europe: the Japanese were forging ahead because of the feudal background which gave them "an aristocracy, and a healthy social hierarchy based on a sound subordination."[15] China had nothing analogous to this.

What exactly had happened, in terms of the social mechanics of the "Meiji Restoration" (Meiji was the reign title adopted by the restored emperor) is still a matter of controversy.[16] There were to be lengthy arguments among Japanese Marxists as to whether it amounted to a "bourgeois revolution" or seizure of power by a capitalist from a feudal class; a baffling riddle, because categories of European and non-European history have seldom coincided exactly. Industry grew up with a markedly feudal-paternal complexion: militarism or army rule was the midwife of capitalism, as in Bismarck's Germany and in a series of Third World countries later on. Capping the whole edifice was the Mikado worship artificially worked up by the tactics well described at the time by B. H. Chamberlain.[17] Japan was traveling backward as well as forward, making far quicker material progress than British India but morally or intellectually developing on less wholesome lines. It was to owe a significant further installment of reform, in the agrarian and political fields, to its defeat in the Second World War and the American occupation. In Korea landlordism was partially disrupted, after the Japanese annexation in 1910, by Japanese settlers and land confiscations and then, after the Second World War, dismantled in the south by American rule, in the north by communism.

In China all peasant risings had failed, for want of a genuinely new program and leadership; the Taiping rebellion, in the mid-nineteenth century, marked the limit of what could be achieved, and its head, the self-defying Hung Hsui-chu'üan, degenerated before long into an imitation emperor. His ideas were partly derived from Christianity; ultimately China would get rid of its *ancien régime* with the help of other Western concepts. Within the bureaucracy no schism or mutiny took place, as it did within Japanese feudalism. Despite its dual Manchu and Chinese composition, the official class was too homogeneous and too much insulated from reality by its antediluvian education. The landowning interests it represented had been ready when they submitted to Manchu sway, and would be ready again when the Kuomintang national party in its later years came under the reactionary despot Chiang Kai-shek and his Western patrons, to welcome foreign power against their own people. No patriotic union against the alien was possible. "What sort of world is this?" the progressive writer Lu Hsün wrote gloomily after the abortive revolution of 1911, which achieved no more than to put an end at last to the derelict monarchy. "The night is so long the way so long, that I had better forget or else remain silent."[18]

Outside the Far East, too, there were, if not nations, a number of political entities having some national character and historical continuance, like Persia, Burma, Siam (Thailand), and in Africa the Christian state of Abyssinia and some kingdoms like Ashanti in West Africa, a region long accustomed to European weapons. A few precariously survived, the rest were swallowed up.

They failed with striking unanimity to meet the approaching menace of Europe; the internal stirrings and discords that prepared Japan for adaptation were not present, or only very inadequately. Asia's efforts to stave off encroachments by timely change spread across the continent from west to east, beginning with Turkey and reaching Persia and India, then Burma and Siam, and finally the Far East, with Vietnam the first in the field. Most effort went into attempts to improve armed forces, with foreign equipment and training; but human material to form effective officers and soldiers was often lacking, and by itself such a program was in any case too narrow.

Nowhere was there any breakaway from old ruts of Oriental government. This can be seen in two widely removed instances, the two most feverish endeavors at building an efficient war machine, those of Mehemet Ali in Egypt and Gia Long in Vietnam. Both were new men, usurpers, conscious of changing times, the one an Albanian soldier of fortune in Turkish service, profiting by the chaotic aftereffects of Bonaparte's irruption into the Near East, the other the first head (1802–20) of a new dynasty which forced its path to power through prolonged civil war. Each employed numerous Europeans, chiefly Frenchmen; each set his country to work by conscription of soldiers and laborers. In Vietnam men were dragooned, fortresses built on the principles of the famous French military engineer Sébastien Vauban, warships launched. But the army was intended very largely for purposes of repression, while conscription inflamed the discontent it was meant to counteract. Egypt was caught in much the same vicious circle, even though Mehemet Ali can be said to have understood that bigger revenues required enhanced economic activity and European markets.[19] Both countries speedily lost momentum and before long fell under the foreign yoke, resisted in Vietnam only by the people, in Egypt by the army fighting against the will of its employers.

Among other cases may be noted Afghanistan, where, after the second British invasion in 1878–80, Abdul Rahman sought to establish unity and firm government by methods of coercion so draconic that they must often have done more harm than good, although zealously seconded by a corps of mullahs whom he took care to induct into government service. Their prominence meant that Afghanistan, even if now more cohesive, would be socially and mentally as benighted as ever. In Abyssinia the British punitive incursion of 1868 resulted in Menelik, the future emperor and repeller of Italian invasion in 1896, becoming head of a province, and it must have helped to inspire his modernizing plans.[20] But there was no political or social reconstruction to sustain them. The last Shah liked to style himself "leader of the Iranian revolution" but squandered billions on vast and useless armaments and put his chief trust in an organization resembling the Gestapo.

The extent to which a country was affected by the shock of complete defeat and annexation depended upon a variety of factors. Such factors included the degree of nationalism present; the relation between government and its subjects; the relation of the army to the populace and whether it was an integral part of the nation or society or—as more often—an excrescence. So many lands were under alien or semi-alien rule that the overthrow of thrones might be welcomed as the deliverance which Europeans professed to be bringing. More usually the transfer of power was watched, if ordinary villagers were conscious of it at all, with indifference, especially since the majority of the old rulers offered little or no resistance. It was so over large parts of India as British ascendancy spread.

Regular armies, or what passed for such, in most of Afro-Asia were quickly knocked out. Long-drawn resistance was likely to be of a guerrilla nature, more popular but not on that account more pregnant with ideas of improvement. It was very apt to turn to religion for reinforcement, and religion meant defense of the past, with all its sins. Where leaders might be true innovators was in helping to forge a people out of a scattering of quarrelsome tribes, as Abd el Kader did in the 1830s and 1840s in Algeria, or the "Mad Mullah" before and after 1900 in Somaliland. In the Caucasus the guerrilla chief Shamyl Beg, down to his final defeat in 1858, was uniting tribesmen against the Russians; he and Nicholas I were both in their way agents of revolutionary change, unwittingly aiding each other to dismantle an old order now past its time.

"Can mankind fulfil its destiny without a fundamental revolution in the social state of Asia?" Karl Marx asked,[21] and he thought he saw this under way in India. But a great deal of the past, bad as well as good, survived there. The East India Company stepped into the vacant shoes of the Mughals, taking over many of their institutions; most literally in Bengal where it took over the "Divani" or administration of the province nominally as deputy or vassal of the fainéant Grand Mogul. Tennyson wrote a long panegyric about the British coming to inaugurate the religious freedom and toleration of which Akbar, greatest ruler of the line, could only dream. The fact that British rule was to close in a frenzy of religious passions and massacres is evidence of how far Britain's better intentions fell short of their aim, because they envisaged too little social and economic remodeling. In some important respects things were altered for the worse; in Bengal particularly, by the Permanent Settlement of 1793, which gave the land to a body of great landlords created for the purpose, with a free hand to rack-rent their tenants in Irish style. This could masquerade as an arrangement to improve agriculture but must really have been designed to call into being a class of useful collaborators. Its outcome was a Bengal "revolutionized," but in a deeply morbid way.

The survival of very conservative, aristocratic elements in British public life makes it less puzzling that the most advanced nation of Europe was ready to patronize the most reactionary forces in India. In its later years the British Raj was increasingly willing to make use of stragglers from the feudal past—

princes and landlords—as buttresses, while it looked askance at those who were
learning from the West lessons inconvenient to their superiors. The memoirs
of Sir Norman Stewart, an army man posted at Madras early in this century,
are one faithful expression of this dislike for the "educated native."[22] Colonial
governments were not infrequently disposed to humor the priesthood, as the
British did in India by distributing high-flown clerical as well as lay titles, or in
Quebec by leaving education to the Catholic clergy and so ensuring that their
French subjects would remain illiterate and give them less trouble.

Collaborators firmly moored to the past were everywhere in demand. In
Morocco the French and Spaniards found few to work with them except
the feudal tribal chiefs, the sort of men who provided Franco with 80,000
mercenaries and helped him to win the civil war. In Indonesia Dutch administrators were partnered by a light-complexioned aristocracy long accustomed
to prey on the darker-skinned peasantry.[23] In Africa the Germans professed
themselves eager to "strengthen the authority of the native chiefs and other
natives of rank . . . and to develop them into auxiliary organs of the administration."[24] In West Africa land belonging to a tribe came to be officially vested
in chiefs, who might obligingly alienate it to planters.[25] Where natives of
suitable station were not forthcoming, they could be manufactured: in India
landlords, in Africa chiefs or headmen. Frequently there was manipulation
of the past to stabilize the present: "British administrators set about inventing
African traditions for Africans."[26]

A regular philosophy of Indirect Rule took shape, with Oxford as one center;
Morocco under Marshal Lyautey early in this century was another. It was bolstered by arguments sometimes well meaning, sometimes disingenuous. There
was always an ambiguity between preserving native institutions and culture and
controlling the many through the few. It would mean at best a dilution of the
civilizing mission, at worst its abandonment. To dream of keeping the past alive,
in any meaningful sense, was futile. Tribal society disintegrated under contact
with the white man and his ways, whose good and bad sides were equally fatal
to it. As Leonard Barnes, one of imperialism's most trenchant critics, wrote in
1939, Western economic penetration was irresistibly breaking up the clan, or
social cooperation based on kinship, which could have a "strange fascination"
for Europeans with no equivalent bond of their own but which must give way
now to class division.[27] And this would be a release from the stranglehold of
the past, but a painful one, into a hazardous, uncharted new age. In a story by
an African writer an old man laments the corrosion of custom, the fading of
time-honored certainties.[28] For long to come there might be nostalgic cravings
for a return to them, "projections of recovered social unity in a millennial world
or in a life beyond death."[29]

The West could admire itself at times as a revolutionizer of comatose
communities; but Mark Twain's Yankee in ancient Britain and a Yankee of

Twain's own time in the Philippines were very different personages. Still, with all its hesitations and reluctances, the title of "Revolutionary empire" that a historian of British expansion has given it[30] was not too ill deserved and can be shared by the Western ascendancy as a whole. A decisive break was being made in the history of Afro-Asia. Change, for the better or for the worse, owed less to conquest in itself than to the steady pressures of colonial occupation. Parts of India were under British rule for nearly two centuries, long enough to detach the comparatively few who were brought into contact with Western ideas from some outworn patterns of thought and behavior and to achieve a certain legitimacy. Many possessions snapped up in the riper years of imperialism came too late for this. The French were in Vietnam for barely seventy years, with scarcely any interval of tranquillity between conquest and expulsion, and even this broken in on by the shock waves of the Great War. Administration never lost a strong military flavor; similarly, French North Africa was always under the thumb of the army more than of the government at Paris. In Korea a Japanese college instructor might be seen lecturing in uniform instead of gown, with a sword by his side.

Orderly peace and quiet was always the first reform aimed at; sometimes almost the only one, but an embargo on feuding and fighting could have many repercussions, as in India when blue blood lost ground and lawyers, traders, usurers flourished. This by itself did not ensure progress of a more far-reaching kind. In Western Europe feudalism had given way by degrees to a capitalist order; in Asia there was a risk of nothing better resulting than a broken-backed feudal society. It did at least make possible the emergence of individuals like the reforming Hindu scholar Ram Mohun Roy (1772–1833) and the enlightened Muslim Sir Syed Ahmad (1817–1898), men who genuinely believed that British rule, whatever its faults, was beneficial to India and who were desirous of learning from the West and spreading its lessons among their people. Young men bred in the climate of opinion disseminated by them were admitted by gradual stages to the higher civil service, remained loyal to the end to the British government, and in 1947 took over the running of independent India and helped to put it on the path of moderate progress.

Marx expected Western conquest to be followed by economic rehabilitation. Lenin insisted that capitalism must have time to dissolve all precapitalist economic features before colonies could evolve further, which they would then do on the same lines as his own country, as analyzed in *The Development of Capitalism in Russia*. In reality, in economic as well as too often in political terms, imperialism showed itself more parasitic than constructive and likelier to cripple old forms of production than to generate new ones. On the land the old bullock went on hauling the same plough. Handicrafts suffered, if not quite so fatally as was complained, from Western (in Korea from Japanese) machine competition; though this happened in independent Turkey as well as in foreign-controlled India.

Modern industry was coming in only sluggishly, even in India where conditions were least unfavorable. It was delayed by blockages on the side of both European and Asian enterprise; with the latter it was not capital that was lacking but the true capitalist spirit. In the later years of the Raj there was lively argument within the Third International about the thesis advanced in some quarters that Britain was coming round to a policy of economic "decolonization" and that India was being industrialized.[31] Correctly enough, the thesis ended by being discredited, and Marxists were pushed toward a radical rethinking, a conviction that imperialism prohibits capitalist development in any colony or "neocolonial" dependency. This belief in turn has had to be revised of late in view of the rapid industrial growth of Taiwan, South Korea, Hongkong—one of whose common features is their belonging to the Far Eastern complex.

European investment in colonies showed more inclination to follow on from old proclivities; it set up new plantations with labor forces kept in conditions not far from slavery. Often segregated in out-of-the-way hill districts, workers were largely women and might be partly recruited, as in India, from aboriginal districts. Agriculture on these lines and mineral extraction were what a Boston financial journal advocated in 1901 when the United States of America was entering the colonial field, not, it stressed, "a revolution in the habits and capacities of the people of the tropics."[32] Crusaders had ridden into Asia to liberate holy places, not human beings; their latter-day successors were finding their holy places in tea gardens, gold mines, and oil wells.

Meanwhile, in the concluding stages of empire, the newspaper, cinema, radio, along with railway train and omnibus, were redrawing men's picture of their world, and of their own position in it, more and more quickly. Ideas or indistinct images of change were germinating; but whereas in Europe they had more or less kept pace with economic progress, in the colonial lands they were running well ahead of it, and an uneasy gap between the two was widening.

It was when a colony, or semicolony like China or Mexico, bestirred itself to think of recovery of freedom that the test came of how much it had learned, how far self-examination and preparation for change, for a step forward instead of back, had gone. The character of the ruling power did much to dictate the terms of the contest and whether it would be a trial of physical force. It was one of Marx's grounds for advocating revolution in Europe that nothing could do so much to wipe the slate clean and allow humanity to make a fresh start. Freedom won by armed struggle in colonies, it has been said, has tended to arouse "enthusiasm for drastic social experiment," and this has served as "a kind of mass therapy for a whole people."[33] Frantz Fanon held that some countries might be exempt from the need,[34] but in general he was convinced of the necessity of violence: it meant "man re-creating himself," freeing the individual "from his inferiority complex and from his despair and inaction," and imbuing a people with a sense of collective strength.[35]

There seems, however, no simple answer to the question whether peaceful or armed struggle for freedom has had a more revolutionizing effect. European analogies scarcely suggest that resort to force has, by itself, much transformative virtue. Revolution with no adequate social drive may only stir up dust and leave it to drift down again. Spain came out of its five years' resistance to Napoleon rootedly reactionary; the Irish Free State for years after its start in 1922 made hardly any progress, economic or intellectual. Earlier precedents outside Europe were no more auspicious. Spanish rule in America had imparted little enlightenment to the descendants of European settlers, none to the other inhabitants. In the course of the long-drawn, murderous wars of independence, Indians and blacks were made use of on both sides but rarely as more than tools. Freedom won by, or as in New Zealand granted to, white settlers has always left nonwhite populations worse off instead of better. Mexico was exceptional in its greater involvement of Indians than elsewhere, and independence was to have a sequel in a series of revolutionary upheavals, in part risings of the largely Indian or half-Indian peasantry against feudal landlord and church, and on occasion of the nation against foreign intervention.

North America was exceptional in other ways; its people carried over with them English institutions and axioms, and their "revolution," which cashiered George III much as James II had been cashiered, liberalized rather than revolutionized American society, leaving the incubus of slavery untouched. At the opposite extreme was Haiti, in spite of the fighting qualities displayed in the struggle for independence from France, and the remarkable leadership of Toussaint l'Ouverture until his capture in 1802. Europe was soon able to view the black kingdom, and then republic, as proof of how a native race breaking away from the white man's leading strings must fall back into barbarism. Always fond of drawing direful domestic parallels, conservatives predicted a collapse of civilization in Britain if Chartist or socialist workers should ever be in the saddle.

National consciousness always takes a jumble of forms. In nineteenth-century Russia it could be either Westernizing and modernizing, or Slavophil and reactionary; in Asia it wavered between similar poles. Recoil from intrusive novelty made many hide from it behind the curtain of religion, and social interests formerly upheld by traditional monarchy could turn to religion, always closely associated with it, as a bulwark now still more necessary. An intelligentsia receptive to new ideas might be in existence already or might have to come to birth in the difficult setting of a colony. India had no shortage of intellectuals, and men like Ram Mohun Roy and the idealists of Young Bengal or the Brahmo Samaj, a Hindu reforming sect, undertook the painful early work of clearing out dusty lumber rooms. It would lead on in time to a desire for the country to be set free to go on remaking itself, without foreign meddling. But in the Bengal of the Permanent Settlement, with a bulky but to a great extent parasitic intelligentsia, progressive thinking might be muddled up with other notions. Nirad Chaudhuri recalls a prevalent and strong admiration in his native province, about 1900, for Napoleon and Bonapartism.[36] In western India social strata, mainly Brahmin, which had provided the Maratha empire with ministers and officials were quick to adopt modern schooling, newspapers, printed books, in order to foster hopes of a revival, under their own socially conservative leadership, for Maharashtra rather than for India.

In spite of all heterogeneities, a coming together of Hindu India in a united national front was to prove possible. The longevity of the Raj permitted nationalism a gradual maturing; Britain's moderation and legalism, by comparison with most other empires, made room for a constitutional movement, deviating at most (except in August 1942) into civil disobedience. Like Europe's bourgeois-revolutionary movements, it was not initiated or led, but only encouraged or taken advantage of, by the industrial bourgeoisie, a small but growing class. Under Gandhi's management there could be a limited rallying of popular forces, chiefly urban middle-class: workers and peasants were left for the most part to their own devices, their fumbling efforts to organize and put forward their own demands. Gandhi idealized the old-time Indian village, with richer and poorer living the simple life in fancied harmony; it was a vision more democratic at least than the admiration felt by earlier romantic patriots for ancient heroes prancing on elephants.

His principle of nonviolence, of *loving* the misguided foreigner away, may have had a certain moral effect, by making it hard for Britons not to see that Gandhians were better Christians than themselves. If so, it helped—the Second World War helped still more by using up Britain's strength and will for power—to make a peaceable settlement feasible. The upshot was a liberal India, where British investments could feel safe, but where reforms impressive compared with those in many other former colonies have been carried out. In addition, there have been remarkable increases in both agricultural and industrial production. India has not fundamentally broken with its old social order, however, and still faces problems seemingly insoluble within the existing framework. Indians, not only of the far left, have sometimes asked themselves whether it would have been better if British rule had provoked them into full-scale rebellion and a more sweeping social revolution.

Muslims everywhere, disgruntled at their sudden precipitation into a new epoch, were left sullenly impervious to any new thinking. Ages of warfare between Islam and Christendom had left tenacious memories, and in many places Muslims were dislodged by European conquest from their dominant position in mixed communities. Some of their writers in India depicted

Europe as a den of monsters, its history a long catalogue of horrors;[37] they saw it in fact very much as Europe saw Asia. Syed Ahmad wanted his coreligionists to wake up and open their windows, but he also wanted them to repose their trust in the British government, as their protector against the bigger and richer Hindu population. In this century the Muslim political movement, after a brief spell of alliance with the National Congress, turned away toward the mirage of an "Islamic State," the reality of a Muslim instead of a less unprogressive Hindu ruling class.

Harshnesses inseparable from imperialism combined with the painful disruption of old habits to turn many others against not only Westerners but everything Western, good or bad. In China the Boxer Rebellion of 1900 was an explosion of such animosity, heightened by rustic superstition. Even among the higher ranks, where religion counted less, confusion and discouragement could bring a turning back to the past; men were trying to polish up old lamps as well as to acquire new ones. Gernet notes a heightened veneration for Confucius.[38] Dostoyevsky, Rabindranath Tagore, in Muslim India the poet Iqbal, exalted spiritual values against Western greed and materialism. By intent or not, their message could be turned into a social red herring, with spiritual blessings to fill empty stomachs. More discriminating critics found fault with Europe's conduct without rejecting its gifts. Fukuzawa Yukichi was the foremost proponent of modernism in the Meiji era, though at the same time he maintained that a true civilization for Japan must be Japanese and denounced Western aggression. "Wherever the Europeans touch, the land withers up, as it were; the plants and the trees stop growing."[39]

A long train of revolts, from French Canada to Vietnam, from the Philippines to Zululand, all failed, as the Indian Mutiny and the Boxer Rebellion failed, against superior arms and discipline. Europeans were beset nonetheless by fears of worse things to come, a Prester John, perhaps, or a Yellow Peril. Worst of all, after the Bolshevik revolution, was the Red Peril. At first its threat was hard to comprehend. A British general campaigning in western Persia late in the Great War saw "revolution" as a strange, demoralizing disease, reducing men to "a dull apathy" in which even the primitive instinct to defend hearth and home was crippled.[40] But it was not long before the spectre of communism was haunting the colonial world as well as Europe.

Marxian socialism could meet needs beyond the purview of romantic nationalism like that of Giuseppe Mazzini, for long in Asia an admired paladin. It was coming from Western Europe, as capitalism had come to Japan; in each case Europe was revolutionizing the outer world less by imposing its rule than by teaching others how to resist it. Sparks from the conflagration of 1917 flew far and wide, but most of them failed to catch. They failed in India, partly from lack of combustible material; it was in the Far East, outside Japan, that they had most success. Acute dilemmas arose over what classes or social forces might be best fitted to absorb Marxism and take the lead in its application, in the absence of a strong industrial working class. Amilcar Cabral in Portuguese Guinea drew his most promising recruits from the petty bourgeoisie, employees or traders with modest earnings, though he was well aware of its ambivalent outlook.[41] With Mao, Marxism learned to appeal to the peasantry as the potential battering ram of revolution. Experience has yet to show whether this could in the long run give socialism a permanent base.

It was just after the Great War, with the "August 4 movement," that modern Chinese nationalism came into being. It had perforce to identify itself with reform and progress; the old Confucian ideology and social order were manifestly exhausted. With enough physical strength to overthrow them, the peasantry had lacked the needful understanding; the nascent bourgeoisie had understanding but lacked strength and was too much tied to the past by its Siamese-twin link with landownership. A small party of socialists can work deliberately to usher in a socialist society; there can scarcely be a similar sense of mission to establish capitalism, and a bourgeois party can only be strong enough to take power when capitalism is already well-developed.

Hence the failure of the bourgeoisie to extend its participation under the Chiang dictatorship;[42] hence also the "masochistic" attitude of middle-class intellectuals who welcomed the Japanese invasion on the ground that in no other way could the old China be demolished and an eventual rebirth ensured.[43] It did help indirectly, by damaging the corrupt and ineffective Kuomintang regime, morally even more than physically, and by stirring up the peasantry. Mass resistance was partly patriotic, partly or mainly long-standing agrarian discontent breaking out once more, but now under the leadership of a communist party. This had persisted in growing, in defiance of ferocious repression and an enormous death toll[44]—in spite also of many baffled gropings amid the confusions of Chinese history and society, in search of the right road.[45]

In the final phases, whether colonies were compelled to fight for independence depended partly on geography. If they were close to the USSR, like India, fear of nationalism turning into communism, as happened in China, might make governments hesitate to go to extremes. None of the Dutch, French, or Portuguese possessions lay anywhere near the Soviet borders. Another factor was the presence of settlers or planters; these were always a potent irritant and had a surprising ability to veto concessions to native feeling that governments would otherwise have been willing to make. When revolt broke out in the post-1945 years it was regularly blamed on sinister communist infiltration, and this could be made the pretext for terroristic methods of repression, which might prosper for a while or might provoke wider resistance and bring into the lead the most determined individuals, often those most indurated by Marxism.

How things turned out depended on many local circumstances and on the leadership available. In Malaya it was the Chinese, or a Marxist-led section of them, that fought a guerrilla war; it was to the tradition-bound Malay princelings that power was eventually handed over. In Kenya the fighting was an obscure episode in the bush; after it was over power went to men who had taken no part in it and whose only aim was to enrich themselves.[46] Indonesians waged a long struggle for freedom ending in nothing much better than the demagogic rhetoric of which Sukarno was an inexhaustible fountain until it was cut off by the army coup, with foreign engineering, in 1965, and the massacre of some half a million real or alleged communists.

China's revolution brought inspiration after 1948 to all militant movements within earshot; above all to Vietnam, whose two or three decades of bloodshed stand in sharp contrast with India's six decades of more or less peaceful agitation. Any nation on the march had to draw on its own collective memories and ideals, though it also had to jettison a great deal of its past in order to lighten the load. Mao found in China's annals a collectivist, utopian tradition;[47] Ho Chi Minh and his party gave close attention to their national history and made much of it in their summons to the masses.[48] Prolonged resistance to French conquest, although defeated, left inspiring memories to patriots of the next century. Vietnam was a rural society, and its literate class was close to the people; it may always have had something of the mixed feeling of the lower clergy in medieval Europe, attached to the governing interests but at times impelled to take sides with the poor. Foreign domination had a polarizing effect on this intelligentsia, part of it joining hands with the aliens, another part helping to preserve national consciousness by composing histories and patriotic poems. At a later stage some would join in the liberation movement[49] or even go over to Marxism.

Away from the Far East, the protracted Algerian war was the salient case of freedom won by an armed rising. Algerians drew some encouragement from the example of Vietnam, but they set out from a lower cultural level, with a nationhood only recently and imperfectly conjured up by the guerrilla fighting against the French occupation. Fanon had high hopes of the transforming effects of the uprising. When it was decided to enroll women as auxiliaries, there was a striking response from them. Soldiers were ready to adopt medical and hygienic practices they had been reluctant to learn from the French.[50] Aware of the disharmonies between semi-Westernized townmen and the more backward but more rebellious countryside, Fanon counted on battle and shared danger to bring them together as a single nation.[51]

Very much was indeed achieved. One handicap, which an Arab writer has emphasized, was the French army's determination to wipe out all elements capable of leadership,[52] though some officers liked to indulge in a bizarre theory of "revolutionary war," or winning over the masses by blending persuasion with brutal coercion.[53] Of necessity the struggle developed too one-sidedly on military lines. In turn, partly for this reason, military activity could not rise much above the guerrilla level, whereas in Vietnam, fused with political activity, it moved on to the building of a regular army capable of fighting pitched battles. It is still not clear in what direction free Algeria is evolving or what will be its reward for the sacrifice of a million lives. For ideas some Algerians still look, it appears, to France, others to the Middle East.

By whatever route freedom has been achieved, there are always residues of former days still to be shaken off. A society is never fully external to the individual; it can subsist only because its humbler members accept much of the mentality of their betters (the converse may also be true in some measure). The new man has to escape from himself as well as from his environment.[54] Mao in his declining years was obsessed by fear of bourgeois cravings and illusions surviving to infect his communist utopia, the fantasies of a defeated class outliving their social base.

One important test of the thoroughness or incompleteness of change is the status of women. They played an appreciable part in freedom movements; in armed revolts they undertook, as in occupied Europe during the Second World War, many unaccustomed duties, but they found little place in the leadership. They could come to the front more easily in countries like India or Ceylon, moving toward a parliamentary pattern. But male love of dominance seems tenacious in all emerging societies, not to be ended in any such summary fashion as colonial or feudal ascendancy.

For many other failings colonial rule can partly be blamed, among them, some of the senseless feuds widespread in the Third World. There was indignation in the Indian press when an outbreak of rioting in Southall in April 1979, set off by a National Front demonstration, caused a death and numerous arrests; but a Hindu-Muslim riot in Jamshedpur a few weeks earlier had caused a hundred deaths. Many Indians accuse British rule of worsening communal relations; it would be hard to assert that it did much to improve them or tried to do much. Clashes between peoples or states, as well as communities, were endemic in old days outside as well as within Europe. National sentiment always present, if latent, in the Far East facilitated new initiatives but also made for pugnacity once it came to be aroused. If China can claim to have created a novel form of socialist society, Japan of capitalist, the one has been guilty of aggression against its fellow-communist neighbor Vietnam, the other of imperialism on a grand scale at the expense of fellow Asians. There have been many symptoms lately of a rebirth of the chauvinist military spirit in Japan.

It was Lenin's hope, from before 1914, that colonial liberation movements would help to undermine capitalism in Europe and that colonial masses and industrial working classes would press onward shoulder to shoulder. When revolution in Europe hung fire, it came to be widely believed that socialism could seize power only in backward countries.[55] More recently, euphoric dreams of salvation from the Third World, under Maoist watchwords, have receded; it may be time for Marxists to recall the Leninist principle that socialism cannot win the day anywhere before some minimum level of economic development has been reached.[56] At present capitalism is still very much with us, technically resilient if socially obsolescent and therefore unstable. As directed from Washington, it has less to offer than in colonial days in the way of progressive thinking, far more in the way of material satisfactions for the few able to scramble for them. So heavily have burdens of poverty and "unfreedom" continued to weigh on vast areas that restless spirits have sometimes thought world peace a lesser good than collision and chaos, to shake the old fabric of things to pieces and open a door out of their prison.

Many ills are clearly connected with bad leadership, by individuals or groups among whom army bosses have had a deplorable prominence. Where freedom, or the nominal freedom of neocolonialism, came with little exertion or sacrifice, power was likely to fall to men reared in and molded by the colonial system. Lurid examples have been the tyrant Francisco Machia Nguema in Equatorial Guinea after it ceased to be a Spanish territory, whom it is not hard to see as an understudy of Francisco Franco, and Idi Amin of Uganda, an erstwhile mercenary soldier serving against rebels in Kenya. Among colonies that really fought for freedom, saddest have been the fortunes of Portuguese Guinea. Its socialist founder Cabral had warned of the necessity of *"struggles against our own weaknesses* . . . this battle against ourselves—no matter what difficulties the enemy may create—is the most difficult of all."[57] He was murdered in 1973; after his brother and successor Luis was turned out by the soldiers and charged with corruption and mass killings, a visiting journalist reported that foodstuffs in the shops were scarce, whiskey and expensive cars plentiful.[58]

For more than nine-tenths of a colonial population, Fanon wrote, "independence brings no immediate change," and disillusion may be quick to set in, coupled with disgust at the affluence of a new-rich "caste."[59] Western rule fortified class division in Asia and crystallized it in Africa; those at the top today do not often appear to feel more responsibility or benevolence to their subjects than Western officialdom did. Egotism is not confined to them; a jostling eagerness to get on, a restless individualism, is liable to pervade all ranks. Multitudes suffer from an itch for the possessions which they know to be abundant in happier lands, wristwatches for instance, and which they covet also as "status-symbols." In the absence of economic expansion this breeds what Spaniards call *empleomanía,* hunger and thirst for government jobs of any sort, and education degenerates into a grabbing at any qualifications that can bring a salary within reach.[60] Contact with the West and its tempting wares, useful or frivolous, can frustrate socialist movements by starving them of idealism, without promoting any local capitalism.

"The people that walked in darkness have seen a great light": it was some such image that Europe cherished of the blessings bestowed by it on the outer world. At any rate it could hug the notion that the world's people had been *shown* a great light, whether they turned their eyes toward it or not. From the other side of the fence the picture has often looked very different. African and other Third World writers have complained that imperialism cut short their unfolding cultures and replaced them with something worse; they reject "the essential barbarism of the 'civilizing' hordes."[61] Truth must be sought not between these antithetical views but in a complex interweaving of them. It is open to Westerners to assert that many ex-colonies have proved unfit for self-rule; and equally open to their peoples to ask why Western rulers, having come uninvited to drag them out of their yesterdays, did so little to guide them toward tomorrow.

Notes

This chapter originally appeared in Roy Porter and Mikulás Teich, eds., *Revolution in History* (Cambridge University Press, 1986).

1. Samuel Johnson, *A Journey to the Western Islands of Scotland* (1775), sections entitled "Aberbrothick" and "Inverness."

2. John Milton, *The History of Britain,* in *Prose Works,* ed. J. A. St. John (London, 1848), vol. 5, 197–98, 214. For a spirited defense of the ideals attributable to modern British empire building, reference may be made to A. P. Thornton, *The Imperial Idea and Its Enemies* (London, 1959). D. K. Fieldhouse gives a scholarly survey of European expansion, with its better and worse features, in *The Colonial Empires: A Comparative Survey from the Eighteenth Century* (London, 1965). A variety of opinions will be found in M. Barratt Brown, *After Imperialism* (revised ed., London, 1970). Marx's views are collected in the anthology *On Colonialism* (Moscow, 1960); see also "Imperialism," "Colonialism," etc., in *A Dictionary of Marxist Thought,* ed. Tom Bottomore (Oxford, 1983). D. R. SarDesai, *British Trade and Expansion in Southeast Asia, 1830–1914* (New Delhi, 1977), is a good example of how Western motives have come to be seen by many Indian and other Afro-Asian scholars.

3. Fernand Braudel, *The Perspective of the World* (1979; English ed., London, 1984), 64.

4. Syed Husain Alatas, *The Myth of the Lazy Native* (London, 1977), 238.

5. J. F. Davis quoted in Leila Ahmed, *Edward W. Lane* (London, 1978), 112.

6. Lord Hardinge, *Old Diplomacy* (London, 1947), 67.

7. *An Embassy to China: Lord Macartney's Journal, 1793–94,* ed. J. L. Cranmer-Byng (London, 1962), 103, 239–40.

8. William Pitt (the Younger), *Orations on the French War* (London, 1906), 301.

9. On the Marxist attitude, see, e.g., U. Melotti, *Marx and the Third World* (London, 1977), 114ff. 121–22, 194.

10. See P. H. Lee, *Poems from Korea* (London, 1974), 64.

11. Yosoburo Takekoshi, *Economic Aspects of the History of the Civilization of Japan* (London, 1930), vol. 3, 282.

12. *Cambridge History of China*, vol. 12, Part 1, ed. J. K. Fairbank (1983), 19, 721–22.

13. Eijiro Honjo, "The Transition from the Tokugawa Period," *Kyoto University Economic Review* 1932.

14. Fairbank, *Cambridge History of China*, vol. 12, Part 1, 725; A. L. Sadler, *Short History of Japan* (Sydney, 1963), 229.

15. A. Krausse, *China in Decay* (London, 1900), 263.

16. The question is surveyed by G. D. Allinson in *E. H. Norman: His Life and Scholarship*, ed. R. W. Bowen (Toronto, 1984), 99ff.

17. B. H. Chamberlain, *The Invention of a New Religion* (London, 1912).

18. Lu Hsün quoted in J. D. Spence, *The Gate of Heavenly Peace: The Chinese and Their Revolution, 1894–1980* (London, 1982), 238.

19. R. Owen, "Egypt and Europe," in *Studies in the Theory of Imperialism*, ed. R. Owen and B. Sutcliffe (London, 1972), 198ff. This writer considers the label "oriental despotism" unsuited to the Egyptian state of those times.

20. See H. G. Marcus, *The Life and Times of Menelik II: Ethiopia, 1844–1933* (Oxford, 1975).

21. Karl Marx, "The British Rule in India" (article of 10 June 1853); reprinted in K. Marx and F. Engels, *The First Indian War of Independence, 1857–1859* (Moscow, 1959), 14ff.

22. See General Sir N. Stewart, *My Service Days* (London, 1908).

23. C. R. Boxer, *The Dutch Seaborne Empire, 1600–1800* (1965; reprint, Harmondsworth, 1973), 213.

24. German Colonial Office, *How Natives Are Treated in German and French Colonies* (Berlin, 1919), Part 1, 7.

25. D. K. Fieldhouse, in *Oxford and the Idea of Commonwealth*, ed. F. Madden and D. K. Fieldhouse (London, 1982), 154.

26. T. Ranger, "The Invention of Tradition in Colonial Africa," in *The Invention of Tradition*, ed. E. Hobsbawm and T. Ranger (Cambridge, 1983), 212.

27. L. Barnes, *Empire or Democracy?* (London, 1939), 161.

28. James Ngugi, "A Meeting in the Dark," in *Modern African Stories*, ed. E. A. Komey and E. Mphahlele (London, 1964); cf. Chinua Achebe's novel *Things Fall Apart* (1958; reprint, London, 1962).

29. Barnes, *Empire or Democracy?*, 160.

30. A. Calder, *Revolutionary Empire: The Rise of the English-Speaking Empires from the Fifteenth Century to the 1780s* (London, 1981).

31. See S. D. Gupta, *Comintern, India, and the Colonial Question, 1920–37* (Calcutta, 1980), Chapter 4.

32. N. Etherington, *Theories of Imperialism: War, Conquest, and Capital* (London, 1984), 17.

33. P. Calvert, "On Attaining Sovereignty," in *Nationalist Movements,* ed. A. D. Smith (London, 1976), 145.

34. Frantz Fanon, *The Wretched of the Earth* (1961; English ed., Harmondsworth, 1967), 155.

35. Ibid., 18, 74; cf. 28–29, 118, 237.

36. Nirad C. Chaudhuri, *The Autobiography of an Unknown Indian* (London, 1951), Book 1, Chapter 4.

37. Aziz Ahmad, *Islamic Modernism in India and Pakistan, 1857–1964* (London, 1967), 92–93.

38. J. Gernet, *A History of Chinese Civilization* (1972; English ed., Cambridge, 1982), 580.

39. Fukuzawa Yukichi, *An Outline of a Theory of Civilization,* trans. D. A. Dilworth and G. C. Hurst (Tokyo, 1973), 188–89.

40. General L. C. Dunsterville, *The Adventures of Dunsterforce* (1920; reprint, London, 1932), 4–5.

41. Amilcar Cabral, *Revolution in Guinea: An African People's Struggle* (London, 1969), 88–89.

42. See M.-C. Bergère, "The Chinese Bourgeoisie, 1911–37," in *Cambridge History of China,* vol. 12, Part 1.

43. Dick Wilson, *When Tigers Fight: The Story of the Sino-Japanese War, 1937–1945* (Harmondsworth, 1983), 3–4.

44. See Spence, *The Gate of Heavenly Peace.*

45. See Arif Dirklik, *Revolution and History: The Origins of Marxist Historiography in China, 1919–1937* (Berkeley, 1978).

46. *Petals of Blood,* by the Kenyan novelist Ngugi wa Thiong'o (London, 1977), gives a graphic account of this.

47. M. Meisner, *Marxism, Maoism, and Utopianism* (Madison, Wis., 1982), 214.

48. Thomas Hodgkin, *Vietnam: The Revolutionary Path* (London, 1981), 186ff.

49. See D. Hunt, "Village Culture and the Vietnamese Revolution," in *Past and Present,* no. 94 (1982): 131ff.

50. Fanon, *The Wretched of the Earth,* 51ff., 142.

51. Ibid., 86–89.

52. E. Hermassi, "Impérialisme et décadence politique au Maghreb," in *Sociologie de l'impérialisme,* ed. A. Abdel-Malek (Paris, 1971), 137.

53. E. R. Wolf, *Peasant Wars of the Twentieth Century* (1969; reprint, London, 1976), 242–44.

54. There is much of relevance to this in Paulo Freire, *Pedagogy of the Oppressed* (Harmondsworth, 1972). Cf. A. Memmi, *Portrait du colonisé* (Paris, 1973).

55. Cf. Franz Marek, *Philosophy of World Revolution* (London, 1969), 102–3.

56. This principle is restated in V. V. Zagladin, ed., *The World Communist Movement* (Moscow, 1973), 112ff.

57. Cabral, *Revolution in Guinea*, 74.

58. Jill Joliffe, in the *Guardian*, 6 December 1980.

59. Fanon, *The Wretched of the Earth*, 58–59, 134. Cf. V. Schwarcz, *Long Road Home: A China Journal* (New Haven, Conn., 1984), 44, on "that hard, awful question that every revolutionary must ask: 'What has changed, after all?' "

60. See Ronald Dore, *The Diploma Disease: Education, Qualification, and Development* (London, 1976).

61. T. Hodgkin, "Some African and Third World Theories of Imperialism," in Owen and Sutcliffe, *Studies*, 102–3. Cf. Ad'Obe Obe, in the *Guardian*, 26 October 1984: "The British are now seen as those who culturally 'raped' Nigeria." Judith M. Brown, *Modern India* (Oxford, 1985), argues that old India was *not* standing still and that British rule *could not* have brought about a social transformation.

6

EUROPE IN THE COLONIAL MIRROR

Introduction

In the Strachov monastic library at Prague is a fanciful map of Europe in the likeness of a female figure whose head is Spain, with Italy for her right arm, and so on. To personify a country or region (or constellation) is the simplest way to think of it as a familiar whole, and from the sixteenth to the eighteenth century, while figures like Britannia were growing up, it was also a common artistic convention to depict Europe as a female figure, together with the other continents by way of contrast. In such groups the evolving concept of Europe and its place in the world can be traced. An early example is the decorative group on the street wall of the "Ancient House" in the Butter Market at Ipswich, built in 1567. Europe and Asia are both elaborately costumed, Africa and America nearly naked and savage. Asia, or western Asia, was Europe's old neighbor and ancient enemy: North Africa was now a battleground between them, but the possession of America could give Europe more confidence as against bigger and richer Asia.

How much in general did the expansion of Europe do to stir up the European mind, to generate novel ideas, aspirations, doubts, as well as material greeds—and how much to strengthen a sense always present, if only flickeringly, of Europe being one region, one civilization? To the thoughtful minority, from century to century, widening acquaintance with the outer world could indeed lend a new dimension to everything—religion, society, government, marriage, law—and most often with the effect of emphasizing the European community of ideas, the greater gap between them and everything non-European. But the process of learning was slow, fitful, cloudy; the record cannot be reduced by the historian, however desirous he may be of giving an orderly, lucid account, to anything like the regular rectangular outline of Edinburgh's New Town; rather, it resembles the higgledy-piggledy lanes and wynds and obscure courtyards of the old town. There was from the first an accumulation of solid knowledge: it is Europe that has made the continents known to one another. But Europe's intrusions into the outer world were coming about in a chaotic, haphazard fashion, and its learning was always mixed up with error, delusion, prejudice. All impressions of the collective mind—as of the individual mind left to its own tuition—are blurred, hazy, contradictory. Europe's pictures of other lands were by turns impressionistic or expressionistic much oftener than realistic. Each nation looked at them differently, some with far keener interest than others. Similarly each class: India meant a great deal to the Victorian middle class, very little to the working class. Europeans were primarily interested in themselves, and much more as Italians or Yorkshiremen than as Europeans: as a rule the outer world was only an amplifier, or a long shadow, making their own sensations more audible or visible to them. There was room for all kinds of fantasy, credulity, deception and self-deception, and the development of stock responses. The vaguer these images were, the more emotive force they could acquire, especially when Europe thought of its identity in terms of race or color and plagued itself with fears of the Yellow Peril or a Black Peril—boomerang effects, as they might be called, of a White Peril from which the other continents were more tangibly suffering.

Europe's Will to Power

Every individual is the center of his own universe, and every community until taught otherwise by rude experience is a Middle Kingdom, comfortably satisfied of its superiority to every other. The narrower the horizon, the easier this assumption: some Eskimos, and many African peoples, call themselves simply "The Men," "The People"—the only truly authentic human beings, that is. Europeans collectively came by stages to regard themselves in something like the same fashion. Along with this they were coming to claim right and title to dominate all the others, more aggressively perhaps than any other people since the Assyrians, except—in their palmier days—the Muslims: Islam and Christendon are half-brothers, as well as for ages sparring partners. Fernand Braudel's conception of Europe is of a region thirsting above all for practical knowledge capable of being used to build and bolster its ascendancy for others.[1] It emerges from his study of the early growth of capitalism over four centuries: we may, if we wish, see in capitalism, one of Europe's many unique and fateful inventions, the mainspring of this self-assertion. Economic competition, national rivalry, class conflict were all growing and interacting and feeding impulses of aggression; consciousness of strength superior to that of all outside Europe was a further stimulus. Nietzsche's cult of the "will to power," at the climax of European imperialism, was the most eloquent expression of this spirit, with a crazy Wagnerian grandeur compared with which the western European outlook was sober and realistic. Britain and France already had empires, and with them problems as well as profits: Germany had scarcely any, and viewed *Weltpolitik* and dreamed of world power more romantically. In sixteenth-century Europe the most stridently bombastic expressions of national chauvinism had likewise come from Germany, because Germany still lacked the national existence that others enjoyed.

Since its earliest formation, however, Europe's tradition had been one of war and conquest, to which Christianity was a reflex or second self or dialectical opposite. Greece was already a microcosm of modern Europe in the intensity of its internecine feuds, combined with a conviction of the superiority of all Greeks to all others. They were always colonists, settlers on other people's land, and ended by combining together for a grand invasion of Asia. Their leader has always been "Alexander the Great" for Europeans, as their first great champion and conqueror beyond their own limits, the first to strike down Asia. It is a curious proof of Asia's far lesser sense of identity against Europe that he has remained a myth-hero in the lands he invaded too, as far off as India, part, as Tarn wrote, of "the dream-world of Asia." No alien invader could ever be so apotheosized in Europe: though the only one after Attila to stamp himself permanently on the European imagination, the sultan known to the West as Sulaiman the Magnificent, was a less hateful figure than his forerunner.

The first Europe was the Roman Empire, whose greatness has always recurred to the memory of Europeans confronting outsiders. Medieval Christendom of the Crusades had its Holy Roman Empire; the Renaissance, with its reverence for everything Roman, its poetic resurrection of the Roman gods and goddesses from their long sleep, owed a great deal to the fact that Europe was fighting its way into other realms as well as fighting on the defensive against the Turks. Luiz Vaz de Camoëns's epic poem on the Portuguese advent in the Indies bears frequent witness to this. British rulers there, whose meager education was mostly fragments of Latin and Greek, saw themselves in their moments of higher consciousness—vital sustainers of men's humdrum toil in any walk of life—as propraetors or proconsuls with seats to return to in the Senate. Mussolini adorned the Forum with an imposing map of the Roman empire and added to it Abyssinia. It was a boast of the early German patriot Ulrich von Hetten, in a dialogue written about 1518, that Rome's legions failed to add Germany to it; but he adds, through his mouthpiece the ghost of Arminius, that "Alexander could not have vanquished the Romans as easily as he conquered the effeminate peoples of Asia . . . and the defenseless nations of India."[2] The notion of Europeans as virile, other peoples as effeminate, was already astir, and warlike Europe found it more and more attractive as its triumphs abroad multiplied. It was a variant of the machismo that men everywhere have cultivated, with the aid of swords, beards, and other trappings and struttings, to impress and overawe women.

Every such European attitude toward outsiders, it must be added, can be paralleled by attitudes of one nation or class toward others within Europe. Kaiser William II assured an Englishman in 1906 that the French were "a female race and a bundle of nerves, not a male race like the Anglo-Saxons and the Teutons."[3]

European Expansion, 1500–1800

When Ulrich von Hutten was writing, Cortés had just conquered Mexico. It does not seem that the discovery of the New World had any such transforming influence as might have been expected on the European consciousness—so far as we can gauge this from the works of the great writers, for instance. The breakout from a Ptolemaic into a Copernican universe may have seemed more momentous. Europe was in some ways more bitterly divided than either earlier or later, too much so to think of any new empires overseas as a European achievement. Feudal Christendom had presented a fairly homogeneous front to the Saracen, though commercial Venice could be seduced into trading with the enemy. From the late fifteenth century the "new monarchies" were building their authority and their national states by chronic warfare among themselves, amid which the Turks could easily find Christian allies, and Christendom was on the eve of splitting into two hostile religions. Some European elation could be felt over the conquest of Granada in the 1490s, as the final liberation of the western lands from the infidel, and again over the defense of Malta in 1565. But between these two events Spain had risen to greatness in as well as outside Europe, and its American resources were adding to the menace of a Spanish of Hapsburg domination, a "Universal Monarchy," which would also be a Roman Catholic juggernaut. To the Counter-Reformation, indeed, Spanish and Portuguese expansion overseas brought an immense reinforcement, not only in the form of silver and spices and the church endowments and armies they paid for but still more in a restoration of confidence in the cause: conversion of fresh millions of souls beyond the seas inspired faith in the conversion of heretics at home, by the same blend of persuasion and coercion; and Jesuit and Franciscan missions in Paraguay or Japan were models for the missionary work of a St. Peter Canisius in Austria or Poland. On this side the expansion had a profound and permanent influence on the emerging European amalgam, some of its lingering effects could be seen until lately in the regime of General Franco.

Among Spain's enemies at least there was a widespread conviction that the country did not really belong to Europe: it was Moorish, African, heroic but barbarous, like an Othello. With this went a greater readiness than Europeans in later times usually showed to sympathize with downtrodden colonial peoples. The horrific picture of oppression in Spanish America, *The Destruction of the Indies,* by the missionary bishop Las Casas, who struggled in vain to secure protection for the natives, had a wide circulation abroad. It did not deter Spain's enemies from following the Spanish example as soon as they had the chance. There was some difference, psychological if no more, in the fact that the British and French for a long time in their colonies were chiefly engaged either in planting settlements of their own people or in extracting labor not from native populations but from African slaves, mostly bought in an honest way of commerce from African chiefs. As to the first type of colony, Bacon could recommend a very edifying native policy. "If you plant where savages are, do not only entertain them with trifles and jingles, but use them justly and graciously, with sufficient guard, nevertheless." They should often be brought to visit the home country, so as to be able to tell their brethren of its superior civilization.[4]

All the early empires were strictly monopolistic, jealously reserved for their own masters. Spanish America belonged not even to Spaniards but to Castilians only. Portugal, small and vulnerable at home, identified itself with its overseas possession with a special warmth and went on down to yesterday hugging—and strangling—them. Not many years ago a Portuguese student was interrogated by the police, and a friend jailed for a month, because the latter was heard quoting a statement of some historian that Afonso Albuquerque was a homosexual.[5] It is hard to imagine even the most fervently loyal British policeman or magistrate being so indignant about a similar aspersion on Lord Clive or General Kitchener. The massacre of Amboina in 1623 was a symptom of how violently Europeans were ready to protect their colonial Ali Baba's caves even against their nearest neighbors and coreligionists. All the same, there was a sense in which all Europeans shared in a heightened sense of power engendered by the successes of any of them, as well as in the pool of material wealth—bullion, spices, and then tobacco, sugar, cotton—that the colonies produced. Even those with the widest differences to separate them had many customs and institutions in common, which, they were discovering, did not exist anywhere else. In particular they shared much the same material equipment, military and naval above all, and a growing certainty that with it, and their own innate qualities, they were irresistible. With 50,000 soldiers, a Fugger correspondent wrote from southern India in 1580, the king of Spain could annex the whole country: Indian rulers had plenty of soldiers, but they were poor fighters. "One Christian can achieve more than six Indians."[6] It has been observed—and it is a dramatic index of this vast disparity of strength—that while Spaniards in America debated whether the natives had souls or were creatures subhuman, the natives began taking them for superhuman beings, the gods of ancient prophecy.[7]

Down into the eighteenth century Europeans overseas were fighting one another more than they were fighting the peoples they overran, whose resistance seldom gave them much trouble. Nor did they hesitate to enter into alliances against one another with Red Indian tribes or rulers of Hindustan.

By the eighteenth century, however, when at war among themselves, they adhered to the rules of "civilized warfare" which were developing in Europe: possibly colonial warfare, where it would hardly do for Indians or Red Indians to see white men treated barbarously, may have given an impetus to the evolution of these rules. There was, moreover, always a cosmopolitan element in colonial enterprise and the building of empires, as, a little earlier, of the national states in Europe. Foreigners wormed their way into the Seville trade with Spanish America. Marranos or crypto-Jews had a big hand in the trade of East and West Indies; Jews exiled in Amsterdam came to control a quarter of the shares of the Netherlands East India company.[8] Numerous Germans and others worked for the Dutch in Indonesia. Huguenot exiles in London were active in the English East India Company, and its soldiers and civilians in India included a heavy sprinkling of foreign names. Dutch publishers in the seventeenth century brought out many Latin and other foreign editions of their volumes of travel and exploration,[9] thus helping to form a *European* consciousness of the other continents. Louis XIV gave wide circulation to the reports of the missionary bodies under his patronage, to the greater glory of God and himself.

All this shared experience or knowledge, however many quarrels accompanied it, must have contributed to the calm self-complacency, the cosmopolitan spirit, of eighteenth-century Europe. There was also the pushing back of the Turks, no longer a menace after the repulse of their final attack on Vienna in 1683. They were still close at hand, still in occupation of the Balkans: the nearness of the frontier was a constant reminder of the line between civilization and barbarism and of Europe's merited place on the right side of the line. A verse in one of Voltaire's epistles to Catherine the Great, where he bestows his approval on her wars with Turkey, reveals how far outside the charmed circle was a sultan who "yawns, and has nothing to do, and never writes to me." If he were civilized he would of course be one of Voltaire's correspondents, like Catherine and Frederick. Equally of course, nine-tenths of Catherine's subjects were equally far beyond the pale, and beneath philosophic notice. There was understood to be one other civilization, the Chinese, too remote to be a rival—as if another planet with intelligent life were being encountered. It soon turned out to be not very intelligent, after all.

Nineteenth-Century Imperialism

Between the aristocratic cosmopolitanism of the eighteenth century and the socialist internationalism of the later nineteenth, there was the John Bright and William Cobden middle-class ideal of a peaceful Europe knitted together by community of economic interest, including interest in expanding outside markets which there was no need to fight over. And in fact after 1815 European governments did not fight among themselves over colonies—

though they were far from renouncing the use of force against Indians or Chinese or Algerians. Here was further opportunity for Europe to contemplate itself with satisfaction in its colonial mirror, or in the colonial wing of its Hall of Mirrors. Traders, diplomats, missionaries, buccaneers from a diversity of countries congregated in the Far East or in Latin America, which was economically on a semicolonial level and in European eyes not more than semicivilized. Here they had common interests, as well as a common desire to steal a march on one another. Even those from second-class countries, like some of the Latin lands, had to be included with the rest, if only as Europeans by courtesy. Malays or Chinese saw not much difference between one European and another, and this had the effect of reminding them of their kinship: even the rugged individualist John Bull, who found that his Indian subjects had little appreciation of his unique British qualities but called him and all other white men "Europeans" or, with more distaste, "Firangis"—Franks, descendants of the Crusaders.

For a long time these descendants, up and down the world, met with so little resistance that they were free to suppose, if they cared to, that their presence was welcome, or not unwelcome. This was not always accurate. When, for instance, a Muslim Indian of the late eighteenth century wrote a history of the age and asked himself why his people had fallen from their high estate, his answer was that Allah had sent British rule as a punishment for their sins.[10] In 1857 the Indian Mutiny left no doubt about how British rule was looked at. It reverberated round Europe, where opinion was mostly sympathetic to Britain. Only fourteen years later, just as the climactic "Age of Imperialism" got under way, there came the thunderclap of the Paris Commune—to conservative Europe a similar portent, a revelation of fires of revolt lurking under the surface of European as well as Asiatic life. It was a warning against empire-building rivalries being pushed too far. Fellow feeling in Europe could be reflected in joint action in the Far East. It culminated in the combined expedition of 1900, with Japanese and American participation, to suppress the Boxer Rebellion. As in India in 1857, the work of suppression was done with savage thoroughness. Faced now with growing unrest and resistance, all Europeans were tempted to react at times with the same freedom from restraint. More generally they were compelled by the challenge to try to appear and feel even more superior than before and to resort to racialist claims, proof against rational criticism and further emphasizing Europe's solidarity.

It was a recurrent paradox that the two great leaders of European expansion, after the Spaniards, were Britain and Russia, both of which were regarded by many other Europeans as not fully or genuinely part of Europe. Britain seemed to have too large a part of its interests outside, to be drawn away from Europe by its growing Dominions and by its "special relationship," already appearing, with the USA. In 1898 all Europe except Britain sympathized with Spain against America; in 1900 all Europe, but not America, sympathized with the Boers against Britain. If Britain was suspected of not wanting to be thought part of Europe, Russia was considered by many liberals as well as socialists not fit to be part of it. European Russia shaded off into Asia, and seemed too much on a level with Asia. It really cannot be doubted that the brutish character of czarist rule in eastern Europe owed much to the fact that the police and army were always engaged in coercion against native peoples next door.

Still, away in the Far East these two questionable countries could be pillars of Europe, as in the fighting against the Boxers. Far Eastern interests helped also to bring Russia and France together, and their alliance was valuable to the czarist regime as a certificate of respectability, bringing it more fully, if also more dangerously, into a European orbit. The Franco-Russian alliance helped in turn to provoke Britain into alliance with Japan, a breach with the united front of Europe of which only semidetached Britain was at this time capable. The Russo-Japanese war two years later was in a way a war of Britain against Russia, fought by proxy. But the perils of this course were soon painfully evident; and the Anglo-French Entente of 1903 quickly led on to the Anglo-Russian understanding of 1908. The Triple Entente, linking together the three biggest colonial empires, was a mutual insurance for its members against Germany, but also against their colonial peoples—at least in a negative way, by keeping them from falling out again over quarrels about odd ports or provinces or bits of uninhabited borderlands far away. Spokesmen of empire were quite clear-sighted about this. Welcoming the Anglo-Russian Convention in the House of Lords, on February 6, 1908, an ex-governor-general of Egypt, Lord Cromer, hailed it as opening "a new phase of European imperialism in which all the major colonizing nations would come together in order to check those nationalist and 'seditious' forces unleashed by the recent victory of yellow Japan over white Russia in the Far East." And the next day the *Pall Mall Gazette* commented: "We, and Russia, and every European Power that has a finger in the Asiatic pie, have to remember that the time is coming when it may be necessary, before all things, to sustain the solidarity of all European interests in Asia."[11]

The Great War and Fascism

The Great War was an ironical sequel to such admonitions. It came about partly at least because of the unevenness of colonial expansion, which had left Germany once more the latecomer. Central Europeans could in a sense regard themselves as the most truly European, because least entangled with the outside world, and Germany's boasts of its "Culture" contained an element of such pride. But Germans were also trading and traveling over the world, proud of their *Weltpolitik,* eager for expansion instead of being content with the role of "Little Europeans." Just as the Thirty Years War, if not a war of religion, was only possible because Europe had been conditioned for it by Reformation and Counter-Reformation, the Great War, if not primarily a war over colonies, was only possible because of Europe's conditioning through imperialism and world power. The white man's accumulated pride in his martial virtues, patriotism, discipline, and so forth—virtues mostly absent in nearly all other races—induced him to submit to four years of stoic self-torture. Each side in the European civil war felt that the eyes of the world were on it, each wanted to be seen as the authentic Europe.

Attitudes acquired during the subjugation of the other continents now reproduced themselves at home: for both sides the contest was one of "civilization against barbarism"—the Western allies had a "civilizing mission" to free Europe from Prussian militarism, the Central powers had a similar mission to free it from czarist tyranny. Incongruously, the Allies were bringing Indian and African troops to fight in Europe, and Germany was trying to promote revolution in India as well as Ireland. Britain was indignant. Before 1914, as a Cabinet memorandum of early 1918 pointed out, everyone took for granted that Asian dependencies and their European rulers "were far apart in political capacity, and were therefore not entitled to the same political rights." No one dreamed of treating Ireland and India, Alsace-Lorraine and Algeria, as questions of the same kind. Since 1914 German propaganda had been trying to blur the distinction and championing self-determination for Muslim countries while denying it to nationalities under German or Austrian rule in Europe.[12]

When Stresemann at Locarno echoed Briand's sentiment that good Frenchmen or Germans or Britons should also be good Europeans, he deplored the millions of dead of the Great War and also the fact that this war had jeopardized the ascendancy in the world to which Europe was entitled "by temperament and tradition." There was very often this other side to the creed of European cooperation, the belief in European domination. Nietzsche had been a "good European," and so in his own way was his bastard descendant Hitler. Nazi imperialism included the grand design of a New Order for Europe, a unified, hierarchical structure which would make the Aryan continent strong enough, under German leadership, to master the world. But the question of how much European domination contributed to the psychology of fascism is a large one, not sufficiently explored. One fascist triumph was the conquest of Abyssinia, and in the Italian case the colonial taproots are more obvious than in the German; but in Nazism there was a much closer fusion of the creed of power and violence with racialism. It represented Nietzsche's hazy "transvaluation of all values" in a brutalized form: its motto was that of Milton's Satan—"Evil, be thou my good!" And this had after all, with or without the aid of any pseudophilosophy, been the spirit of too much European behavior in Africa, Asia, the Pacific, most recently and barbarically in the Belgian Congo. In such colonial areas the dualism latent in European as in all civilizations had gone to extremes, and human beings had been treated in ways no longer permissible in Europe. Nazism practiced deliberately the same dualism, now between Germans (except communists) and non-Germans. Orwell's nightmare of a more sophisticated fascist state of the future—Oceania, uniting all the Western world, and perpetually at war—may have owed a good deal to his own experience in the colonial police service, and he foresaw a revival of enormities that had died out in Europe, through contact with lands where they still flourished. The prisoner about to be devoured by rats is informed by his interrogator: "It was a common punishment in Imperial China."[13]

The Civilizing Mission: Missionaries, Officials

If Europe has an identity, it is hard to find; but a fictitious entity, which every nation partly is, may have a potent appeal; and if Europe has had its civil wars, so have many nations. Northwestern Europe became the home of liberty but also the chief agent in the slave trade, which helped to pay for its progress and freedom. No civilization has been more deeply divided and self-contradictory than the one which invented democracy and fascism, parliament house and gas chamber. With its divided soul, as well as its shallower national divisions, it may have been moving toward some kind of unity under the logic of its own inner development, but it was the contrast between itself and the outer world that enabled it most fully to recognize itself and what it had in common. It saw itself as Civilization confronting Barbarism. This antithesis ran through nineteenth-century thinking; it went naturally with the idea of Progress, the conviction that Europe was advancing while others were at best standing still. The word "civilization" was so often used and misused as to lose a good deal of the meaning it was supposed to have, like Dr. Johnson's earlier term for the same thing, "civility," which descended to the level of politeness. Europeans responded warmly to it, difficult as they might find it to define what they meant by it. In practice it was often equated with pacification, as it had been long before by Virgil in his summons to the Roman nation still unborn to subdue the world. In Africa it could be thought of in simple terms as the habit of wearing clothes, in the Pacific of not practicing cannibalism. Many more complex titles to superior status could be claimed by the European as he went about: the art of politics, for instance, though this like most other virtues was very unevenly distributed about Europe itself. Often Europeans were inclined to hold that they, or cousins of theirs with fair complexions, were responsible for practically all human achievements (though it was not easy to forget the Chinese); they could rejoice at the discovery of rock paintings in the Sahara showing that a fair-skinned people were there in prehistory.

Civilization facing Barbarism could not be content, in modern Europe's expansive mood, merely to contemplate it: it felt the same call that Marx gave to Philosophy, to *change* the world. Hence the "civilizing mission" that all the colonizing countries claimed. This, too, had antecedents and parallels inside Europe. In 1501 a German poet in an oration before the emperor Maximilian boasted of how his people had both conquered and spread Christianity all round their borders: through their occupation of Prussia, for instance, its old inhabitants had been "saved" from the grip of heathenism and made into civilized, Christian men."[14] Three and a half centuries later when the *Ausgleich* turned the Hapsburg empire into the Dual Monarchy, the Austrian representative said to the Hungarian: "You look after your barbarians, and we'll look after ours"—the Slavs and other inferiors.[15] The sense of mission came to each nation in its messianic moments, and Europe collectively inherited it. All its colonial empires, it was agreed, whatever their feuds and rivalries, were spreading the light of civilization; there might be misgivings at times about some of them, it is true—Portuguese, Russian, German, Belgian. This complacency was fortified by the admiration for European ways that many in the colonies felt, for a complex variety of reasons—the early generations of Westernized Bengalis, for instance; it was a more dignified counterpart of the flattery heaped on colonial officials by "natives" hopeful of wheeding favors out of them. It was felt too by imitators more free to choose, notably the Japanese. A share in the civilizing mission came to be a cachet of the respectable European: a country with no black or brown wards to educate lacked a title to self-respect. Even Spaniards as progressive as Castelar or Costa Martinez were anxious to see Spain winning a place for itself in Africa.[16]

Civilization could most conveniently and emotionally of all be identified or at least linked with religion, and with the missionary legions of the nineteenth century setting out on their journeys, Europe could once again be Christendom. Religion (among many better doings) threw its cloak over the slave trade, as over serfdom or capitalism inside Europe, and converted it into part of the civilizing mission: Africans benefited by being transported to the New World because there they could become Christians. "By what means are the Europeans thus powerful," asked the philosophic prince in Johnson's *Rasselas* (1759), "able to travel the world, trading or conquering everywhere?" "They are more powerful, Sir, than we, (answered Imlac,) because they are wiser"; but *why* this is so can only be explained by "the unsearchable will of the Supreme Being." Twenty-two years later, in a stagecoach with Boswell, Johnson read the passage again for the first time and was greatly struck by his own words. "This, Sir," he declared to his companion, "no man can explain otherwise."[17] The Supreme Being was thus called in to underwrite European expansion or furnish it with a certificate of divine right. Success wherever they turned, with no enemies half as formidable as they were to one another when they fell out in India or Canada, might well convince Europeans of being a chosen people: much as a Calvinists's prosperity satisfied him of his own righteousness, of being one of the elect. A good part of the religious revival felt in Britain from the later eighteenth century, and spreading over much of Europe, can be attributed to the conviction of a commission from Providence to civilize the world, though it was also a reaction or antidote to the social perils brought by the Industrial Revolution and the French Revolution. Now as during the Counter-Reformation, the long-flagging religious spirit could be reinvigorated by the achievements of missionaries in far parts. While divine favor guaranteed the success of the empire builder, his success was a guarantee that Heaven was not untenanted.

Conversely, religious faith has waned in Europe with the passing of imperial power; while it has burned brightly (and noisily) across the Atlantic with the rise of American imperialism. At the end of the Great War a Soviet observer rejoiced to see bourgeois Europe reading Spengler on *The Decline of the West,* turning away from its old morality, dabbling in mystic cults or Hindu philosophy.[18] The war had only accelerated a decay of faith already under way and ushered in an age of doubt instead: which might indeed owe something to contact with other religions, realization that Christianity did not have a monopoly of good qualities. A European consciousness cast in religious terms—Europe as Christendom—was bound to be largely a *false* consciousness. The Third Republic was highly anticlerical at home, a great supporter and employer of Catholic missions overseas. Meanwhile missionaries might cut very diverse figures. To the Boers they were, as Livingstone's reports show, renegades, befriending the black man against the white, accused of supplying the black man with guns to defend himself with. To colonial populations they often appeared to be hand in glove with authority. In any case it was very largely their reports that provided many of Europe's millions with their picture of the outside world, their colonial mirror.

Missionaries were among the "men on the spot," Europe's eyes and ears when journalists or other visitors were rare; they were seldom very acute organs, for several reasons. Their own involvement, as officials, traders, soldiers, had its own bias; the peoples they were living among lacked, until the later days of the empires, modern consciousness and articulateness; few of the men on the spot were writers, still fewer thinkers, and when they came home they were usually isolated figures, like the ex-governor in Bridie's play, or sat in their clubs talking to one another. There have been several studies lately of the popular fiction, mostly very third-rate, written by British novelists, mostly women, about the heroic British Atlas holding up the Indian heaven. These Britons were very British, even exaggeratedly so, as the French in Indochina were very French. But after all, the country they called home was one with the great majority of whose inhabitants they had little in common: the nation, as distinct from the state, has always been mainly a creature of imagination. The men in the outposts, whatever their national quarrels, really had more in common with one another: they were in a way the first "Europeans." They shared the same technology and faced the same problems; most obviously, they were men of the same color. Telegraphs and steamships kept them in touch with one another's colonies and with Europe as a whole, whereas in the earlier days Spaniards who crossed the Atlantic to settle for life, or Dutchmen going to Java for a long term of years, had contact only with their home countries, and went on feeling simply Spanish or Dutch.

Intellectuals, Historians

Peering into its colonial mirror, Europe saw itself in a glass, darkly—especially before the rise of colonial movements or parties intelligible to European thinking, because largely derived from it. Even their spokesmen, before socialism entered the colonial world, were of the upper classes and were apt to know very little about their own masses. Hence there was plenty of room for Europe to project its own images onto the cloudy shapes of the world about it. In much the same way, before women lately began to organize themselves and become vocal, men were free to form pictures of them and insist on women outwardly conforming to these pictures—which we now see to have been ludicrously unrealistic. Camoëns's epic the *Lusiads* is a fine example of how one society can look at others through ready-made spectacles, supplied by its own historical formation. It is a glorification of conquest and plundering, gilded with a bizarre mixture of Christian zeal and classical mythology. The moral, however, stands out clearly. Christian Europe is the most civilized and powerful region of the globe. Christians ought to stop fighting one another and join hands to drive back the Turkish enemy or seek wealth by invading Asia or Africa instead of one another.[19] A small country like Portugal was the likeliest to give such a lead, since it lacked strength to fight any of its European neighbors as the French or Spaniards were always doing. Camoëns lived long enough to hear of the defeat and death of his king Sebastian, fighting in Morocco in 1578 at the head of a mixed European army of volunteers and mercenaries.

Camoëns evoked the figure of Alexander, the conqueror of Asia, reading and drawing inspiration from Homer.[20] The *Iliad*, too, is concerned with a war of Europe and Asia; and Victorian empire builders also, or those who had not been too idle at school, reveled in Homer. It must have been easy for them to recognize a likeness between his world and theirs: they were ruling over native peoples much as the quarrelsome, eccentric gods of Olympus ruled over mankind. Between Camoëns and Kipling we can see cosmopolitan eighteenth-century Europe, with its Eastern Fables, Persian Letters, Chinese Travelers, deliberately arranging an Oriental backdrop against which to contemplate itself. All this was primarily the sphere of the intelligentsia and aided in its own attainment of self-awareness and self-confidence. Intellectuals, the thinking section of the developing middle classes, were prominent in molding national feeling, but their outlook was international as well: the two things evolved together in an intricate counterpoint. There was a Republic of Letters of the European scholars and writers before there was a Socialist International. For a time in the later eighteenth century they gathered confidence from the half-illusory spectacle of an intelligentsia in power in China ruling more benevolently and well than any monarchs or aristocrats in Europe. Later on China was lumped—as Turkey had always been—with the rest of a world where nearly everything valued by the Republic of Letters was missing and where, consequently, stagnation reigned instead of progress. Hapsburg and Hohenzollern and the older ruling classes believed in Order: the intelligentsia believed in a reign of Law, under which freedom of thought and inquiry, constitutional right, professional respectability could be enjoyed. None of these things seemed to exist in Afro-Asia: it was all the more incumbent on Europe to cherish them. In so doing it would naturally feel its kinship and its distinctness from all others.

Past as well as present could be looked for in the imperial mirror. Nineteenth-century Europe was going through profound transformations and upheavals, encountering problems—political, economic, intellectual—which again might goad it into wars but which were recognized as generic problems of its civilization, as modified now by steam and electricity. In this condition it needed the kind of reassurance that a long pedigree confers, and it was always peering into its past, inventing scientific history for the first time, seeking the *origins* of all its institutions—parliaments, laws, churches, customs. All this work was stimulated by the knowledge being acquired of the very different history of India or Ashanti or Japan; and empire-building habits abroad colored Europe's impressions of its own past at home. There was a great overvaluation of the Roman empire, a veil drawn over its barbarities and its crippling everywhere of native cultures. The same instinct showed itself in Britain, as lately as 1966, in most of the writings called forth by the ninth centenary of the Norman Conquest: the Normans were extolled as bringers of civilization, and their reduction of the Saxon peasantry to serfdom was seldom recalled. Modern historians generally have been uncritical admirers of the absolute monarchies of sixteenth- and seventeenth-century Europe, and one can scarcely doubt that one reason for this is the fact that nineteenth- and twentieth-century Europe was imposing "absolutist" forms of government on Afro-Asia, establishing "order," bringing feudal barons like the Indian rajahs and nawabs under some sort of restraint. Every schoolboy knows the epigram of the French historian about the absolute monarchs: *Le nouveau Messie est le roi.* Europeans in Afro-Asia did not doubt that they were new Messiahs, bringing law and order to the dark continents.

That order is always better than disorder for the peasant majority of mankind is a dogma seldom questioned by the armchair historian. The European intelligentsia—like the Islamic but not the Chinese—has always been an urban class, and its spokesmen, like Voltaire, thought of the peasant masses—exactly as Europe was always apt to think of the Afro-Asian masses—as mere hewers of wood and drawers of water. But the spectacle offered by most of the outside world, before it came under European sway, seemed very often to be one of feudal anarchy or mass disorder: it could remind Europe of its own murky past, and flatter its pride in having advanced so far since then, but it could also be a frightening warning of what Europe might sink into: not feudal disorder now but social upheaval and anarchy, the civilization of the upper classes destroyed by the barbarous new factory-working classes. Here again Europeans, despite all their quarrels, were conscious of sharing the same achievements and perils; they were all in the same boat together.

Psychology, Anthropology, Darwinism

A kind of Manichaean dualism has run through the European consciousness. It may be inseparable from any society infected with change, instability, whereas conventional harmonies taken for granted between classes, between sexes, and between man's physical and moral being, belong to more static cultures. Any epoch of rapid, painful change, like Hamlet's or King Lear's, sharpens the sense of dualism or division. "But to the girdle do the gods inherit." Middle-class Europeans of the nineteenth century suffered again from this: the Victorians most of all. They struck their French neighbors as prudish; but it was Britain that was undergoing the deepest social, if not political, changes. Civilized man at such times cannot overcome a distaste for what a Victorian diplomat in China called "the lower desires and necessities of our nature,"[21] and contact with the "naked savage" could easily accentuate it. Underlying the antithesis of civilization and barbarism was that of mind and body. Reacting against the debased native, the European was in part reacting against his own baser self. It has been noticed how ready the white man often is to invest the black man with all the worst impulses he is conscious of in himself. Skin color disturbs us, perhaps, because its unfamiliarity forces us into awareness of the physical self that we would prefer to forget, and among people resembling ourselves can forget.

Europe could not help being uneasily aware from time to time that its behavior overseas could sometimes be as primitive as anything it reproached the other continents with. Reluctantly enough, Europe (which again means primarily the intelligentsia) was learning a good deal about itself from seeing what others were like or what it thought they were like: the depths of their benightedness stirred recognition of similar depths lurking in Europe's own soul, as well as in its historical past and in its social order. About a hundred years ago anthropology was taking shape as a science; so was psychology— likewise with many unscientific ingredients, but as a systematic inquiry detached from its matrix of religious self-examinations, another achievement unique to Europe. The founders of psychoanalysis owed much to anthropology; we need only recall Freud's own treatise *Totem and Taboo*. Primordial savagery, still in full sway in black Australia, was being discovered by Freud at the root of the civilized psyche. His theory might be called a poetic if not scientific expression of Europe's forebodings of the forces that were carrying it toward war and fascism. In all these ways the expansion of Europe, on the one hand, bolstered its self-satisfaction and, on the other hand, more subtly, undermined it, reducing the European to the same level as his subjects, or victims, more efficaciously than Christianity was raising them to *his* level.

As usual, these cross-currents can be traced in relations between men and women. Successful empire building gave the European man a fresh title to be loved, honored, and obeyed by his wife as he was—he believed, or deserved to be—by his colonial dependents. At the same time, one grand cause of the ascendancy of Europe was the degree of freedom and social status that its women, compared with all others, had always possessed; and it carried this with it into Afro-Asia as a badge of its superiority, to be given gresh emphasis because it was so much in contrast with the treatment of women there. But—also at the same time—privately, European men were alarmed by the increasing liberty and self-assertiveness of their women, while the new inquiries into the psychology of sex threw doubt on any moral elevation either of man over woman or of European over non-European. It would be interesting to consider whether the rise of colonial nationalism had any influence on the pioneers of women's further liberation movement in Europe or whether suffragette tactics owed anything to the example of Bengali terrorism in the same years. At any rate, Europe's slide toward the final dethronement of Man has gone together with its loss of empire. Fascism endeavored to arrest both processes, to restore man's belief in himself as the superior sex, as well as the white man's belief in himself as the superior race.

More realistic thinking about sex was bound to remind human beings that they were close relatives of the animals, closer very likely than of the angels. Europeans and other master races, like the Japanese, have often treated their native subjects as if they were animals and sometimes have explicitly regarded them as such. There is a parallel between the Roman Catholic argument that animals have no souls and the conviction of the Boers whom Livingstone encountered that Kaffirs have no souls,[22] with the same conclusion drawn in both cases that cruelty to them does not matter. But men—especially when abusing one another, as "swine," "swine hounds," and so on—have always recognized moral as well as physical traits common to them and the beasts, and the popularity of the old animal epics about Reynard the Fox and his ilk shows man contemplating himself in the mirror of the animal world, much as Europe has done in that of the colonial world. While Europe was getting to know this other world, Darwin was introducing man to the other animals, as not merely creatures with some accidental resemblances but as close relatives. The shock was very great and comparable with that felt by the white man (or the Brahmin) at any debasement of racial purity by mingling with inferior stocks. It might lead toward a more modest estimate of himself on man's part, just as recognition of affinities with other peoples might lead the European; but the outcome was more likely to be infection with Social Darwinism, because this had powerful vested interests to favor it. If men and nations and races were part of Nature, they must be as red in tooth and claw as Nature. Nietzsche eulogized the Nordic "blonde beast" in the same spirit in which the Kaiser, sending his soldiers to China in 1900, exhorted them to behave like Huns. Hitler easily induced his men to behave like a combination of animals and Huns.

Luckily for itself, Europe was divided along many different lines besides those of nationality, and rapid and unsettling change brought it face to face with all kinds of contradictions and doubts. Respect for Nature, for what was "natural," therefore "reasonable," had been part of its mental development; but industrialism was making life more and more artificial. Hence there could be an inclination to look to societies outside Europe in search of standards or norms of human conduct: not to elaborated cultures like those of the Far East or Islam, nearly as artificial as Europe's and in that line far behind Europe, but to simpler societies where human nature and its healthy instincts might be most easily recognizable. This was encouraged by the search for historical origins and stimulated by controversies round many questions, all of concern to all Europe. Many of these were connected with religion, others with sex. Writers like Edward Westermarck convinced themselves that monogamy has always been the norm, the natural and proper arrangement of domestic life, to which modern Europe should therefore adhere. A different reading of the evidence might lead to the view that the poor man everywhere has been glad to have one wife rather than no wife.

Of more practical importance was the controversy, growing with the coming of socialism, about whether or not private property was a "natural" institution, rooted in human nature and impossible to get rid of.[23] On this the haughtiest European landowner or capitalist was happy to call the humblest Hindu or Hottentot as a witness. The argument for private property could be given another turn: if it *was* found to be absent in some societies, this could be taken, not—as by the socialists—as a summons to abolish private property in Europe, but instead as the cause of these other societies remaining backward, whereas Europe had advanced thanks to its firm establishment of property rights. Oriental despotism could be linked with their absence, as it was by the Dutch in the native kingdoms they encountered in Java.[24] Marxism, it may be added, was able to make use of both sides of the argument.

Literary and Cultural Impressions: Elitist and Popular

In *Othello,* and still more in *Anthony and Cleopatra,* Shakespeare was inspired by the contrast between European civilization and the other continents and by the flux of feeling that Europeans have often experienced between attachment to their own values, as the highest, and the appeal of other modes of being, less rigid and constricting (as every other mode of life appears to us, compared with our own). Othello is noble and heroic, though an African (or Moorish) barbarian; Cleopatra is a fascinating and in her way heroic woman, though the epitome of Asiatic decadence. Not many others among the geniuses of European literature, in the early age of expansion, shared this interest, this worldview, which is one reason why Shakespeare towers so high above them all. A good many of the foremost writers of western Europe in later times had connections of one sort or another with the empires, but they very seldom made these their theme; they might at most choose a returned Nabob as one of their characters, as Scott or Thackeray or Daudet did. Scott did indeed set one of his novels in India, to take advantage of the notoriety of Tipu Sahib, but it is very far from being one of his great novels.[25] It may not always be remembered that Bertie Wooster had a married sister in India;[26] the empire has an even smaller place in the works of P. G. Wodehouse. Perhaps more is to be found among the great Russian writers—Pushkin, Tolstoy, Lermontov—than any others, because Russia and its colonies shaded into one another, and Bashkirs and Kalmucks and Tatars had been as intimate as a part of Russian history as Irish or Scots of English history. As for European writers drawing inspiration from alien literatures, the *West-Eastern Diwan* of Goethe and the *Rubaiyat* of Fitzgerald were very lonely examples, though they were followed by some remarkable translations of, notably, Chinese poetry. Discovery of things like Chinese poetry might have been expected to blur the line between civilization and barbarism, and so for a few Europeans they did. But the practical men who ran things in Europe, and most of all in England, were accustomed to regard artists in general as vagabonds, eccentrics, no less irresponsible than women or natives, and to keep practical matters in a separate compartment. They did this the more easily because Europe had always professed a religion totally at variance with its practical management of affairs. Chinese porcelain was known and admired in the West long before the West embarked on its opium wars and gunboat policies.

In general it was the visual arts of the other continents that influenced Europeans most (that is, a handful of artists and their admirers), from Chinese and Japanese styles to the grotesque masterpieces of West African sculpture, in which again Europe could glimpse things in itself that it had not yet found any means of expressing. Music, too, was free of linguistic barriers, but the barriers against any crossing or mingling of the world's musical regions have for some reason been more obstinate than with any other art. The sole exception, on the lowest possible level, has been the synthesis of debased African and debased European music, which took place in America and has flooded Europe. Its mass popularity has not made white men any more friendly to black men, but it has given Europe (or capitalist Europe plus the USA) an unprecedented degree of cultural unity, of a certain kind. It appeals to Britons or Germans as working masses uprooted from any native culture of their own by industrialism, adrift in the new world of the big city; it can do so because jazz was the joint product of Africans and Europeans uprooted from their own continents and thrown together in North America.

Fiction is the other popular art, and the encounter between Europe and the outer world supplied plenty of scope for what the man in the street wanted, adventures and hair-breadth escapes like Othello's, in which he could recognize himself—as a bold, dashing Briton or Frenchman, but also as a European. Far from home, distinctions of national character become less significant and less within the reach of popular novelists equipped only with a few simple stereotypes: it was the confrontation of European and non-European that counted, and that was always likely to take on the still simpler form of white men and colored. No doubt expansion, battle, imperial rule did make room for many good qualities, virtues that humanity needs. Gramsci admired Kipling and wanted his young sons to read him.[27] Kipling was the prophet of these qualities and virtues for the middle classes, of Europe and the USA as well as of Britain. For the semiliterate public something more elementary was required, and free from the occasional twinges of doubt that might make a reader of Kipling uncomfortable. Kipling himself was an appreciative reader of Edgar Rice Burroughs, whose *Tarzan of the Apes* came out in 1914 and sold millions of copies in no time.

Burroughs was an American, but he was gathering up and continuing a long accumulation of European notions about primitive lands and peoples, and he could make his leading figures a composite group, with an English hero, French allies, an American heroine. Burroughs had never been in, and knew nothing about, Africa, a fact suggestive of how much of fantasy has entered into the Western image of the backlands. Tarzan owed his immense appeal to his combining in himself both civilization and barbarism: he is a free, wild, uninhibited creature of the jungle, as we would all like to be in our daydreams, but he is also a nobleman in disguise, and a white man, somehow endowed with the instincts of an English gentleman. He is the natural conqueror of all the other jungle denizens, animal or human. He fights his way to the leadership of his tribe of apes, and tries to give it wise guidance, but gives up the task in disgust and goes off in search of his own kind. Not, that is, of fellow humans, but of fellow white men: he has always been in contact with the blacks, but they—and their women—arouse in him no feelings except of hatred and contempt; he is always robbing and killing them.

Tarzan was soon multiplied and magnified by film versions, which brought all the absurdities into prominence—but no absurdity could be too glaring for the film audiences of those years. The cinema was being built up chiefly in America, but largely by producers and actors from Europe, and it helped greatly to fix common conventions and ideas for the mass mind, including those connected with the white man and his place in the world. Like religion, art may prove a double-edged weapon, and it may less easily be kept under control than religion. In 1922 the British government, faced with mass resistance in India, felt obliged to protest against films pouring out of Hollywood which it felt to be subversive of the white man's prestige and his empires.[28] One might speculate about how much cinema visions of bathing belles in Hawaii and the like have done to subvert the white man's own standards since then. By those old standards, twentieth-century Europe has become more the same, more one whole, but also less European; it has been "going native," most of all in its morals, as illustrated by the near nudity of the modern white woman by contrast with the missionary horror of unclothed native life a century ago.

Racialism, Imperialism, and Their Critics

Still, Europe's image of itself in the colonial world easily took on a crudely racial complexion. Skin color was the lowest common denominator easiest to find. It is maintained by some that racialism did not exist before the rise of the modern national-imperial state. The proposition raises many questions, about, for instance, how Brahmins thought of their fellowmen. As for Europe, it must be remembered that there were confrontations between Europeans and others on its own soil, when its expansion had yet scarcely begun. It is true that if Shylock is the villain of his play, his daughter is the junior heroine and marries a Christian.[29] But there were no Jews in Shakespeare's England, and his picture of both was merely fanciful. In Spain Jews and Muslims had been banned a century before, and their nominally converted descendants were still being hounded; the Moriscos were about to be finally expelled to Africa. In the course of the persecution the notion of *limpieza de sangre,* purity of blood, became firmly fixed in the Spanish mind, and it survived to be one of the taproots of modern anti-Semitism. It may be conjectured that the Christian doctrine of original sin, the state of corruption transmitted hereditarily to all the descendants of Adam and only partially removed by baptism, made it easier for Europeans to attach a permanent stigma to other peoples. It may have helped them also think it right to impose perpetual, hereditary slavery on Africans, quite unlike the temporary servitude which in Muslim lands soon ended in assimilation.

In sixteenth-century Spain with its rage for titles and status there was much talk of preserving the pure blood of aristocratic families, and *limpieza de sangre* was a democratized, vulgarized form of this snobbery, nobility for the common man. Demos was aping his betters, as he has so often done; race and class feeling have always had common roots. The more democratic, or demagogic, modern Europe grew, the more it needed some common bond among the classes, some way of flattering the lower into an illusion of being accepted as equals by the higher. Nationalism no doubt supplied this, but it also imposed heavy burdens, of taxation, conscription, chronic danger of war; racialism, the common pride of the white man, floated blissfully above all such mundane things. It even held out a hope of peace and good neighborliness among the white peoples; it was, in a debased form, a *European* sentiment, a cheap substitute for rational conviction or a common program. Attempts were made to give it a more practical turn, like the Kaiser's Yellow Peril propaganda in favor of European solidarity under German leadership. The rise of Japan, its defeat of Russia in 1904–5, was damaging to the white man's pride and his imperial prestige in Asia; it was disconcerting to come on a non-European race which seemed to possess most of Europe's boasted qualities, such as patriotism, and to carry some of them, like suicidal courage on the battlefield, still further. There was consolation in thinking of these yellow men as not really human beings of the same order as the white man but as aliens, travesties of him, with the courage of automata. In more sober terms, however, the Kaiser's talk ignored the Anglo-Japanese alliance and the fact that, although Britons might be highly sensitive to color, half their army was composed of "colored" men.

It is a remarkable tribute to Europe's self-complacency that even while still carrying on the slave trade, it was preening itself on its moral superiority and sending out missionaries to reclaim others from their darkness. There were always critics here and there and moments when Europe came face to face— in situations like the one depicted in Joseph Conrad's *Heart of Darkness*— with its own depravities instead of its virtues, its barbarism instead of its civilization. On the whole such revelations did little to shake European confidence. There was no European authority to be blamed, no collective responsibility. The opium trade was the fault of the British, the later slave trade of the Portuguese; the Congo atrocities, as brought into the open by individuals like E. D. Morel, were not even the fault of the Belgians but only of King Leopold and his fellow racketeers. Only an odd philosopher like Tolstoy was likely to see in these things an indictment of the European ascendancy altogether.

Similarly, not many saw abuses in coal mines, underground labor of women and children, as an indictment of capitalism. Such things, when they became impossible to ignore, could always be put right. Europe's faith in progress, with itself in the vanguard, which owed so much to its sense of moving ahead of the rest of the world—all motion is relative—was not shaken. What shook it was the two world wars and the nightmare experience of fascism, the eruption from somewhere in Europe's own depths of worse barbarity than it had ever encountered anywhere else. This has compelled some Europeans to recognize likenesses between their crimes against one another in the twentieth century and their crimes of genocide, mass enslavement, and so on, against other peoples in earlier times. Much of what we now feel about the imperialist age may be said to belong to this delayed-reaction order. So far as a common European consciousness is concerned, such a feeling of partnership in guilt can be a contribution to it, just as shared self-satisfaction has been. Christian brotherhood rests, in doctrinal terms, on the acceptance of a total depravity shared by all and a need for expiation.

Socialism and the Working Class

Underpinning any moral unity of imperial Europe were the large economic interests it shared. Capitalists might wrangle fiercely over their respective shares of colonial profit, but it was flowing into the pool of European prosperity. Indian jute found its way to Germany, Indonesian coffee to Italy. Cause and effect were not always apparent; critics of imperialism might be conservative at home, like W. S. Blunt, or only as mildly reformist as Cobden. It was the socialists who were offering a radical criticism of Europe's economic and social system and with it a new internationalism, a new form of European consciousness in place of the aristocratic cosmopolitanism of the eighteenth century. Socialism was in principle for all mankind, like Christianity; in practice, like Christianity, it was to remain for the most part a thing of Europe until taken up independently by peoples outside. Its founders and some of its consistent upholders condemned capitalism to no small extent because of the crimes they saw it committing outside Europe. But Marx and Engels also saw even these crimes as part of a regeneration of the world, because they goaded old, torpid societies into new life. They had a very strong sense of the relative progress Europe had already made, of the degree to which it represented civilization against barbarism: they felt this quite strongly even of industrial western Europe in their time as against backward eastern Europe, and these Germans were not always careful enough to avoid saying things reminiscent of the old German contempt for Slav peoples. They, too, could equate Europe's past with Asia's present and see Western capitalism in India carrying out something like a bourgeois revolution, part of a civilizing mission, if a brutal one. They were inclined to think the worst European colonial regime less bad than the best native government. In 1975 an Indian historian reproached Engels for still, in his older years, expecting Europe and North

America would lead the way to socialism—and the "semi-civilized countries" would follow, holding on to their coattails—and has called this "a condescending attitude to non-European civilizations and an implicit assumption of leadership."[30] To lesser socialists a comfortable feeling of superiority to non-Europeans often came almost as naturally as to Christians. One feature of Eduard Bernstein's Revisionism, at the beginning of this century, was his claim for Germany of a part in the civilizing mission, which Hitler was to call a place in the sun.[31] Speculations about "ultraimperialism," as developed by Karl Kautsky and others, might be seen as socialist acquiescence in a cartel of colonies, a Europeanization of imperialism. It has a more tangible counterpart today in acquiescence by right-wing socialism within the (European) Common Market in the rule of multinational corporations.

With the aid of socialist thinking, the working masses in Europe might have been expected to see their own existence reflected, and magnified, in the spectacle of colonial poverty. In reality the worst off, such as the eastern European peasantry, knew nothing about the colonial world: those who did know something, like the workers in Britain, knew themselves to be better off than the colonial masses and naturally wanted to remain better off. This spectre of colonial poverty can be seen haunting the Western mind from quite early: it made still more vivid the abyss always waiting to engulf the unlucky. A pamphleteer in Philadelphia, during the radical ferment which preceded the Revolution, accused the rich of wanting to get the whole wealth of the province into their hands—"and then the people will be nearly in the condition that the East-India Company reduced the poor natives of Bengal to."[32] European workers might sympathize at odd moments with colonial workers, but more often they saw them as competitors, sweated labor whose products would force down living conditions elsewhere. Fellow European workers, too, might be competitors, but could be accepted as reasonable ones, with an interest in maintaining the European standard of living. In Lancashire or Glasgow memories of cheap Irish labor brought in as blacklegs in former days could be stirred into fresh life. All these reactions were part of the struggle of labor in Europe for its place in the sun; in the imperial context this necessarily meant a claim by labor to be accepted as part of a superior race or civilization, entitled to a better place in the sun than others.

Democracy, thus refracted, was gaining ground in most of Europe before 1914, but not in Russia, where autocracy was still intact and saw no reason for giving concessions or privileges to its humbler Russian subjects, any more than to its subjects in Asia. Serfdom had been imposed in former days on Russian peasants and on Bashkir or Kalmuck tribesmen at the same time; and the two lived side by side, joining together in rebellions like Pugachev's against czar and landlord. Nothing like this could happen in any other empire; in India there were occasions when British soldiers, in Company days, would suspend a mutiny of their own in order to help to put down mutinous sepoys.

This special Russian tradition of fraternization gave Bolshevism part of its special character, and leaders like Lenin and Rosa Luxemburg saw the crimes of imperialism in Afro-Asia as confirmation of their case against capitalism as brutal and predacious.

Self-Images of Other Regions

Europe, or some Europeans, have learned something about themselves from criticisms by outsiders too, men like Gandhi or Nehru. But all Europe's responses to the outer world might profitably be compared with those of other regions to the pressures of Europe. Islam, the oldest enemy, produced in the later nineteenth century a Pan-Islamic movement against Western imperialism. There was a Pan-American movement intended to keep European meddling out of the paradise of the New World, and a surprisingly early Pan-African movement. Of these two the first was too obviously sponsored by Washington, the second by a handful of intellectuals. Another regional image was too obviously congenital to the idle rich: it was the Theosophic vision, worked up by the feudal landowner Rabindranath Tagore, of all Asia as a *corpus mysticum,* sharing in a spiritual insight, an absorption in the things of the soul, that marked it off from materialistic Europe. On this view, while Africa worshipped stocks and stones, Europe was worshipping stocks and shares—and Asia its transcendental self. All these dreams of unity proved shadowy; and if Europe's sense of unity has often seemed more myth than reality, it has had more substance than any others. Europe is after all the only great region whose parts have always been interacting with one another, whether peacefully or not. India, indeed, with a population comparable to Europe's, has moved ahead of it to political unity. This was forced on it originally by British rule, but it must have been cemented by the spectacle of Europe's national conflicts, in which India was twice involved by the British connection. China's far older unity must have gained new force in this century from the lesson of Europe's quarrels, which a progressive Chinese writer in the 1890s was comparing with the anarchic period of the "Warring States" in China two thousand years earlier.[33] But China has gone through a period since then of profound self-criticism, as well as criticism of the West, and of radical self-transformation; India has not; and in general the images or ideologies conjured up by Western pressure in the old continents, whether national or religious or regional, have contained too little self-criticism and too much self-flattery, whose effect in practical terms has been to leave the ascendancy of obsolete ruling classes uncompromised and undiminished.

Something of this sort has happened to western Europe as well, but the loss of its empires leaves the West far ahead of the rest in wealth. In material terms this wealth was built up to some considerable extent on colonial exploitation; it leaves the West free now to look down pityingly on its former colonies and thank Heaven that it is not as other regions are. The antithesis of civilization and barbarism is increasingly replaced by that of affluence and poverty. In 1976 the Indian government justified its restraints on foreign journalists, under the new special powers, by complaining that they always report bad news from India with additions, while saying little or nothing about India's achievements. This might be said still more strongly of Western reporting of Africa. The effect is to reinforce Western conservatism and self-satisfaction (under some strain at present from economic crisis); it is one of the reasons why such unity as Europe has so far achieved has a dangerous resemblance to its organization into two rival coalitions before 1914. But in seeking to trace such causes and effects, we are entangled in the frightful complexity of history, which puts so much more strain on the historian's mind than on the botanist's or mathematician's and ages him so prematurely. What he can find in the colonial mirror, or hall of mirrors, is no single clear-cut image of Europe, but a swirl of dissolving pictures, fleeting shapes, such as the clairvoyant may be supposed to see when peering into his crystal or his magic bowl. All the same, whatever Europe is, it owes in part to its imperial adventures.

Notes

This chapter originally appeared in the journal *History of European Ideas* (1980).

1. See F. Braudel, *Capitalism and Material Life, 1400–1800,* trans. Miriam Kochan (London, 1973).

2. G. Strauss, *Manifestations of Discontent in Germany on the Eve of the Reformation* (Bloomington, Ind., 1971), 79–80.

3. *Old Diplomacy: The Reminiscences of Lord Harding of Penhurst* (London, 1947), 128.

4. Francis Bacon, "Of Plantations."

5. I owe this anecdote to my friend Bruno da Ponte of Lisbon.

6. *The Fugger News-Letters,* ed. V. von Klarwill (London, 1928), 47.

7. An observation of my colleague A. J. A. Malkiewicz in a seminar at Edinburgh University.

8. C. Roth, *A History of the Marranos* (New York, 1959), Chapter 9.

9. C. R. Boxer, *The Dutch Seaborne Empire, 1600–1800* (Harmondsworth, 1973), 181.

10. Ghulam Husain Khan, *Seir Mutagherin* (Calcutta, 1903).

11. I owe these two references to Dr. J. G. Oswald, author of a Ph.D. thesis entitled "British Public Opinion on France, the Entente Cordiale, and the Anglo-Russian Entente, 1903–8," Edinburgh University, 1975.

12. Dept. of Information, January 1918, CAB 24/39, Public Record Office, London. I owe this reference to Mrs. T. Brotherstone.

13. George Orwell, *Nineteen Eighty-Four* (1949; reprint, Harmondsworth, 1954), 230.

14. Strauss, *Manifestations of Discontent*, 68–69.

15. H. W. V. Temperley, lecture at Cambridge, 1934.

16. See G. J. G. Cheyne, *Joaquín Costa, el gran desconocido* (Barcelona, 1972), Chapter 12.

17. James Boswell, *The Life of Samuel Johnson*, under June 2, 1781.

18. E. Preobrazhensky, "From N.E.P. to Socialism" (Moscow, 1922; unpublished translation by Brian Pearce).

19. Luiz Vaz de Camoëns, *Lusiads;* see especially Cantos 7 and 10.

20. Ibid., Canto 5.

21. Sir Rutherford Alcock, *Life's Problems* (1857).

22. *Livingstone's Missionary Correspondence, 1841–1856,* ed. I. Schapera (London, 1961), 232. Cf. Olive Schreiner, *The Story of an African Farm* (1911), Chapter 5.

23. See P. Grossi, "Un Altro Modo di Possedere" (Milan, 1977).

24. Boxer, *The Dutch Seaborne Empire*, 214.

25. Sir Walter Scott, *The Surgeon's Daughter* (1827).

26. P. G. Wodehouse, *Carry On, Jeeves* (1925), No. 10.

27. Antonio Gramsci, *Lettere dal Carcere* (Turin, 1965), 783n.

28. Jean A. Ellis, "The Structure of Politics in South India, 1918–39," Ph.D. thesis, London University, 1975, 82.

29. Cf. H. Sinsheimer, *Shylock, the History of a Character* (London, 1947).

30. P. S. Gupta, *Imperialism and the British Labour Movement, 1914–1964* (London, 1975), 8.

31. See E. Bernstein, *Evolutionary Socialism,* trans. E. C. Harvey (New York, 1961), 172ff.

32. G. B. Nash, "Up from the Bottom in Franklin's Philadelphia," in *Past and Present,* no. 77 (1977): 81–82.

33. D. C. Price, *Russia and the Roots of the Chinese Revolution, 1896–1911* (Cambridge, Mass., 1974), 67.

7

ANTONIO GRAMSCI AND THE OTHER CONTINENTS

In a letter from prison in 1927 Gramsci wrote that his mind was in a state of frozen calm, like Nansen's ship drifting imprisoned for months in the polar ice. That fantastic and truly epic journey had always fascinated him, he said.[1] His own life as a thinker was another voyage of exploration. It might be said to have begun in boyhood, when he was stirred to imaginative picturing of things far away by storybook reading. He reckoned this a genuine part of learning. He read *Robinson Crusoe* and *The Mysterious Island* at the age of seven, he recalled, and he lamented that childhood enjoyments like these seemed to have dried up: children were born nowadays, like the Chinese philosopher, eighty years old.[2] One favorite he reread in prison was *The Last of the Mohicans*.[3] He was familiar with Jack London, including his dog stories; he was indignant at the faulty Italian translations of Joseph Conrad.[4] It is disappointing that he did not care for H. G. Wells's marvelous science-fiction tales, which he condemned as mechanical.[5] But science came within his horizons, as from his cell his mind roamed far afield in space and time. He knew Eddington's *Nature of the Physical Universe* and commented on how it brought Idealism into physics; he wanted to read Sir James Jeans's *Mysterious Universe*,[6] another book that was making a stir in the 1930s. He welcomed a new edition of an old work on capitalism in the ancient world, as in agreement with Marxism in rejecting the habit, introduced by Mommsen and now being made fashionable by Rostovtsev and others, of classing any growth of money economy in any social context as "capitalistic."[7]

With a thirst for information extending to the other continents, and hence to Europe's relations with them, it would scarcely have been possible for Gramsci not to be drawn to the subject of imperialism. There were pressing practical motives as well. Mussolini was banging all his drums in an effort to hypnotize his Italians into feeling Roman and imperial. In his brief years of active politics Gramsci never missed an occasion to draw parallels between the exploited peasantry at home and the colonial peoples abroad; and he identified colonialism, for instance in a speech in the Chamber of Deputies in 1925, with export of capital.[8] This was of course the keynote of what has been known as the Marxist theory of imperialism ever since Bukharin and Lenin, during the Great War, gathered together ideas long afloat on the Left and put them into definite shape. Gramsci inherited a well-established doctrine.

His own preoccupations, however, when his thoughts turned to the outer world, did not lie on the same axis. True, the prison notebooks are a vast heap of fragments whose underlying connections are not always clear. Gramsci was reading very widely in several languages, but also very discursively, dependent to a great extent on the accident of what books or magazines happened to be available. He could not, as Marx did in the British Museum, follow up any subject systematically; what he was thinking, when he copied out this passage or that, often has to be guessed from the mere fact that he judged it worth copying. Still, it can be said that his scattered commentaries do not point toward any distinct innovation in the theory of imperialism, though they contain ideas which could be made use of to enrich the Leninist thesis, clothing its bare economic bones with the flesh and blood of social activity, human thoughts and feelings. Those who contributed most to the Marxist, or "Hobson-Lenin," theory were British, German, Russian; they belonged to the powerful nations of Europe, and the focal point for them was the imperial relationship in itself, the exercise of power by stronger countries over weaker, Gramsci's Italy, despite its precocious jackal hunt for colonies, had till yesterday been one of the weaker, itself under foreign tutelage. His concern was not primarily with the fact of domination but with the birth and growth of resistance to it: not with what Austria got out of its Italian possessions, but how the Italians reacted to its presence. It was the same when he had in mind such a case as that of Britain and India. More generally, he was interested in the peoples of other continents in themselves, on their own merits; their social order, their acquired mentality, their religion and culture; all as facets of the experience of the human race, capable of reflecting light on one another and on Europe.

H. G. Wells's, *Outline of History* Gramsci liked not very much[9] (but far better than his fantasies). The salient merit he discovered in the *History* was its breaking away from the old custom of attributing to Europe a monopoly of meaningful events or movements. Wells put old India, the medieval Mongols, China, on the same plane as Europe—"He shows that from a world point of view Europe can no longer be a province which thinks itself the repository of all world civilization."[10] To Gramsci it came quite naturally to think of all regions as having a past worth studying, a significant evolution. It has been argued, by contrast, that "Gramsci thought European civilization and culture very superior to that of other peoples."[11] In various particular aspects no doubt he did, and nearly everyone, European or not, must agree. But of the passages cited to prove his belief in a general, all-around, intrinsic superiority, the only one of any weight is his statement that elements of other cultures have attained universality solely by virtue of incorporation into that of Europe. But this must be taken to refer to no more than the recent centuries of Western ascendancy, founded on a sudden long lead in technology and political techniques, while Gramsci's curiosity extended much further back. As to the present, that ascendancy, he observed without regret, was crumbling. Men talked now of "the West" as they used to talk of "Christendom": it really had achieved a new homogeneity during the past two centuries, but its inner contradictions were reducing it now to a state of crisis."[12]

Externally the balance of power was shifting. Gramsci took note of the newly hatched science of geopolitics, pioneered before the war by a Swede and now being taken up in Germany.[13] He saw that the vital decisions lay with London, Moscow, Washington, Tokyo; no longer with continental Europe.[14] He anticipated a time when India and China would be modern industrial nations and would break away from European leading strings; with their preponderance in population this would remove the earth's center of gravity, the Pacific would supplant the Atlantic.[15] To many Europeans all this was bringing a mood of self-doubt, loss of confidence. A book of that period mentioned by Gramsci was about "the twilight of the white nations."[16]

At the same time there was an "unpleasant sensation of Europe being overshadowed by the USA. Gramsci read whatever he could lay hands on about America, including current novels by writers like Sinclair Lewis and Upton Sinclair, and never underestimated its coming importance. Britain, though victorious in the war, was tacitly having to admit the American hegemony, and economic statistics convinced Gramsci that it had no choice.[17] It might talk of its big navy—but what if the USA grew big enough to swallow up Great Britain and its whole empire?[18] He made notes on the outlines of US history leading up to its modern expansionist phase,[19] others on the rise of US power in the Caribbean region and in the Far East.[20] He came on suggestions that America might take over European possessions in the West Indies and Africa in settlement of war debts and perhaps use them to repatriate its black population to Africa.[21]

Gramsci was critical of the USA, not hostile to it: in his opinion there was a great deal to be learned from it, though only in the material sphere. He looked to the impact of its economic and technological energy to compel Europe to renovate its comparatively antiquated social and economic structure—much as Europe, he might have added, was compelling Asia. If this happened, it would bring about a new European civilization, and at no very distant date, because nowadays everything takes place more quickly.[22] Britain, though thanks to its empire still important, he regarded as very much a part of an obsolescent society. One of his remarks on it has a topical sound today: he was querying the notion that Britain's return to the gold standard meant a harmful sacrifice of industry to finance and pointed out that by keeping up the value of the pound it might have averted dangerous class tensions. "In a country as traditionalist, conservative, ossified in its social structure as England, what results might inflation have had . . . ? Much graver ones certainly than in other lands."[23]

Seeing in America the rise of a new species of imperialism, and recognizing in it, we might say, some of the features of what has come to be called neocolonialism, Gramsci contemplated in the British empire the biggest of the old type. There is a reference to Carson and the Ulster rebellion of 1914 in his jottings on an article by Ramsay Muir about the British form of government.[24] Another on British naval policy he docketed briefly as "useful," and he read about the politics of oil and its place in imperialist ambitions both British and American.[25] Predictions of war between Britain and Soviet Russia are recorded at several places in the notebooks.[26] Two of his longer passages are devoted to the complex political composition of the British empire. In one of them he pays tribute to Disraeli and his vision of an Imperial Parliament: this empire could not be run on Roman military-bureaucratic lines, and what it required was an amalgamation of all its local ruling groups into a single imperial class. Disraeli penetrated this with the clear eye of an outsider, but he had no successors; his vision was frustrated by the narrow outlook, the *inglesismo,* of the English, who could not imagine an Imperial Parliament making laws for England.[27] They have lived to see a Western European bureaucracy making laws for England instead.

A second train of thought was suggested by an article of 1927 on the prospects facing the British empire since the latest imperial conference in view of the centrifugal tendencies at work and colonial nationalism, tinged in India with industrial unrest. Dominion status for the more advanced components seemed to him an instructive concept and reminded him of Lenin's dictum that national issues might find a peaceful solution even within a capitalist framework, as in the case of Norway's separation from Sweden. How any sort of common foreign policy could be agreed remained a riddle, all the same.[28] A 1929 article about US tariff policies made him wish for a comparative study of all national tariff policies, past and present, and speculate about a tendency for each powerful state to group all its political "vassals" into an economic bloc. The world might come to be made up of a series of Zollvereins; one such might be the "Pan-Europa" that the French statesman Aristide Briand was propounding; another might form the empire free trade preached in England by " 'Lord Beaverbrook' (or some such name)."[29]

Gramsci's impressions of the world outside Europe were colored by his being an Italian, and a Sardinian, which from some points of view made it easier for him than for socialists in more advanced Western countries to enter into the human condition in "undeveloped" lands. Sardinia was only half Italian in speech and character, and it was notorious for its poverty, which pushed some of its inhabitants into banditry, many into emigration. In his boyhood there things were little changed from a century before when Arthur Young deplored the great estates belonging to spendthrift or absentee land-lords, and peasants living in miserable cabins, and M'Culloch described the inhabitants as reduced to "the lowest point in the scale of civilization"[30]—a kind of phrase ordinarily used by Europeans about the recesses of Africa or Asia. Italy was always a mixture of nationalities; Gramsci credited his countrymen with freedom from national, even racial antipathies—a seafarer of the Genoese coast might bring home a colored wife, he said, without fear of protest by his relatives.[31] In Gramsci's opinion, the overthrow of feudalism by the northern Italian towns in the Middle Ages had left no room for the myth, patronized by the French aristocracy, of Gothic or Nordic superiority;[32] he was showing his awareness of how prejudices of race grow out of those of class. Touching on a book by the American racist Madison Grant, who maintained that his country's blood was being poisoned by the influx of inferior stocks from southern Europe, Gramsci remarked that it was poetic justice for Europeans to be looked down on as they so often looked down on others. But all theorizing about races or about national destinies was absurd, he added: some observations of a quite secondary character were all that could have any validity.[33]

Italy's recent history had a special relevance to Gramsci's scrutiny of an Asia where national movements were rife. It was one of struggle for both national liberation and unification, amid which Italian socialism had to make its first painful start. Its crushing defeat now by fascism threw Gramsci back on an attempt to explore the nineteenth-century movement and explain why the united free Italy it brought about was so little capable of progress. What he was compelled to realize, more and more sharply, was that the Risorgi-mento, or national revival, was a half-baked enterprise in which the people played only a minor part, not by its own fault but because of "the scanty effectiveness" of the dominant groups.[34] These were more anxious to hold the masses in check than to arouse them; they were bent on keeping all the gains of freedom for themselves, and afraid that the masses, if stirred up, would demand a program of social reform as well as patriotism.

The two outstanding figures—Mazzini, who preached armed revolt, and Cavour, who wanted to build up economic resources—were alike in not wanting to mobilize and arm the people. Both seemed to Gramsci very inadequate. Mazzini's spasmodic insurrections, with small bands of enthusi-asts, he felt could not possibly have succeeded, at least without "long ideologi-cal and political preparation," slowly permeating the mass mind.[35] Cavour was a man of property as well as a patriot; he was addicted, as Gramsci said, to "prodigies of subtlety and intrigue,"[36] and his real strategy was to enlist foreign aid, to get the French to drive out the Austrians. He accomplished this, but the Italy which resulted in 1861 was not a nation newly made by struggle: it was only an artificial enlargement of the small conservative king-dom of Piedmont.

In examining the Risorgimento, Gramsci was acutely conscious of the gulf between northern and southern Italy, a dichotomy akin, as he said, to that of town and countryside. Southern leaders were the most determined of all to prevent social emancipation from accompanying national unification. Peasant revolts which broke out in Sicily were ruthlessly crushed. To far too many of the bad old Bourbon kingdom of Naples and Sicily, the coming of Italian unity seemed less a liberation than a conquest by Piedmont and the northerners. Not only was the new nation emerging with a very unreformed social structure, especially in the south, but its heterogeneous provinces, each with a historical evolution of its own, were very imperfectly fused. In Sardinia a separatist movement appeared, to which Gramsci was drawn for a short time in youth; memories of a rising in 1906 and its brutal suppression were still alive. He soon outgrew this localism, but as an Italian leader he advocated regional autonomy for areas like the south and the islands (as he would presumably have done for Scotland and Wales). Such a reorganization has been accepted since 1945, though only grudgingly implemented. Sardinia is still miserably poor and badly run.[37]

Southern Italy and the islands, Sicily and Sardinia, were only corners of a poverty-stricken southern fringe of Europe, all the way from southern Portu-gal, where the Algarve province (*al-gharb,* "the west") was long Moorish and in the sixteenth century imported large numbers of African slaves to Greece, last of the chain of peninsulas to throw off Muslim rule. All this belt had closer historical links in many ways with Afro-Asia than with northern Europe, and northerners often thought of it in that light. "Asia begins at the Pyrenees." One of Gramsci's obsessive problems was the semicolonial relationship ex-isting between northern and southern Italy, both in economic terms, with northern industry treating the rustic south as a captive market and source of cheap labor, and in psychological terms, a contemptuous attitude which the workman shared with his employer in manufacturing centers like Turin, the town where Gramsci studied and practiced politics. He found its working class conditioned by the subtle influences of the bourgeois state to think of southerners as ignorant yokels, shiftless and irresponsible.[38] This situation confronted him and his party with an acute form of the dilemma of how to bring workers and peasants together under Socialist guidance. It is in fact the fundamental dilemma of all developing countries and has everywhere proved an intractable one. To put hammer and sickle side by side on a flag is easy, to combine them in reality is another thing altogether.

Paradoxically, while southern Italy was regarded by the north as something like a dull, stupid colony, its own poverty and land hunger helped to make Italy, scarcely arrived at independence, turn imperialist and go greedily search-ing for colonies outside Europe. Imperialism offered a substitute for self-improvement; it was (or sometimes only seemed) easier to overrun patches of Africa than to grapple with feudal landlords at home. Eritrea was occupied in 1890, in 1896 there was a disastrous failure to conquer Ethiopia, in 1911 Turkey was defeated and Tripoli seized. These efforts got under way at a time when industrial capital in Italy was too little mature to require colonial outlets. They were instigated, rather, by political demagogy, which could make a peculiar appeal to the famished south. Francesco Crispi, the prime minister who did most to push them on, was a Sicilian, a fiery nationalist with no inkling of the need for agrarian reform, who harshly suppressed disturbances at home and turned to jingoism to provide a synthetic unity and national purpose. He played on the southern peasant's land hunger by conjuring up the mirage of farms for all to be won by conquest overseas.[39] There was a strong dash of this spurious—or un-Leninist—imperialism later on too, in Mussolini's renewal of the onslaught on Ethiopia near the end of Gramsci's life. Not much of the promised settlement of surplus population on new land followed. As Gramsci knew, emigration is governed by demand for labor: capital, not population, determines the need for colonies.[40]

Some likeness or other can be deciphered between almost any pair of countries, but between Italy and India there is more than most couples so far apart could show. Marx once made a comparison between them, as two mountain-crowned peninsulas.[41] Italy is exceptional in Europe, India in Asia, both having been until lately politically fragmented and under foreign ascendancy. A great deal in Italy's social structure and the social psychology that goes with it, notably in the south, has its counterpart in India. Gramsci was not unconscious of this. When he wrote of the unwholesome proliferation of social strata merely parasitic, or engaged at best in trade instead of production, in Italy and other parts of Europe, he went on: "it exists in an even worse form in India and China, which explains the historical stagnation of those countries."[42] China was to go another way, but India's national movement bore unmistakable resemblances to Italy's. Its leadership, too, was elitist, reluctant to summon mass forces to any more realistic action than a breaking of Salt Laws. In Gramsci's words, "similar situations almost always arise in every historical development."[43] Indian independence owed nearly as much to foreign intervention, the crippling of British power by the Second World War, as Italian to the Franco-Austrian War. When it came, the National Congress Party took over the British-trained army, police and bureaucracy intact, much as the Piedmontese army and bureaucracy took over Italy.

Some of the affinities between Italy and India have been pointed out by Rosselli in his biography of Lord William Bentinck, who went to Madras as governor in 1803, was British commissioner in Sicily and its virtual ruler during the Napoleonic occupation of Italy, and in 1828 became governor-general of India. Rosselli finds it natural that early Indian national feeling, about the mid-nineteenth century, should have drawn some of its inspiration from Mazzini's writings,[44] whose influence lasted long enough to give Lala Lajpat Rai his youthful ideal of liberty.[45] There was opposition to imperialism in Italy after unification, and the most famous Italian of the age, the then old composer Giuseppe Verdi, was expressing it when he talked about India to an acquaintance in 1896: "Here's a great and ancient people given over as prey to the English . . . and the English are sons of bitches. . . . Unfortunately we, too, are in Africa now playing the part of tyrants; we are wrong and we will pay for it. We say we are going there to bring our civilization to those people. A fine civilization ours, with all the miseries it carries along with it!"[46] In 1911 Italy's seizure of Tripoli outraged India, or at least Muslim India, whose poet Iqbal denounced it, as he later denounced Mussolini's invasion of Ethiopia, along with Western imperialism at large, as Nehru also did.

Between Gramsci himself and India one surprising link was the admiration he felt for Rudyard Kipling. From his student days he always attributed to Kipling's works a character-building quality. They were "imperialistic," he held, only when read in a certain limited context; taken more broadly, they could lend courage to "any social class fighting for political power."[47] In the early days of his captivity, when he and a dozen comrades were being taken to the convict island of Ustica, he had an eerie sensation of reliving the adventure narrated in the story "The Strange Ride of Morrowbie Jukes."[48] When he heard of his young son wanting to read *Uncle Tom's Cabin,* he urged him not to waste time on such sentimental stuff but to read *Kim* and the *Jungle Book* instead.[49]

His own early reading of such books had been in Italian or French translations. But at the end of 1928 he was asking for an English grammar, and by mid-1931 he reported that he could read the language fairly quickly, much more easily than German.[50] He was able to get copies of the *Manchester Guardian* and *Times* weeklies, sometimes even of the *Labour Monthly,* edited by the half-Indian communist Palme Dutt.[51] Any of these would give him plenty of current information about Indian events. He can scarcely have known Marx's writings on India, and, unlike Marx, he had no very compelling incentive to study Indian history. A systematic study of the national movement there, if he had been in a position to undertake it, would have produced invaluable ideas about it and might well have helped him in his own task of analyzing the Risorgimento.

His odd jottings are always worth reading. An article of August 1929, "Rebel India," during the agitation before the second Civil Disobedience movement, furnished him with some of the statistics he wanted[52]—however far he might wander in hypotheses he always liked to feel solid ground under his feet. Late the next year he was reading an interview given by the novelist Aldous Huxley, who had been visiting India and was asked his opinion about the disorders. Huxley's explanation was that the British had gone astray by opening universities instead of primary schools, and it was the unemployed graduates who were now discontented and wanted to get power. There was some truth in this, was Gramsci's judicious verdict, but not much. Loria, too, had theorized about jobless intellectuals, but such groups could not by themselves create a state of affairs like the actual one in India; they must be serving as mouthpiece to all the middle-class elements which economic development had been forming in India.[53]

Gramsci was clearly intrigued, like everyone else, by the enigmatic personality and tactics of Gandhi. He was not inclined to dismiss him, as the Indian communist party then just getting on its feet did, as a mere humbug and false prophet. His picture of Gandhi fitted into his distinction between "active" and "passive" resistance, such as Mazzini and Cavour epitomized in Italy, and between the phases of a long-drawn revolutionary struggle which he called, in military parlance, "wars of movement" and "wars of position"—neither necessarily armed conflict. He mentioned "the current phenomenon of Gandhism in India" and the ideas of Gandhi and Tolstoy as "naive theorisations of the 'passive revolution' with religious overtones."[54] Gandhi's passive resistance is a war of position, which at certain moments becomes a war of movement, and at other times underground warfare." By this last he meant secret preparations for revolt. "Every political struggle always has a military substratum," he remarked in the same context.[55] But just as he looked back on Mazzini's insurrections as futile, he seems to have surmised that it might be a mistake for Indian nationalism at present to challenge the government to a trial of armed strength; and if the British thought themselves faced with a plan of large-scale rebellion, they would be likely to try to provoke a premature local rising, in order to nip it in the bud.[56] One may wonder whether the strategy he thought the British might resort to really was in the minds of some of them in 1919, at the time of the Amritsar massacre, and again in 1942 at the time of the August rising.

For several years after the unification of Italy the south was in a chronic condition of agrarian revolt, the outcome of peasant frustration worked on by reactionaries. It was officially designated "brigandage" and put down by military force. A parallel between this and the harsh suppression of the communist-led peasant rising against landlordism in Telengana, in southern India, just after India became independent, would be easy to draw. It might be said too that Italy's failure to absorb the south into a genuine union has an analogy in India's imperfect assimilation of some of the semifeudal territories of the ruling princes of British days, those Oriental Bourbons, and other pockets of backwardness. Obviously in Pakistan, where the "national movement" had far less still of transforming energy, the incompatibility of the eastern and western wings was beyond remedy.

Many of the same obstacles have beset Italy and India since the one began a new existence with the expulsion of fascism and the German army in 1945, the other with the withdrawal of the British in 1947. Ever since then they have had governments of about the same political complexion, so far as home affairs are concerned, oscillating between center-right and center-left and both heavily loaded with careerists and corruption. Under these auspices each country has had some economic growth and some social reform, but uneven and inadequate, at any rate as regards southern Italy and the islands and most of India. In southern Italy as in India the old feudal estates have been broken up, under peasant pressure, but the misery of the poorer peasants and landless laborers remains. Naples city and its rat-haunted slums, as vividly depicted a few years ago by a woman communist in an election campaign, is a worthy compeer of Calcutta.[57] Pressure of population is a menace hanging over each country. Its basic causes are social and economic, but religion helps to aggravate them. Fresh miracles and cults still blossom in Italy, as holy men and sects mushroom in India. So do the schemes of the extreme Right for playing on mass discontent and disillusion, those of neofascism in Italy, RSS or Shiv Sena in an India which contains a perilous quantity of material for fascist-type organizations well able to borrow from European models.

Gramsci, fascism's foremost opponent and victim, can have known little about the early gropings of the communist movement in India; if he had been in touch with it, he could scarcely have failed to recognize in it some of the same failings that he was conscious of in his own party: what he called 'Byzantianism," or "scholasticism," a habit of treating questions of theory in abstraction from reality,[58] and what he condemned as "blind, unilateral 'party' fanaticism" or sectarianism.[59] They were weaknesses of a left-wing intelligentsia too little in contact with ordinary people, too much a self-contained conventicle. They were worsened by a party structure taken over too uncritically from the Bolshevik pattern, whose defects Gramsci was uneasy about during his time in Moscow. For all these reasons it is not surprising that his writings have begun to attract the attention of the Left in India, as they have far more widely in Western Europe.

If India about 1930 was suffering from an overdose of British "law and order," China was only just leaving behind the anarchy of the "warlord" period which followed the fall of the monarchy in 1911. Gramsci's omnivorous curiosity made him wish for a book he heard of—a big collection of statistics about China under Kuomintang rule published at Shanghai.[60] His notebooks reveal no detailed acquaintance with what was going on, but he knew of Sun Yat-sen (whom he oddly calls 'Suen Uen') and his progressive plans, and of the superficial reuniting of the country by a Kuomintang party turning against the people after Sun's death. Nothing had changed since 1911, he felt, except that generals had replaced mandarins, each in turn trying to get the upper hand.[61] He seems to have been impressed by China's regionalism; he thought of the local warlords as a primitive expression of this, as against the "cosmopolitanism" of the old imperial order,[62] and may have been looking, as in Italy, to a federative solution. This might indeed have come about, in a very crude form—Chiang Kai-shek's system was a kind of warlord federation—if the hammer blows of Japanese invasion had not fused the nation into a far closer unity than ever before.

Already, the foreign danger, Gramsci pointed out, was much more threatening than the Muslim pressures which helped to give medieval Christendom a rough sense of identity. He was depending on the common people both to rescue the country from this and to reunite it more organically than the Kuomintang ever could.[63] Instead of trying to rouse the people, Sun's reactionary successors were refusing to summon the democratic constituent assembly he had looked forward to, and wanted to preserve the archaic military-bureaucratic framework.[64] Nationwide elections, Gramsci believed, would bring the millions of the interior into a national agitation hitherto confined to the coastlands and river valleys and thus compel both social reforms and federal union.[65] Clearly he did not despite "parliamentarism" as a form of struggle. But as things were, he concluded, "it appears to me that it will be hard to re-establish any lasting order without a profound national revolution of the masses."[66] As to China's external position, he noted an Italian writer's forecast of an east-Asian bloc of China, Japan, and the Soviet Union, against an Anglo-American combination.[67]

Among scattered reflections on other parts of the world, it is characteristic of Gramsci that when he asked himself in what sense "Latin America" was really *Latin* and counted up its diverse components, one that he, unlike the majority of writers, discussed was its Amerindian population. He saw correctly that they must have a marked, even if only passive, influence on various of the states and wanted to collect information about their status, for instance in relation to ownership of the soil.[68] There are one or two allusions to Africa and mention of a book on linguistics with some lessons in an African language[69]—a Zulu saying copied out of some English journal, which must have appealed to him; it is better to go forward and perish than to stand still and perish.[70] But his other non-European references cluster round the neighborhood of northeastern Africa and the Middle East, containing a large part of the Muslim world, with which Italy and its ambitions were most closely involved.

Thus he made notes about Ethiopia and its recent history and conjectured that it might one day be the center of a clash of great-power rivalries; also that, as the sole free country of the continent, it might find itself at the head of an "Africa for the Africans" movement.[71] A generation later Addis Ababa did become the headquarters of the Organization of African States. Eritrea, the Red Sea colony bordering on Ethiopia, was valued by Italy partly as a point of contact with the Arab countries.[72] Gramsci made detailed notes in 1927 about Yemen, its treaty with Italy, and the rivalry between it and the Saudi kingdom for primacy in Arabia.[73] Other articles he read at this time dealt with Italian interests in Asia Minor, including Mosul and its oil, and in Egypt, where he noted that Britain was trying to humor the nationalists at the expense of other foreigners, like the Italians long settled there, who for their part wanted to be friends with the nationalists and leave all the odium to be borne by the British.[74] One of the books he was trying to get in 1929 was T. E. Lawrence's *Revolt in the Desert*.[75] A year or two later he found food for thought in a set of writings on the influence of Arab civilization in former days on the West and told himself that this was a subject he ought to follow up.[76]

A high proportion of Gramsci's notes and ponderings about the other continents (as well as about Italy and Europe) concerned cultural and religious matters rather than political or economic, though to him all these were but different aspects of the same thing. Typical of his approach are some remarks on a survey of religion in India by an Italian scholar who rejected the conventional image of a spiritual race of mystics and asserted that material concerns were what Indians cared most about. This writer pointed to a moral crisis, a modern critical spirit impotent to defeat the old beliefs, and as a result "superstition among the lower classes, hypocrisy and lack of character among the higher, or so-called cultured classes." Clearly this crisis would be long drawn out, Gramsci commented, in view of India's age-old torpor and ossified social order and of the accumulation of "intellectuals," mostly of the priestly sort, as in all big agricultural countries. His conclusion was that (as in China) "a great revolution will be necessary as the starting-point for a solution."[77] A meditation in an earlier notebook may reflect something of the conventional image, here discarded, of a spiritual East contrasting with the materialistic West. Gramsci had heard of a lecture by Bergson whose theme was that if mankind had devoted itself to studying its own inner being instead of the external world, matter instead of spirit would have acquired the aura of mystery. 'Mankind,' Gramsci appended, "means the West; the East has stopped at the stage of turning its eyes inward."[78]

No doubt religion bulked large in his reading partly because church journals were more accessible in jail than some others. But it had also a vital significance for him. In his *integrating* concept of Marxism, ideas represented an incalculable, though not an independent, force. On a more practical level there were many topics connected with religion that he had to take into account. He was aware of an organization set up by Italian industrialists to support Catholic missions, with an eye to economic as well as cultural penetration of backward lands.[79] Political control was clearly intended to follow. Twice, he noted ironically, in an article in a clerical journal in 1929 on Italian colonies, Albania was referred to as one of them.[80] It was indeed part of Mussolini's destined prey, and imperialism was promoting the cordial harmony between him and the church that showed itself over the conquest of Ethiopia.

Gramsci attached particular significance to what the Jesuits might be thinking; for example when he came on some Jesuit essays of 1930 on Hindu sects and philosophy, because, he remarked, they were grappling with practical problems of the church's missionary work and hence had an objective meaning and could help toward an understanding of "the structure of cultural and moral hegemony" in a big Asian country. No converts were being secured in India except among the low castes, while intellectuals were resistant, and it was they whom the pope was anxious to win, and the masses through them.[81] Elsewhere Gramsci referred to a celebrated Hindu *sanyasi,* or holy man, turned Catholic, Upadhyaya Brahmabandhav, who was censured by Rome for wanting to convert India by adopting whatever ingredients of Hinduism could be absorbed into Christianity. "I fancy," he added, "that today the Vatican would be more tolerant."[82]

A comparable issue was coming up in China—as it came up long ago, in the eighteenth century, when Voltaire joined in the debate on it. The Kuomintang, paying loud lip service to the memory of Sun Yat-sen, ordered a ceremony in his honor every Monday, and study of his Three People's Principles, in every school, Christian included. Gramsci copied out at length a letter from the apostolic delegate in China to the Jesuit translator of Sun's book, pronouncing that parts of this could be reconciled with modern Catholic social teaching, that the Monday ceremony was not idolatrous, and that therefore no objection should be raised. Clearly, Gramsci commented, this opened the door to a Chinese "national Catholicism."[83] It must be supposed that he had in mind also the task which communism in Italy would one day have to face—the converse of the church's task in Asia—of finding some modus vivendi between itself and Catholicism.

When Gramsci read about Arab or other Muslim lands, it was the spectacle of Islam, a religion and culture in crisis, that riveted his attention most. In his notes on Yemen the background of the Wahhabi movement of Islamic revivalism and fundamentalism found a place. He came on another survival from the past in a 1929 article on the *merabouts,* or martial saints, most numerous in northern Africa, above all in Morocco where they were leading the fight against European occupation. They were described as representing the popular mystique of Islam, in which pre-Islamic traces lingered, as distinct from its scriptural orthodoxy, the two being brought together periodically by outbursts of fantacism. Gramsci laid stress on the lack of a regular priesthood, to keep orthodox doctrine and popular credence from drifting too far apart (a function of the Christian clergy to which he gave great weight), and on the need for a close study of the organization of religion in Islam, and the part played by theological institutes like Al-Azhar at Cairo. "The mental gulf between intellectuals and common people in the Muslim world must be very wide, especially in certain quarters of it."[84]

On contemporary trends in Islam he read a mediocre sketch by an Afghan diplomat which drew from him the comment that "among Muslims there

exists a jesuitry and casuistry as well developed as in Catholicism." More
noteworthy was an introduction to it by a Professor Guidi, who raised the
question of whether Islam was capable of evolving and coming to terms with
modernity, now that it could no longer abide in "splendid isolation." Gramsci
drew a comparison with Christianity, conventionally accepted as part of
"modern civilization" because it had little by little adapted itself to capitalism.
Contradictions between the two were glaringly obvious to outsiders, hence
the little headway made by missionaries; at home in Europe they passed
unnoticed—"Christianity has undergone a molecular adjustment and has
turned into jesuitry, that is into an elaborate piece of hypocrisy." Why, then,
could not Islam do the same? The absence of a hierarchy ought to facilitate
the process. Against this was the fact that instead of being allowed plenty of
time, like Christianity, Islam's fossilized feudal society, long insulated, was
being dragged suddenly into intercourse with an advanced though already
decadent Western civilization. At bottom, all the same, he judged it to be
reacting in the same fashion, exchanging the old "theocratic cosmopolitanism"
for the heresy of nationalism, while attempting by way of compensation to
recapture its ancient purity of faith.[85] A figure of that day like the poet and
religious revivalist Iqbal, now looked back on by Pakistan as its spiritual
founder, could hardly be better summed up.

It was a sound maxim of Gramsci's that in studying any religion one must
reckon with the divergent conceptions of it held by priests, by intellectuals,
and by ordinary people—divergences marked everywhere, widest he supposed
in eastern Asia.[86] Whether Shinto was an authentic religion or a crude mythology struck Gramsci when he read something about it as the primary enigma
of modern Japanese culture. He was puzzled by its similarity to the pagan
cults of ancient Europe and the anomaly of a deity like Ama-terasu, of the
same family as Osiris or Apollo, being worshipped in a modern industrial
country—though he added the sage caution: "Perhaps however things are
not as simple as they may appear." Shinto as state cult seemed to him akin
to that of the deified Roman emperors and not at all the same as Shinto as
a religious sect; and he surmised hopefully that although the latter was still
potent, modernization must be ushering in a secular consciousness. Political
life, with parties and newspapers and elections, would dissolve old theocratic-
absolutist modes of thought. In short he hoped that Japan was entering a
stage like the Enlightenment in Europe.[87] One would like to know whether the
"running amuck" of the Japanese army in Manchuria, and the recrudescence of
absolutist and obscurantist ideas, dashed his hopeful expectations.

Gramsci's underlying aim here was to reach an understanding of what
Japanese intellectuals stood for. At this and several other points he seems to
have in mind a collection of material for an all-around study of intellectuals
and their place in the world and in history. Had he lived to write such a

work, it would have been his magnum opus; it is one of the great unwritten books of our century, a lost Atlantis of the mind. It was a subject that always preoccupied him, and how he looked at it in non-European settings does something to elucidate his leading concepts. In both Japan and the USA, for instance, he found illustrations of how impulses barred from political expression may spill over into a multiplicity of religious sects—as in czarist Russia where such sects took a morbidly extravagant shape because political blockages were so rigid.[88]

An acute sense of historical continuity as well as change enabled Gramsci to detect in the functions of the priest the matrix of the intellectual, and the one evolving into the other. In China the two could be watched side by side through the ages. Gramsci came on a study which contrasted rationalizing Confucianism with mystical Taoism,[89] and a second of the history of Chinese thought which stressed its ethical bent, the lesser prominence it gave to logic. He agreed with the author of a German book on Chinese literature that to comprehend China today and its collective psychology, it was essential to know its past, and he held that scrutiny of a nation's literature could throw much light on its mental makeup.[90] He disagreed with this writer's contention that China had possessed for millennia a kind of "Confucian communism": collectivist elements could be pointed to in any preindustrial country.[91] Gramsci felt a good deal of curiosity about the peculiarities of the Chinese language and its method of writing;[92] he regarded this—wrongly, it would now appear—as making any broad popular culture impossible and thought an alphabetic script, though he appreciated the technical impediments, would be required to liberate the spoken language and allow new intellectual strata to develop. In the old Chinese script he saw the chief factor which had molded the traditional intelligentsia and its social functioning; this whole subject he believed to deserve very careful study because of its unique features.[93] Max Weber's sociological studies of Chinese history and religion,[94] it may be remarked, had looked for answers to similar riddles and would have been absorbing to Gramsci if they had reached his cell.

Gramsci's estimate of the importance of "intellectuals" was extremely high, though his definition of the term was so very flexible as sometimes to appear loose.[95] They had for him two main and opposite spheres, as conservators and as innovators. In the first of these guises an intelligentsia shades off into a bureaucracy, and Gramsci wanted these two things to be investigated together.[96] On the other side, that of the intellectual's function of spreading new ideas, we find him curiously close to sundry other practical men, in walks of life remote from his, in holding that new ideas cannot reach the mass of mankind directly but can only be filtered to it through an intelligentsia of some kind. When he was reviewing Catholic missionary tactics in India, he gave the pope credit for taking clearer cognizance than many on the Left did of "the mechanism of cultural change among rural masses . . . people in the mass cannot be converted *molecu-*

larly, or individual by individual; it is necessary, in order to hasten the process, to win over the natural leaders of the multitude, that is the intellectuals.[97] Nearly a century earlier a British governor in India used exactly the same argument in favor of higher education, in English, in preference to primary teaching. Doubly cut off by class and race from the Indian masses, Sir Erskine Perry might well feel the impossibility of any direct approach to them. "In order," he declared, "to make a permanent deep impression on the Asiatic mind, . . . we must apply our chief endeavour to the cultivation of the higher branches of learning and of the superior order of minds. The growth of opinion in nations appears to us exactly analogous to what takes place in small circles . . . the majority have no opinions of their own, they take them from the original mind, from the man who thinks for himself."[98]

Gramsci was prepared to indulge in the improbable speculation that Africa might one day be regenerated and united by black intellectuals (he meant any educated blacks) from the USA either utilized by Washington to promote American influence there or driven to leave home by racial prejudice.[99] On a more practical plane his concern with the intelligentsia stimulated his always keen interest in education. This and his interest in the colonial world came together when he read a report of a big British Commonwealth conference in London in 1931 on the theme of education in a changing empire, with much talk about "interracial understanding." Indian representatives, he noticed, complained very frankly of British incomprehension of the Indian mind and racial arrogance. There was lengthy discussion, as a century before in India, about whether African peoples ought to be taught in English or in their own languages. Gramsci was conscious of nationalist feeling, tinged with race pride, in the declaration of one African speaker that they had no desire to be Europeanized.[100]

Gramsci's Marxism and his universality of mind as a human being enabled him to compose all his multifarious inquiries into a single intricate harmony. He has been described by an admirer as the Lenin of our day, of an industrialized world.[101] It might be more accurate to say that he belongs both to the industrialized and to the newly modernizing worlds, to the realm of Marx and the realm of Mao, and forms a bridge between them. With this duality we may associate his gift for bringing together fact and idea, matter and mind, in his complex understanding of history; the gift praised by the same admirer when she speaks of his teaching that ideas as well as material forces go to make up action, that Marxism is *not* "the science of the infrastructure" but of base and superstructure always interwoven.[102]

Notes

This chapter originally appeared in the *New Edinburgh Review* (1975).

1. Antonio Gramsci, *Lettere dal Carcere* (Prison Letters) (collected ed., Turin, 1965), 78–79 (18 April 1927).

2. Ibid., 287 (1 January 1929).

3. Ibid., 168 (30 January 1928).

4. Ibid., 119 (29 August 1927).

5. Ibid., 885 (n.d.).

6. Ibid., 474 (31 August 1931) and 475n.

7. Ibid., 323 (10 February 1930).

8. See A. Pozzolini, *Antonio Gramsci: An Introduction to His Thought,* trans. A. F. Showstack (London, 1970), 121. Cf. J. M. Piotte, *La pensée politique de Gramsci* (Paris, 1970), Chapter 6.

9. Gramsci, *Lettere,* 885 (n.d.).

10. Ibid., 498–99 (28 September 1931).

11. Pozzolini, *Antonio Gramsci,* 122.

12. Antonio Gramsci, *Passato e Presente* (Past and Present, a volume in the collected edition of the *Quaderni del Carcere,* Gramsci's prison notebooks) (Rome, 1971), 265.

13. Antonio Gramsci, *Note sui Machiavelli, sulla Politica e sullo Stato Moderno* (Notes on Machiavelli, on Politics, and on the Modern State, another volume in the *Quaderni* series (Rome, 1971), 291.

14. Ibid., 229.

15. Ibid., 238.

16. Gramsci, *Lettere,* 365 (25 August 1930).

17. Gramsci, *Note sui Machiavelli,* 231.

18. Gramsci, *Passato e Presente,* 273–74.

19. Gramsci, *Note sui Machiavelli,* 231–34.

20. Ibid., 235–36, 236–37.

21. Gramsci, *Passato e Presente,* 273–74.

22. Gramsci, *Note sui Machiavelli,* 442–44.

23. Ibid., 224.

24. Gramsci, *Passato e Presente,* 168–69.

25. Gramsci, *Note sui Machiavelli,* 291.

26. See Gramsci, *Passato e Presente,* 272–73.

27. Ibid., 271–72.

28. Gramsci, *Note sui Machiavelli,* 224.

29. Ibid., 234–35.

30. M'Culloch quoted in A. R. Wallace, *Land Nationalisation* (2d ed., London, 1882), 154.

31. Gramsci, *Lettere,* 507 (12 October 1931).

32. Gramsci, *Passato e Presente,* 242–44.

33. Gramsci, *Note sui Machiavelli,* 229–30.

34. See Q. Hoare and G. N. Smith, eds. *Selections from the Prison Notebooks of Antonio Gramsci* (London, 1971), 89.

35. Ibid., 110.

36. Ibid., 84.

37. In regional elections in Sardinia in June 1974 the communist vote rose from 19.1 to 26.8 percent, while the Christian Democrat majority fell, and the central government was galvanized into promising a big ten-year subsidy to improve the island's economy.

38. Gramsci, *Passato e Presente,* 31.

39. Hoare and Smith, *Selections,* 67–68.

40. Gramsci, *Note sui Machiavelli,* 273.

41. Karl Marx, article of 10 June 1853, in Marx and Friedrich Engels, *The First Indian War of Independence, 1857–1859* (Moscow, 1959), 14.

42. Hare and Smith, *Selections,* 285.

43. Ibid., 108–9.

44. J. Rosselli, *Lord William Bentinck: The Making of a Liberal Imperialist, 1774–1839* (London, 1974), 108.

45. P. Mudford, *Birds of a Different Plumage: A Study of British-Indian Relations from Akbar to Curzon* (London, 1974), 208.

46. Giuseppe Verdi quoted in V. Sheen, *Orpheus at Eighty* (London, 1958), 171.

47. Gramsci, *Lettere,* 783n.

48. Gramsci, *Passato e Presente,* 272.

49. Gramsci, *Lettere,* 10 (9 December 1926). Gramsci's reference is inexact: the Kipling story is in *The Phantom Rickshaw and Other Tales.*

50. Ibid., 579 (22 February 1932); 791 (11 June 1933).

51. Ibid., 245 (December 1928); 449 (29 June 1931).

52. Ibid., 379, 421, 454.

53. Gramsci, *Passato e Presente,* 274–75.

54. Antonio Gramsci, *Gli Intellettuali e l'Organizzazione della Culture* (The Intellectuals and the Organization of Culture, another volume in the *Quaderni* series) (Rome, 1971), 109–10.

55. Hoare and Smith, *Selections,* 107.

56. Ibid., 229–30.

57. Ibid.

58. See Maria Antonietta Macciocchi, *Letters from Inside the Italian Communist Party* (trans. S. M. Heilman, London, 1973).

59. Hoare and Smith, *Selections,* 200–201.

60. Ibid., 266–67.

61. Gramsci, *Passato e Presente*, 292.

62. Gramsci, *Gli Intellettuali*, 117.

63. Ibid., 113.

64. Ibid., 112.

65. Ibid., 112–13.

66. Ibid., 117.

67. Gramsci, *Note sui Machiavelli*, 236–37.

68. Ibid., 455–57.

69. Gramsci, *Lettere*, 134 (3 October 1927).

70. Gramsci, *Passato e Presente*, 179.

71. Gramsci, *Note sui Machiavelli*, 262–66.

72. Ibid., 266.

73. Ibid., 257–59.

74. Ibid., 259–61.

75. Gramsci, *Lettere*, 283 (17 June 1929).

76. Gramsci, *Gli Intellettuali*, 109.

77. Gramsci, *Note sui Machiavelli*, 391–92.

78. Gramsci, *Passato e Presente*, 266–67.

79. Ibid., 166.

80. Gramsci, *Note sui Machiavelli*, 398.

81. Gramsci, *Gli Intellettuali*, 110.

82. Gramsci, *Note sui Machiavelli*, 391.

83. Gramsci, *Gli Intellettuali*, 188–20.

84. Ibid., 105–6.

85. Ibid., 107–9.

86. Hoare and Smith, *Selections*, 23.

87. Gramsci, *Gli Intellettuali*, 120.

88. Gramsci, *Passato e Presente*, 269.

89. Gramsci, *Gli Intellettuali*, 117–18.

90. Ibid., 115–17.

91. Ibid., 115.

92. Ibid., 113–15.

93. Ibid., 110–12.

94. Max Weber, *The Religion of China* (trans. H. H. Gerth, New York, 1951).

95. Cf. V. G. Kiernan, "Gramsci and Marxism," in *History, Classes, and Nation-States: Selected Writings of V. G. Kiernan*, ed. H. J. Kaye (Oxford, 1988).

96. Hoare and Smith, *Selections*, 186.

97. Gramsci, *Gli Intellettuali,* 110.

98. Sir Erskine Perry, quoted in A. J. Roberts, "Education and Society in the Bombay Presidency, 1840 to 58", Ph.D. thesis, London University, 1974, 121.

99. Hoare and Smith, *Selections,* 21.

100. Gramsci, *Gli Intellettuali,* 102–3.

101. M. A. Macciocchi, *Pour Gramsci* (Paris, 1974), 14. Chapter 4 of this work concerns the problem of the south in the Italian national movement.

102. Ibid., 13–14.

8

AFTER EMPIRE

Poor Old England

Virgil's Trojans in exile could be cheered by the thought that all the world was ringing with their deeds; Englishmen of not long ago could feel that the whole world was witness to theirs. England's name, like its language, has traveled far and wide, after first being brought by the Angles from Denmark, and has undergone odd mutations; American Indians turned "English" into *Yengeez*, Hindus into *Angrezi*. For generations, while Englishmen were taught to think of themselves as guardians of an empire that would never stop expanding, to be a "little Englander" was to be stamped as decadent or only half an Englishman. It is still hard to comprehend that all this should have disappeared so swiftly, like the baseless fabric of a dream.

The First World War was followed within a few years by a grand operation to restore morale and confidence, the Empire Exhibition at Wembley. This was accompanied by what must have been the most elaborate and massive scheme of indoctrination, through the schools, ever undertaken in peacetime. A sometimes reluctant Prince of Wales was kept touring the colonies and being photographed among elephants, kangaroos, and other picturesque denizens; in every way the empire and its glorious past and future were dinned into every ear. In reality it was already entering its final twilight; after 1918 it no longer had any aim beyond moneymaking, and colonial nationalism, loudest in India, was challenging all its pretensions. During the long years of the Slump people had time to feel that their boasted possessions were doing them little good, even if profits from them may have been cushioning the economy in ways the ordinary man failed to recognize.

Still, it had a very long history and may well have molded the ordinary man in ways he was equally little conscious of. To measure how such an experience as three centuries of world power may sink into national character is scarcely feasible, and many other factors of social structure and psychology are involved in the complex outcome. It has at times helped nations to stiffen the sinews and summon up the blood in face of disaster, with a potency only paralleled in religious fanaticism. It may long outlive the circumstances which gave rise to it: Spain's dominance in Europe, for instance, lost in the seventeenth century, and in the Americas, lost in the nineteenth. Without this, and the inflexible Castililan pride which grew with it, one may wonder whether Spaniards would have been capable of such prodigies of endurance in their last civil war. When Britain's turn came in 1940, its rulers were fighting to preserve their empire, the common man was far more concerned with the survival of his own native land and, gropingly, with the defeat of fascism; yet they had something, some inherited temper, in common. To this writer, long an adherent of what was then the furthest Left, it did not occur as a remotest possibility that his country might follow the French example and surrender.

During that war very large numbers of Britons saw their empire, India in particular, for the first time and were seldom much impressed by the accomplishments of British rule. A few years after it was over, at the time of the coronation in 1952, the country was treated by its mentors to another and far sillier deluge of ballyhoo, like the Wembley exhibition but limited now to the merely personal symbol of a juvenile monarch. India had already gone, and in retrospect the emotional orgy may be viewed as a requiem for the empire which England felt in its bones it was losing, along with its former high estate in the world. However much or little the emotional orgy affected the workers, for the middle classes it was a last feast of fantasy, like a school boy's blowout of pastry at the end of a holiday. Newspapers and orators poured out floods of rhetoric about the nation going through a grand spiritual revival, a rededication to its faith—in conservatism, presumably. One editor commissioned a well-known artist to draw the archiepiscopal hands which were to place the crown on the royal head. Of all that outburst of absurdity a good quantity can be charged to the contagion of a hundred years of imperial drums and dreams, or dram drinking. It is agreeable to suppose that we have grown sober since then, though an uneasy doubt may obtrude: it may be that there is a more or less constant ratio of imbecility in the human species at the stage of evolution where it now is, which when not canalized by Church of England or Tory Party will meander into table rapping, astrology, occultism, all now doing a flourishing trade among us. *Populus vult decipi*— people may need their doses of freak ideas as much as their annual millionfold pill swallowings.

Rearguard actions were fought in Malaya and a few other territories, but on the whole the dismantling of the empire went on smoothly enough, far more so than those of the Dutch or French. Having fought its way through the Second World War with credit, Britain could depart with dignity. Africa was quietly abandoned, bit by bit, mostly by Tory ministers,[1] flag-waving to the end as they marched their bemused followers backward. The rapid fading of empire seemed to disclose that in spite of so many lifetimes of drilling by schoolbook and newspaper, most Englishmen were too sensible—or too parochial—to care much about it; they as well as their Asian and African wards had outgrown it. There was no such political or constitutional crisis as Irish Home Rule caused in the late nineteenth century, or Ulster in 1914. Ministers, Tory or Labour, and admirals and generals, have pined for lost grandeur, because they would like to cut more of a dash at international conferences, and they attribute to the man in the street their own longing for a voice in the world, a special relationship with the USA, and so on. The attack on Suez in 1956 incited the middle classes to a brief fit of hysteria, undoubtedly shared by some older workingmen.

In spite of this fiasco, the Tories, who only a quarter century ago were calling themselves "the great imperial party," have lost surprisingly little ground with the vanishing of their old soapbox or thumping tub, as abrupt almost as that of Aladdin's palace. Labour was in a poor position to claim the forfeit, because its own colonial policy has usually been a bipartisan one. Also, Tories who used to feel they were doing quite enough by spreading, or purporting to spread, enlightenment through Asia and Africa, now began to see that they would have to find something to say about progress for Britain. It was they who expanded higher education, no doubt counting on it to strengthen their middle-class base, as so far, despite salvoes of left-wing fireworks from the universities, it may have done.

The New Insularity

Empire was a poor substitute for a genuine, open-minded interest in the world, and if England had been discovering such an interest since 1945, it would be a big step forward; instead there seems, rather, to have been a relapse into insularity. Membership in the Common Market has done nothing to counteract this. It was too palpably a Tory maneuver, even if some young hopefuls welcomed it at the time as a move toward European and world union. Englishmen by and large have continued to think of the outside world like seamen in a tranquil harbor contemplating the sad lot of those tossing on stormy waves. To them the outside has looked disorderly and unpleasant; formerly wide stretches of it were "policed" by their fellow countrymen, but now it is best left alone, except for vacations on sunny beaches. It is much the same point of view as Baldwin preached during the Spanish civil war, that England should thank God for not being as other nations are and find sufficient excitement in the affairs of Mrs. Simpson. Economic failure may have begun to erode this complacency at last, while foreigners have come to regard England with the same patronizing pity that Englishmen have felt for them. Diminished self-confidence shows itself in sundry odd ways. Before the last war an Englishman said bluntly, "I think . . ."; today he is learning to say, "I would have thought." This silly periphrasis, formerly heard only in Oxbridge commonrooms, would have puzzled Descartes. "I think, therefore I am"; "I would have thought, therefore . . . ?"

Everywhere the old nationalism was fed on aggressive, jingoistic ideas, and the nation was too often a Moloch, demanding sacrifices—in its last, fascist form, most barbarously of all. Today we think of nation or state in more utilitarian terms, as an arrangement for providing us with hospitals and old-age pensions. It is a change like the earlier one from the walled city, miniature fatherland and emotional focus, to an urban area whose dullard councillors and officials ought to be providing better drains. This earthier attitude is a great deal more sensible than the old romantic flag-waving. Yet a nation, while it remains a sovereign entity, cannot altogether be reduced to a joint-stock company and can scarcely function without a dash of idealism, which in most English people in this generation has found little means of expression. Sporadic appeals for moral revival and unity, from archbishops and suchlike, fall on deaf ears.

To Scots of all classes, with their fewer resources and opportunities, the empire meant proportionately more than to the English, and its loss would hit them harder in a number of ways, unsettling their junior partnership with England. Scotland after the Union, with its upper classes leading the way, was happy to be linked with an England far richer than itself, and rapidly expanding in the world, with its colonies as a very special attraction. Those who went out to manage them were largely Scots or Ulstermen, who must have contributed several traits to the composite image of the imperial Briton: his taciturnity, for instance, was more Scottish than English. It must have been out there, where English, Scots, Welsh, Irish, were mixed up as in Henry V's army at Agincourt, that the expression "Briton" came into use most readily. There was always a touch of the laughable about it, partly because "ancient Britons," painted blue, were somehow ludicrous, and this *may* denote a certain unreality in the union of hearts thus expressed. In the form "Britisher," in vogue when the empire cult was at its height, it took on a stronger flavor of the ridiculous. In the title "Britannic majesty" it had a special royal guise. At home, until lately, Englishmen thought, as foreigners did, of "English" and "British" as meaning the same thing. Thomas Campbell the poet, a very Scottish Scot living in England, used the two words inter-changeably. Scotland was "North Britain," a phrase Scots began at some date before 1945 to repudiate.

Scottish peasants and workers, only less willingly than Irish, flocked into the army, whose main occupation was in the colonies. Military habits may foster militancy of other sorts, as the story of Irish nationalism demonstrates: less patently, but on a higher level, the militancy of the Red Clyde in its great years may have owed something to the same source. This socialist dawn faded into the light of common day; and after the empire was shaken to its foundations by the Second World War, there was a brief phase of romantic Scottishness, when a "literary renaissance" sputtered for a moment and went out, because too few Scots cared about it, and when some youthful enthusiasts stole (or liberated) the Stone of Scone. This prompted Churchill to one of his wittiest parliamentary replies, beginning, "When I call to mind the great qualities and deeds of the Scots . . ." and ending, "I think they ought to be restrained from making fools of themselves."

At that time a separation of the two countries seemed barely thinkable. Since then Scottish nationalism has ebbed and flowed by the moon, its fits and starts never seeming to come to anything. Now there is a new Eldorado, under the North Sea, to take the place of the old one represented by the empire. With the whiff of oil in their noses Scots have been remembering their national selves with slightly comical suddenness, as the Bavarian general Wrangel heard his German blood calling to him when Napoleon was defeated at Leipzig and made haste to change sides. Or so the French saw it in 1813, and the English can hardly be blamed for seeing it now, when they trouble their heads about it at all amid a throng of more urgent perplexities. Familiar old symptoms of national vanity have been quick to show themselves. A Scots student came back lately from a short visit to the Continent convinced that all Europeans hate the English but love the Scots. Probably people do feel a trifle more amiable toward foreigners who belong to minorities—Scots, Bretons, Basques—simply because they are not identified with the big neighbors we grow up to feel mistrustful of.

Polydore Vergil, the Italian humanist in Tudor England, noted with surprise how many languages were current in the British Isles.[2] Today Wales has a language and a national movement interested in literature; Scotland has oil and a movement of quite other complexion. It is certainly far better that Scots should be eager to extract wealth from the sea waves than, as formerly, from Bengalis or Zulus. Cupboard love for a native land is far preferable to the archaic poses of IRA men avenging the wrongs of bygone centuries by exchanging bombs with Cromwellian troopers disguised as their fellow workers. Still, a patriotism which does not—to English eyes at least— appear to rise much above a thirst to turn oil into beer as fast as possible, lacks something. Ideals and utility look as if they were diverging further and further in our corner of the world, and it is only from an alliance between them—they can never be altogether one and the same—that true progress is to be expected.

England lost most of Ireland long since, after violent conflict, without suffering any of the dire harm prophesized by Unionists, while Eire has turned out to be neither a spectacular success nor a dramatic failure. What aches and pains were left behind are due to the part of Ireland that England kept; some of which, though not all, it had and has no choice but to keep. This writer recalls the historian Sir Lewis Namier, in a talk to a college society in the 1930s, raising a laugh by declaring that "if only we could tug Ireland out into the middle of the Atlantic and leave it there, how happy we should be!" Most Englishmen today would heartily agree. Scotland is a very different matter. England may be supposed (one can only conjecture what a country is thinking, and a collective mind does not work on the same lines as ordinary logic) to have watched the recent growth of Scottish separatism with a blend of bewilderment, regret, and—always the commonest sensation, collective as well as private—boredom.

On a planet in peril of extinction either by capitalist war or by capitalist peace, the devolution and independence debate must often seem parish-pump stuff, especially as, whatever flag flutters over the North Sea, most of the profits from its plundering will go to the same bevy of capitalists, mostly American. A caricature version of a national movement is on view in the Isle of Man, made up of a few idealists and a lot of shopkeepers who want to "develop" the island into a tax haven and tourist paradise, or bear garden. Happily for his peace of mind, John Bull is too phlegmatic to take all this tragically, or cry out like King Lear:

> The little dogs and all,
> Tray, Blanche, and Sweetheart, see, they bark
>   at me.

And to lose Scotland or the Isle of Man after being deprived of the biggest empire ever known would be scarcely more than losing Elba after losing Europe. It might even seem a logical completion: England has been the grand nation builder of the modern world, both by attraction and by repulsion, and the time may have come for Scotland to reemerge, fashioned by the long English connection into the stable, viable nation it never was before.

John Bull was genuinely surprised, though, at India, or any other possession, wanting to get away from his leading strings and cannot help feeling more astonished at Scotland wanting to do so. Scots have been a good deal admired, and looked upon as very creditable members of the family. This has only been so for the past century and a half or so, it is true; there was a long epoch before then when Scots were derided, and Scottish fortune hunters detested. Irritation over the long-drawn nuisance of devolution, with the far sharper irritant of Ulster in the background, might conceivably resurrect some old acrimonies, making England all the more inclined to turn its back on an ungrateful world and retire into its shell—though a shell now, so to speak, tumbling about its ears.

The Membrane of Englishness

Many over the ages have tried to paint England's portrait, or capture its essence, in one way or another, with the compilers of Domesday Book leading the way. Defoe wrote a description in the seventeenth century, the Honorable John Byng jotted down fragments of one in his tour journals in the eighteenth; William Cobbett's *Rural Rides* and Dickens's *Uncommercial Traveller* were attempts to weigh up the state of the nation in the nineteenth century, J. B. Priestley made another during the Slump years of the twentieth. Very diverse have been the methods of exploration. About the beginning of this century two Americans were in London studying its life, Henry James by dining out every evening in the West End, Jack London by disguising himself as a workman and plunging into the "abyss" of the East End.[3] Tom Harrisson endowed himself with a thousand eyes or antennae by inventing Mass Observation.

Anyone setting out to scrutinize his impressions of his fellow countrymen with any precision is likely before long to feel puzzled. What we know of them is fragmentary, nebulous, as is most of what we know about our near neighbors. Few individuals seem to know their wives or husbands at all well. Emotionally our reflexes about our compatriots are highly ambivalent; when we are with foreigners we think our own people splendid; at close quarters with them, as within the family where most of our stock responses are molded, it is quite another thing. And even if there seem to be characteristics prevalent among them individually, there may not be any close correspondence between these and the temper of the nation collectively, which incorporates psychological elements that may show little in private life; the converse must be equally true. All surmises are subjective, and as years pass, humanity at large comes to appear less and less familiar or comprehensible; though this dimmed perception may be more, not less, realistic than the plain clear sight of earlier years.

"England" and "France" have always been more fiction than fact. What does have some real meaning is a country's institutions, and the conventions or habits of mind that grow up round them; it is the institution, political or other, that lends a degree of consistency, some firmness of outline, to a people, or a class, itself amorphous, capable of drifting or being steered in many directions. To put it in another way, what counts is the network of relationships prevailing among individuals, groups, classes. Workers and employers, voters and politicians, teachers and taught, the lettered and the unlettered, spiritual flock and shepherd stand variously to one another within these frontiers or those, and the sum of such attitudes makes up the life of the commonweal.

Not long ago, as inquirers like Jack London discovered, East End and West End were as completely apart as Black Town and cantonment or "civil lines" in India. Since then there has been rather more contact, hence friction as well as some leveling, but in England as a whole the old bulkheading remains intact. Social groups learned, and in many ways have not forgotten, how to keep away from each other, meeting only at fixed points, on opposite sides of the House of Commons, for instance, or of the racecourse, where behavior is regulated by custom. Snobs and Londoners are as painfully lost in the north of England as in Scotland, while on a more objective view London today looks about as English as San Francisco. Traditional English society, still only gradually fading away, had a noticeable resemblance to the caste system in India; like Hindu society also, it has had a peculiar sort of coherence, or integration, along with extreme discrepancies, as though held together by a tough transparent membrane.

Educated Englishmen have been fond of mild jokes against themselves, not often meant very seriously, though even this extent of self-criticism betokens a tradition of free speech unknown to most lands. (Scotland's sense of humor belongs to another species.) At the Festival of Britain held to celebrate the emergence from the Second World War, there was a life-size White Knight on horseback, typifying England, who every ten minutes recited a little speech of ironic self-praise. A real exercise in national self-examination is much harder to envisage. Every people is an enigma to itself as well to others, its history a succession of enigma variations in the course of which it rises higher and sinks lower than could be predicted by itself or by anyone. Nations, like individuals, are only aware of themselves in any critical sense at times of intense experience; wars and other ordeals can engender such a mood, which artists and politicians set themselves to interpret or to falsify. England may have been compelled too seldom to embark on any searching self-scrutiny because it has scarcely ever lost a war, and because although for two hundred years it was in the vanguard of human progress, transformation came over it slowly, almost imperceptibly.

Many other countries have found themselves on the switchback railway of modern history far more abruptly. That foreigners are erratic, excitable creatures, unlike his own sober self, must be one of the convictions that have sunk deepest into the Englishman's mind. Such fixed beliefs may, like sunken hulks across a harbor entrance, block the passage of new ideas—even when, like this one, they are not entirely false, as one need only glance across the Atlantic to realize. Neither slump nor war in the 1930s and 1940s could shake up the public mind in any fundamental way, or rather, it may be, in any way that it could translate into political terms: the effects may have to be sought more deviously elsewhere, in the sexual revolution, for example. It was scarcely to be expected, then, that the passing of empire would bring much conscious, reasoned change of thinking.

Compared with forty or fifty years ago, England today exhibits a bewildering mixture of progress, retrogression, and stagnation, with ideas ranging from the most advanced to the most childishly superstitious jostling in its head; a medley where any distinct tendency seems missing. It is a bizarre confusion of prosperity, drugs, ignorance, welfare, and crime, the product of progress of a lurching, piecemeal sort, brought about by reluctant Tory or Labour reformism and sectional pressures by trade unions, with exasperated planners trying to get a word in here and there. No real drive (though much talk about it) toward overhauling and modernizing the country has taken place, only a sporadic patching up and pasting over. Most of Britain's competitors may have undergone no social renovation either, but at least in economic terms some of them have been compelled since the war to put themselves in better order.

Of all alterations of the past half century the vividest is, of course, the shrinking of poverty. In the writer's native city of Manchester, in areas like those round the docks, it was common fifty years ago to see barefooted children in the streets. It was the same, one is told, in Edinburgh, which had a "boot fund" for the unshod.[4] A quaint illustration of how the hardships of one age may turn into the fashions of the next is the spectacle today of young women parading our dirty streets in bare feet, in order to feel like Marie Antoinette among the milkmaids or obeying (more literally than usual) an obscure *nostalgie de la boue*. Improved living standards for most seem an undeniable as well as highly welcome fact; even if a high proportion of what we have gained consists of rubbish we would be better off without. Yet we are told that we have a million illiterates, and four million on or below the poverty line.

We can see, hear, smell, without being told, that affluence has not been matched by any similar blossoming of "culture," in most of its meanings, or diminution of nuisances. Forty years ago, out in the country, a cyclist hardly needed to know which side of the road he was on; the road was his; now he carries his life in his hands at every turn of the wheel. There is a prevalent frowsiness, outside the home, which does not go unnoticed by visitors from more up-to-date lands. Armies of dogs are kept to satisfy a morbidly obsessive desire in their owners to foul the streets; there are chronic reports of insanitary hotel, even hospital, kitchens. Urban solitariness, unlike that of the fields, generates a craving for the mass life of football crowds and pop festivals, and with this a passion, faster-growing than any other, for noise. The Englishman of legend, sparing of words, is being displaced from our railway carriages by a distressingly loquacious type, as the native red squirrel was dislodged by the gray species from North America. Modern industrial environments have much in common everywhere, and must be smoothing over national diversities; not many of these, between countries on the same level of technology, may run as deep as the gap between generations. Young English folk roam the Continent and get on more naturally with young Germans or Rumanians than with their elders at home.

In elementary schools down to well after 1918 caning went on incessantly and was submitted to as an unquestionable fate, just as the solders in the trenches submitted to being massacred. Today we hear of pupils terrorizing their teachers; this is on balance a change for the better, but not much better. Juvenile crime and street violence seem to come and go in mysterious ways, from epoch to epoch. A character in Scott says that in his (and Scott's) youth "men would have sooner expected to meet with the phoenix than with a highwayman."[5] This was Scotland, but England was not less orderly; a hundred years later Dickens was indignant about bands of young ruffians in London jostling and insulting anyone in their path,[6] and Carlyle learned to carry a big stick and keep his eye open on his nocturnal rambles.[7] As a child, just after the Great War, this writer was solemnly warned not to take anything from strangers, because Fenians were supposed to be going about with pocketfuls of poisoned sweets. But as he grew up, he went about at all hours and in all seasons, in town and country, including midnight London, without any thought of molestation ever crossing his mind. This was well before poverty began to give way to affluence. It might be worth while to speculate about how these ups and downs may have been related to phases of empire history and to colonial warfare as an outlet for aggressive impulses. At any rate, it is an unpleasant part of the seamier side of our new life, a sinking toward an American level, that it is becoming an adventure to walk about one's own city alone at night.

A consequence of the end of empire may have been to deprive young progressives of one motive for joining left-wing parties. Immigration from former colonies, and the dilemmas arising from it, ought to offer them a new incentive to activity, less colorful but more urgently practical. It is not untypical of the wisdom with which the empire was run that when rules for immigration and naturalization came to be revised in this century, the English climate was assumed to be an adequate deterrent against anyone from the tropics settling here.[8] Now, while the old nationalisms of Great Britain are reviving and drawing apart, a dozen new communities make confusion worse confounded. That the British Isles are now well stocked with Chinese restaurants is one of the salient novelties of our time and among all immigrant phenomena may be the only one commonly regarded as a good thing. The rest are taken as so many more of life's sournesses, to be swallowed as philosophically as may be. On the whole this undesigned and hazardous experiment has been faced with a surprising degree of good humor. Labor has a fund of tolerance, or pococurantism; the middle classes have been less directly exposed to contact. It may be that real awareness of the new situation has yet to dawn. Newcomers have been entering England all through the ages, but until lately nearly all were of kindred stock, fairly easily assimilated, and until the eighteenth century they were protected by authoritarian government. For a democracy to come to terms with unmistakable aliens, all of a sudden in its midst, must be much harder. Here may be one of the problems destined, along with economic crisis, to jolt the country out of its comfortable somnolence.

With this large infusion of new blood, the quality or sensation of Englishness will be further modified. At the worst, old-style nationalism might take on a new, racialist lease on life. One prophylactic against this is the new sexual permissiveness, making interracial marriages or liaisons less horrific (though not to old-fashioned immigrants) than they would have been not long since. The time is coming, however, when the old license for all couples to reproduce their kind ad libitum, at the expense of the community, will not and should not be allowed to continue. Most of our settlers are here because their own countries are drowning in the misery of overpopulation; they will stand out invidiously if they persist (as some Irish Catholic settlers have done) in the same old-world habits here, just when this country has, wonderfully, begun to achieve a stable population level.

In some other ways the England of today has tastes oddly congenial to those of some incomers, especially from the West Indies. Our popular "culture" is Afro-American (if Scottish nationalism can build a dam against this evil, it will have justified itself, but it is far likelier that oil and more affluence will only mean more saxophones). Love of noise for its own sake seems a bond between rustic Caribbean and neourban, the latter by now half deafened and, if the sufferings of the older are anything to go by, at least a quarter crazed by the ceaseless bedlam of sound that it lives and wallows in from morning till night. To a haunter of the cricket ground, with its ancient peace and quiet, which brought together—the reverse of the racecourse—the cream of every class, it is a sad change to see the stands invaded by spectators who seem to be obeying the summons of Keats's Titan—"Speak, roar, shout yell!" Yet West Indians play cricket as well as anyone, and perhaps it is only to such an accompaniment that cricket, that fine flower of English civilization, can now survive, away from the village green.

More generally, what may be foreseen is a further strengthening of today's utilitarian, matter-of-fact attitudes to the res publica. With a brown or black neighbor one may perfectly well share a rational interest in local drains or transport, but one cannot share with him patriotic transports about heroic Elizabethan sea dogs and slave traders, or William Wallace or Clive or Winston Churchill (Americans were able to romanticize their national self because they made no pretense of racial democracy). Old-style love of the motherland was always very much an abstraction, since it never included real regard for more than a small number of the patriot's fellow countrymen; when a good many of these are of a different color, the illusion is broken. Arithmetically they may not be very numerous, but by standing out so visibly they can intensify a remolding of the community consciousness already in process.

With any significant antithesis of political principle frittered away between the big parties, and with the rise of regional feeling, British politics may be on the way to a regression from national level to a squabble among local and sectional pressure groups, on American lines. Trade unions have been pushing this on, and the new ethnic minorities may give it an extra push. Utility means by itself only getting as much as one can out of the pork barrel for oneself and one's group. A danger increasingly distinct is of more and more pressures being organized on religious lines. Jews have been urging their claim to more state aid for their schools, and arguing, what is undeniable, that what Catholics are entitled to they must also be entitled to. Muslims, now said to number more than a million, have taken up the cry and started to ask for—or more often *demand*—separate schools, separate abattoirs, and a long list of other things.

All these *demands* are to be paid for by hard-pressed taxpayers most of whom have no religion, and some of whom object strongly to religion in general and to certain Catholic doctrines and Jewish-Muslim practices in particular. We should be all the more wary about Muslim agitation because it has a long background of agitation in Indo-Pakistan, habitually stirred up by individuals desirous of pushing themselves forward in their community and raising religious grievances as the easiest means. What they can do, Hindus and Parsees can do, and if Catholics or Anglicans are entitled to subsidies there is no reason why Primitive Methodists or Mormons should not be subsidized, and all the rest of the dozens of cults and sects now rooted in our soil. Giving public money to religion almost inevitably means backing the more obscurantist against the more enlightened; the Catholic hierarchy, for instance, against the sensible middle classes who practice birth control in defiance of it. Muslims, if their self-appointed guides have their way, will be kept shut up in a mental backwater, cut off from any meaningful intercourse with the rest of the country.

Against segregated education, Ulster is a dreadful warning. There is another weighty point to be considered, namely, that granting a privileged, protected status to religious bodies may insidiously circumscribe the area of academic and public freedom of speech. Lately the Muslims of Merseyside were being worked up into a fit of indignation because the Epilepsy Association included Muhamad among famous epileptics of history. This, it was preposterously asserted, revealed "immoral, undignified, and deep-rooted hatred and prejudice" against Islam. All through Muslim history everywhere the faintest breath of criticism has been enough to raise the cry of "Islam in danger," much to the advantage of the rabble-rousers and to the jeopardizing of public peace and common sense. It is disgusting that a profiteer should plan a film about the sex life of Jesus; but his right to do so ought to be upheld, and equally his right to make one about the sex life of Muhammad—a more promising subject—because any kind or degree of censorship on free speech about religion may very well, as England now is, turn into a padlock on scientific discussion or history writing. There are too many Holy Prophets, Holy

Fathers, Holy Saints, holy panjandrums of every description. It is high time for Britain to follow the USA and India and declare itself a secular state, put an end to old subsidies, refuse any new ones, and thus make it considerably harder for any government or politician to be seduced into seeking votes by pandering to sectarian "demands."

The Left-Wing Alternative

A strong socialist movement in England in the late nineteenth century, it has been said, could have won the mass of the Jewish refugees from eastern Europe to socialism; as it was, they were left to be shepherded by their conservatives into Zionism. A strong movement now, with a vision of progress for all irrespective of race, could lift the country above the sordid prospects of competing and maneuvering groups and interests, and of minorities huddled in on themselves and their private ideologies and grudges and rancours, and lead toward a new nation and national consciousness, with a harmony of feeling and purpose not to be achieved by mere inert coexistence. Among the younger immigrants and their children born and growing up here, a good number of individuals capable of sharing in and working for such a vision might be looked for; but it is the coming generation of white Britons who will have to show the way. This calls for rational idealism. It must be added that a handful of jangling ultraleft groups, each more sectarian than the other, offers a very unsuitable medium. Nor will any good be done by the shallow philanthropy which shuts its eyes to all the problems brought about by immigration and condemns a Labour MP who ventures to allude to them as a reactionary. Migrants have quite as much to learn about how to live and behave in a new country as its old inhabitants have to learn about getting on with *them*.

About an entire class, as about a nation, only tentative judgments can be made. Nobody, in or out of it, can pretend to read it like a book. Still, if we are to have any hypotheses to work on, we must be content to go by the aspects and verisimilitudes of things. Labor in England (and Scotland) has an élite of politically conscious and active men and women, the true aristocracy of labor, and indeed the salt of the earth, but they are unfortunately a small, unrepresentative, frequently isolated minority. In the mass, labor seems still not to have escaped, or felt any desire to escape, from its old slough of "Laborism," that peculiar English version of a workers' movement which consisted of shutting itself off within its own trade-union entrenchments, like an island within an island, and leaving nation, empire, and world to go their own way, or leaving them to the handling first of Liberals, later of Bevins and Wilsons. Its origins must be sought in the fact that industrialism came in first in this country, before any socialist theory was to hand, and developed very slowly. It must have been deepened by an excessive part of the labor force consisting for a long time of women and children; we should ask what philosophy of life those hapless forerunners handed on to their descendants. A large part again consisted of Irish immigrants, segregated and self-segregated from the rest.

So far as there was any looking outward, it could sometimes be diverted to the empire, that is, the white settlement colonies to which so many workers were removing. Empire sentiment was preached up as an alternative to international solidarity, as by Viscount Milner, that blend of jingo and paternalist, in his writings at the end of the Great War when he was alarmed to see some workers misled by the will-o'-the-wisp of socialist internationalism.[10] When labor did begin to acquire some political ambitions, these remained timid and fumbling, partly because the immense complexities of the world empire meant responsibilities which it felt unequal to.

Another thing which must have some relevance is that while newcomers have been flowing into Britain all through history, in modern times its own people have been flowing away, all over the world. More thought should have been given by historians to the motives of those who left and—more puzzling—those who stayed. Emigrants are apt to be young, energetic, individualistic. The ones who stayed behind might be called stick-in-the-muds; but they were sometimes men and women with roots in their native soil, an attachment to their own community and its struggles. These might in some ways be deemed the most valuable type, but they were liable to the defect of being more than usually indrawn, turned away from things beyond their own horizon.

During the Second World War a Mass Observation report on one war factory gave a graphic picture of "laborist" introversion. Among the workers in the whole area could be detected no sense of involvement in the conflict. Men were heard to express satisfaction at the fall of Malaya, as fresh proof of upper-class bungling (as of course it was); only a political few felt any spur of urgency after the invasion of the Soviet Union, while the rest were simply relieved (like their bosses) that Hitler had gone away eastward. Tom Harrisson commented on *"the dangerous decline in positive citizenship,* especially among the young."[11] Whether there was really a decline from any previous higher level may be queried; whether there has since been any improvement must be doubted still more.

Laborism has been very much an English phenomenon, part of the continuum of English society and mentality; it exhibited in the most obtuse form a national philistinism, or disregard for ideas about everything except money-making and amusement—about applied science, for example. This, too, owed something to empire and the Kiplingesque ideal of strong silent Britons directing weak silent natives. Scotland, or at least Clydeside in its great days, stood apart; it was preserved by the Scots intellectual (including theological) tradition, more widely shared than any systematic thinking in England. But the Red Clyde of 1915–20 found itself isolated (the other most militant area was South Wales), and thereafter Scottish labor was to relapse, along with Scottish education, toward the English average. Mental inertia in England owed much also to the bureaucratic, authoritarian, birch-rod mode in which their respective shreds and crusts of culture were rammed into public schoolboys and elementary schoolchildren alike. For the working class the outcome has been—in today's world where so much and varied knowledge is a necessity—a standard only barely above illiteracy and very little inclination to take advantage of the channels by which knowledge is now accessible.

The working class greedily swallows, by contrast, the entertainment provided for it by capitalism, however trashy; far more readily than it accepted bourgeois religion while the bourgeoisie still had one. Football must represent an enormous diversion of vital energy into thin air and must have instigated more defiance of law and order than all Good Causes put together. There are forty-seven British comics, with a vast circulation. One of the notes they strike, it has been pointed out lately, is an imbecile echo of imperial clichés; their Africa is still full of wild animals and wild tribes, "blacks still dress like cannibals and go in for nigger minstrel talk."[12] Capitalism discharges its waste into our minds as well as our rivers. This pabulum is not consumed by the working-class youth alone, but it is a sad symptom of how the alienation of labor from the rest of the community has banished it also from the realm of ideas. There can be no such thing as a "proletarian culture," except on the humblest level, but there could have been an appropriation and development by labor of things belonging to the common stock. The absence of any such intellectual or artistic growth may well be a fatal impediment to any interest in socialism or conception of a new order of things.

Make-Believe Class Struggle

England is in the doldrums, with more good will and good intentions scattered about than ever before but as little clarity as ever, or less than ever, about what is to be done. One curiosity of our time is the perpetual use of the word "compassion," never heard until lately outside religious circles. Even allowing for its not seldom hypocritical use by politicians, it is a sign of Christian ethics escaping from the decaying churches which kept them locked up in their sacristies and becoming part of workaday life. (A more strictly theological term in common use, though strangely misconstrued, is "charisma.") Officially, too, a democratizing tone, often but not always bogus, is expressed in the polite practice of the "media" of referring to a lorry driver or street sweeper's *colleagues,* instead of mates, as if he were a professor or a cabinet minister. Officially the nation is one happy family; the BBC makes a point of telling us the name of every news reader, by way of helping to give our impersonal existence a synthetic neighborliness. Christmas trees and

Christian names are among our few outward relics of Christianity, and we have been falling into the bad American habit of using first names with all and sundry. Parliamentary leaders write to each other as "Dear Ted" and "Harold," an informality which would have disgusted Benjamin and William and does less to convince us of their mutual affection than to mark the diminishing content of party principles.

All this fraternizing is oddly contradicted by the atmosphere of class strife or hate, the running dogfight between capital and labor, which strikes foreign observers, Americans above all, so forcibly. By an unforeseen reversal England, in the nineteenth century the citadel of class collaboration, now stands out as Europe's firmest stronghold of class consciousness and class strife. Laborism has proved more stubborn and resistant than Continental social democracy, although it may also look more and more like a blind alley instead of a way forward. It makes for chronic deadlock, not without some redeeming virtues on the moral side. American labor, so willing to endorse Vietnam wars and CIA crimes, shows how a working class degenerates when it comes to equate its interests with those of capitalism. British labor, in spite of its Bevins, has never sunk so low. Again, trade-union loyalties draw on real fraternalism, even if this may often seem to take futile shapes or be carried to ridiculous lengths; one man sneezes, five hundred others troop off to hospital with him. Worse, solidarity tends to be highly restrictive and exclusive, and strikes over interunion disputes to be marked by a mulish obstinacy, as of so many Hotspurs caviling on the ninth part of a hair.

Man does not live by bread alone, and in such behavior can be recognized an assertion of notions, fossilized as it may be, which have come to be bound up with self-respect, something like the *pundonor,* the point of honor, that a Spanish laborer of old would draw his knife over. When a working class has failed to reach or get close to political power, or rather has long since abandoned any ambition of it, it must find what makeweights it can. Then again, recurrent strikes in the motor industry, with its deadeningly mechanical routine, may be taken as an inarticulate protest against the whole system of industrial capitalism, part of a Luddite or anarchist spirit which has lingered on here after being exorcised abroad and which contains a salutary force of change, if so far only elementally. Harold Wilson observed that many strikes and sit-ins express embitterment of workers who crave for a more responsible, intelligible part in what they are doing.

All this, for want of any definable goal, is wastefully dissipated and mixed up with manifold contradictions. Bristol workers call on the country to go on paying them to make Concordes that nobody wants, and that ought not to be wanted, so that it would make more sense to pay these men to dig holes in the ground and fill them in again. Far worse, many others are content to have well-paid jobs making guns and tanks for sale to any customer with money to buy them, obvious though it is that as a rule the richer the customer the more villainous his reasons for wanting them. (This is one area where left-wing leadership can at times impose some restraints.) And in practice, whatever our punctilios, we are left scrambling for the shoddy goods that capitalism, really still paying in truck instead of good money, finds it convenient to supply us with and can hypnotize us through its battery of persuaders into believing that we need or want: imitation beer, poisonous nicotine, dangerous cars, useless pills.

In the absence of any vision of radical change, the hubbub of class strife retains a flavor of make-believe. Labor may be forgiven for not caring much about the rest of the nation, because the rest of the nation has never cared much about *it*. But the most powerful interests within labor appear to care little for the rest of their fellow workers and certainly are not prepared for equality with them. Hence the laborist outlook is something lower, and more inchoate, than authentic class consciousness; this requires a common animating ideal, a magnetic north or polestar, which socialism alone can supply. The spirit of the age is against fidelity to remote goals, to planning for a better collective future; it is an existentialist spirit, fostered by the experiences of the war, by the uncertain tenure of human life on the planet since atom bombs came in, by the waning of religion and of the family.

Individuals and groups today want a better place, however illusory, for themselves here and now and are less disposed than their ancestors to forego present gain for a happier kingdom on earth for their grandchildren who may never be born. Leyland toolmakers on strike lately to recover their "differentials," at the cost of massive unemployment for other workers and grave damage to a tottering industry and national economy, were not more than ordinarily egotistic. A bishop wrote to the *Times* to commend their praiseworthy defense of the sacred principle of inequality. After all, if toolmakers were to get no more than less skilled men, it might soon come to bishops getting no more than curates. Extremes meet; and while for capitalism such wage claims are inconvenient, in broader terms they are welcome as indicating acceptance of the capitalist creed of every man for himself and as a safeguard consequently against socialism. For most immigrants all this holds out cold comfort: their place is clearly at the bottom.

Parasitic Capitalism

Those countries where there has been a dynamic expansion of production since 1945 are the socialist lands, and some others, Germany and Japan above all, where the economy was in dire danger of collapse and had perforce to turn over a new leaf. It is still capitalism, and very much what Mao might have called *goulash* capitalism, but it has reached a stage far higher than the one Lenin mistook sixty years ago for its highest. If empire, in the old guise of direct colonial rule, turned out when lost to have been much less lucrative than it was advertised as being, capitalism has proved vastly more capable of "delivering the goods"—largely shoddy or ersatz goods—than seemed conceivable before the last war. In the prosperous industrial countries headed by the USA, history has neatly stood Marx on his head by transforming the working class from gravedigger of capitalism to its staunch supporter.

British industry has accomplished far less, and part of the cause must lie in the aftereffects on it of the long imperial sway. Empire encouraged the parasitic, get-rich-quick proclivities that businessmen contracted through too much mingling with the nobility and gentry, and with the new gentry of the stock exchange, largely foreigners and the most undesirable immigrants England has ever had. Britain, the pioneer of industrialism, was still very imperfectly industrialized by 1914, and bigger fortunes were always made out of finance and trade than out of production. Manufacturers could not be a genuine ruling class and were too weak and muddleheaded to sweep away landlordism with its close links with the City and its colonial bulwark. Henry James found a deeply decadent upper class in the West End he combed so diligently, and the decadence of some of its branches went on worsening. There has never been any grand social crisis to compel their jettisoning, as so many Jonahs, by the more active, constructive forces.

Empire must have given labor as well as capital a tincture of laziness; how should the owners of a quarter of the world be expected to work hard? Happily the blight affected labor less. Yet the secondary role of industry in the economy gave a further dimension to labor's isolation in its north-country fastnesses; while something of the City's old security of financial and imperial dominion seeped down to the workers, and has helped to puff up trade unionists with their present lordly indifference to what the rest of the world thinks, despite the fact that Britain is now abysmally in debt to the rest of the world and has spent half of its pot of oil at the foot of the rainbow in advance. Our grandfathers would have been ashamed of such indebtedness. But the imperial turn of mind, when colonial gains dwindle, seems to favor borrowing habits, as it did with nineteenth-century Spain: it is the world's duty to support us, by giving us loans if it cannot be made to pay tribute. Colonial sterling balances kept in London, a disguised forced loan, helped to put England on the slippery slope.

Our trade unions have signally failed (unlike popular opinion in the USA) to recognize the distinction between creative and parasitic capitalism, the same kind of distinction that the colonial nationalist movement learned to draw between "national bourgeoisie" and feudal reactionaries. Industrialists with a constructive bent, who really want to make something, belong to the same genus as the enterprising managers who will be indispensable to socialism. They, too, have souls to be saved and need opportunity and encouragement to perform well. Hitherto labor has in effect been harassing and hobbling these men, while leaving landlords and City slickers and racketeers to collect their effortless millions without let or hindrance. Everyone, farmers included, agrees that the farm laborers on whom our survival largely depends, are underpaid and hence are leaving the land; but posterity will read with wonder (if it cares to read about us) that while Britain sank into bankruptcy it went on paying toll to the landlords who had been fleecing it for centuries. Daniel O'Connell thanked God that he lived in a country whose inhabitants would rather perish by famine than fail to pay their rents; he would be quite at home in our England.

Management has its own ailments and shortcomings, but labor has been falling between two stools by being, or appearing, so obstructive as to push business energies back into atavistic speculation and sharking. Thus while in the factories the whistle blows for managers and shop stewards to scrum down and shove, the ball may have been whisked away to the other end of the field. Trade unions win many skirmishes and some battles, but they are not winning any war, because laborist historical conditioning allows them to think in terms neither of an advance to socialism nor of partnership with a prosperous capitalism. They have been hearing for years of economic miracles in West Germany and Japan and suppose that their own employers can perform similar wonders if only life is made sufficiently unpleasant for them. In reality, while in the past quarter century they have been more militant in England than almost anywhere else, their winnings have been relatively meager.

Communists and Affluence

Forty or fifty years ago neophytes in the Communist Party were taught that the working class might be a sleepy giant but would soon be awake and astir—as it seemed to be for a moment in 1926—and would be guided infallibly by class instinct in the right direction. Clearly instinct is not enough, and clearly the CP has not learned how to remedy the deficiencies. Its loss of so many of its intellectuals in 1956–57, after the Hungarian rising, unbalanced it, giving too much weight to its industrial wing, men engrossed in day-to-day local strife over wages and conditions. Failing to make political headway, the party, without realizing it, has come to share a good deal of "laborist" thinking, and its lead, for practical purposes, has been far more "economist" than socialist; it has consisted of supporting all wage claims indiscriminately. Its watchword is free collective bargaining, in other words, economic anarchy. This faith in the ability of capitalism to pay out higher and higher wages, whenever any Moses of a shop steward strikes the rock, is a remarkable reversal of the classical Marxist doctrine of "increasing misery": we now have in its place a dogma, likewise too simple and sweeping, of increasing affluence.

No doubt in economic terms the rights and wrongs of the inflation question, the stumbling block on which in recent years the national consensus or torpor has shown most signs of coming to grief, are exceedingly mysterious. Little can be made of modern capitalist economics except by professional economists, who invariably disagree. No doubt also wage earners (and salary earners) are tired of the admonitions that have been dinned into their ears ever since 1945 about "too much money chasing too few goods," "limited shares of the national cake," and these metaphors have been too grossly manipulated by capitalists busy gobbling their own lavish slices. All the same, *ex nihilo nihil fit*, cake cannot be conjured out of thin air. Clamorous wage demands have no direct connection with socialism, and a fixed determination to raise them in season and out of season would make the task of a socialist government, if we ever had such a thing, hopeless. All socialist countries go in for strict wage limitation; none of their governments emulate the jolly monarch in *The Gondoliers* who wished all men as rich as he. Backing and organizing wage demands, moreover, though it has given the CP industrial influence, has brought it no political standing whatever, no reward in votes. The best that can be said is that, on the tacit assumption that socialism in England is out of the question, it is better to have trade unions led by Marxists than by Bevins who would, like their counterparts in America, align them with reaction and imperialism.

It is because CP strategy no longer seems to be leading toward socialism (though it may lead toward or away from a number of other good and bad things) that parties further to the left have been capturing the enthusiasm— very briefly as a rule—of the young. There is evident risk here of hope and energy being squandered on petty sectarian squabbles, an opposite mischief to the steamroller weight of the CP in the days of monolithic left-wing unity. These sects, to gain an industrial foothold, have no choice but to echo wage claims even louder, and they can afford to do so even more irresponsibly. At times a political calculation seems to underlie this, the thought that wage inflation will sooner or later make capitalism unworkable. But a revolution by sleight of hand, socialism smuggled in as it were in a warming pan, would not last long. Grass-roots leaders have usually been firm in disclaiming any political motives, like the one in a car plant strike in May 1975 who declared, "It would have been impossible to get the support of the workers on anything other than a straight pay issue."[14] In all likelihood, only too true.

That the socialist or any other progressive idea cannot gain ground without mass forces behind it remains as axiomatic as ever. In modern industrial society, however, the middle or middling classes or strata are also a mass force, not without some potentiality for progress, and one whose existence the Left has been apt to overlook. It has argued in the framework of a neat antithesis between shirt-sleeved workman and top-hatted boss, that archetypal pair who were always confronting each other across the boss's desk in the old *Daily Worker* cartoons. Early Marxism forecast a disintegration of the

middle classes as industry developed. Nowadays even Marxists of the more
fundamentalist persuasion no longer assert that the middle classes have evapo-
rated, but too many Marxists go on behaving as if they believed it. The CP
has yet to find an apostle to the Gentiles, or middle classes (the Labour Party
has only too many). Socialism cannot be built without the working class,
which is not interested in it; it cannot be built against the middle classes,
which are hostile to it.

Earthquakes or Monsters?

Nowadays puzzling features of relations between the classes abound. Workers have taken on middle-class characteristics, such as ownership of cars: a
class or race emulating a "higher" one is likely to start by adopting its worse,
not its better proclivities. Workers have been leveling themselves upward by
learning to eat and drink, smoke and gamble far too much, while continuing
to read and think far too little. Meanwhile the middle classes have been
acquiring traits—carefree hedonism, easygoing sexual conduct, irreligion—
which they used to despise in the workers. All the same, they keep their
innate feeling of separateness and superiority, and the same conviction of
being entitled to their "differentials" that trade unionists feel against one
another. They share foreign impressions of "the English disease" and hold,
in spite of all statistical disproof, that English workmen value jobs chiefly as
enabling them to go on strike. To them it is as clear as daylight that Labour
ministries and the national fortunes are far too much in the hands of voters
who take far more interest in the fortunes of their football clubs.

At moments when Englishmen are compelled to glimpse their unpromising
situation, they all blame one another for it. Low output can be put down
either to inefficient management or to uncooperative labor; probably it should
be ascribed to both. Criticism of trade unions has been blunted by their
grumbling submission to pay restraint in the past couple of years, but middle-
class sentiment continues firmly in favor of the Tories, destitute of ideas and
leadership but at least staunchly antiunion and a memorial of what can be
looked back on, with the aid of pride and prejudice, as England's better days.
An economic crash which on the most sanguine guesses of the furthest Left
would precipitate us through a trapdoor into socialism, and metamorphose
football fans into revolutionary Ironsides, would simultaneously drive the
middle classes the other way. The penalty would be a light one if it proved
no worse than another decade of "National government." No one can tell
what earthquakes or monsters may be lurking under any country's placid
surface. Lately Mr. Jack Jones told us that two years ago the Labour government and the trade unions had to fend off a threat of a right-wing coup. If
this is accurate, as it may be, a conspiracy of silence has descended, and
nothing is known of any care taken to prevent the threat recurring—unless

the "social contract," or agreement to reduce real wages, has been the required sop to Cereerus.

"Amidst some patriotick groans, somebody . . . said 'Poor old England is lost.'" This was in 1776, at the famous dinner when Joshua met Wilkes, and the Doctor responded with a joke about poor England having been *found* by the Scots. Of course the country has always been going downhill, just as *Punch* has never been as good as it used to be. Nevertheless, today by most tests, there is plenty of room for pessimism. What may matter more, England has been losing faith more and more in its ability to master its own destinies. There is a worsening of a mood of helplessness which in one way or another has infected all the "advanced" countries since atom bombs came in. Anybody who has taken part in CND (Campaign for Nuclear Disarmament) demonstrations must have been struck by the commonest reaction of bystanders, a blank stare, neither approving nor disapproving, as of sheep paralyzed by foreknowledge of the knife.

Conservative Revolution?

If, in our apparent deadlock, we look around for a way out, a program capable of rallying adequate support from more than one class, we cannot as things are look to socialism. But we may look to something—what has come to be known as "conservation"—which points circuitously in its direction and will be resisted by Tories and by many nominally socialist trade unionists. This new philosophy has a growing appeal, and not only here, as the success of "Ecologist" candidates in the French municipal elections of March 1977 showed. Britain has done very laudably of late in stabilizing its population, even if this has been inspired only partly by rationality, realization that ours is a small and horribly overcrowded country, and partly by national discouragement, fading of the delusions of Magna Britannia. A logical next step would be to make another virtue of necessity by taking "zero growth" as the economic ideal.

England's economic and social life, like its political life earlier, is clogged by a proliferation of checks and balances which keep it standing still. But for an industrial nation to learn to stand still, in terms of use of irreplaceable resources and reduction of inequalities between rich and poor nations, is exactly what human evolution now calls for. Heredity and environment may be combining to make England the first to achieve it. Lack of growth hitherto, haphazard and unwelcomed, has meant unemployment and waste of all kinds. Accepted and rationalized, it could go with a sweeping improvement in life, private and social, by a shifting of production from cosmetics, patent drugs, and miscellaneous rubbish, produced for the sake of profits and jobs, or guns and bombs sold to pay for imports there is often no real need of, to better-equipped schools, better housing, and many other blessings.

Any such program would have to be built on maxims as diverse as restoration of the railways, controlled imports, no more growth of numbers, and therefore no more immigration except for specific individual cases, with priority for political refugees. Its long-term ideals would include rendering England more capable of giving aid to developing and deserving countries, and this would reduce the overspill of population there seeking a new home. It would call for many adjustments and a good many sacrifices, which would have to be as equitably distributed as possible. It could only unfold at the same rate as a mentality rising above sectional egotism. There would be no Lakeland by now if its scenery were left to the custody of those who make their living there. Such a mentality can only have its rise among men and women prepared to make the effort of thinking and acting intelligently; whereas the intensifying complexity of national and world affairs may year by year be widening the gap between these and the mentally inert. Barratt Brown has claimed a "rich vein of support" for conservationist views in the working class.[15] It must devoutly be hoped that he is right, but it must be feared that he is only right about the élite; also that the more rewards come to be equalized between manual work and mental—teaching, for instance—the less respect for mental exertion will the rank and file of labor feel.

This means in turn a further prospect of members of the working class who take to education and qualify for professions drifting away from their class, for want of binding ties. By now an appreciable part of it must have gone over into the middle classes in this way—another kind of emigration. Yet, given a program capable of winning and holding it, it may not be fanciful to hope that this lost legion might remember old allegiances and an ancestral longing for progress come back to life in it, freed from the dead weight of Laborism. If so, it might at the same time have a leavening influence on the middle classes, in alliance with a growing weight of professional and technological opinion pushed by experience toward a search for a more rational stewardship of collective resources. Much might be expected too from the multitude of ex-students, middle-class or working-class, with a program which would give them something to go on working for after they leave college and disperse. Clearly the wild oats from which their fiery potations of college days are distilled do not provide this: most left-wing graduates become political dropouts very quickly. So far the expanded graduate population has made very little difference to the dulling, muffling quality of English life which—for both good and ill—deadens every "explosion."

An odd intellectual or two "going to the workers" makes no more dent on them than the Narodnik students on the peasants of old Russia. A progressive movement of this composite order might gradually carry with it the more thoughtful, older and younger people alike, of working class as well as middle class. If England can make a change in the next generation on lines like these, it will once again be giving a lead to the world, as momentous as when it got rid of Charles I or when it started the Industrial Revolution.

Notes

This chapter originally appeared in the *New Edinburgh Review* (1977).

1. See D. Goldsworthy, *Colonial Issues in British Politics, 1945–1961* (Oxford, 1971).

2. D. Hay, *Polydore Vergil* (Oxford, 1952), 92.

3. Jack London, *The People of the Abyss* (1903).

4. I owe this and other recollections of Edinburgh to a French observer of the scene, Mrs. A. Geddes.

5. Sir Walter Scott, *St. Ronan's Well* (1823), Chapter 15.

6. Charles Dickens, *The Uncommercial Traveller* (1861), Chapter 30, "The Ruffian."

7. See D. A. Wilson, *Carlyle to Threescore and Ten (1853–1865)* (London, 1929), 487.

8. H. Tinker, *Separate and Unequal: India and the Indians in the British Commonwealth, 1920–1950* (London, 1976), 37.

9. Reported in the *Guardian*, 6 January 1977.

10. See Viscount Milner, *Questions of the Hour* (London, 1923), especially 135.

11. T. H. Harrisson, ed. *War Factory*, a Mass Observation report (London, 1943), 9 and Appendix, by the works manager.

12. N. Tucker quoted in the *Guardian*, 7 December 1976.

13. Speech at Blackpool, 17 March 1973.

14. Barratt Brown, *Guardian*, 22 May 1975.

15. Barratt Brown, review of F. Hirsch, *The Social Limits to Growth* (London, 1977), *Guardian*, 24 March 1977.

INDEX

Page numbers in italics indicate central discussion of the item.